RESERVATION
PROBLEMS AND PROSPECTS

Book by the Same Author
Tribal Education in India

Reservation
Problems And Prospects

SHYAMA NAND SINGH
Associate Professor in Political Science,
Department of Political Science,
University of Ajmer-355006
Rajasthan (India)

UPPAL PUBLISHING HOUSE
NEW DELHI—110002

UPPAL PUBLISHING HOUSE
3, Ansari Road, Daryaganj, New Delhi-110002

First Edition 1991
ISBN 81-85024-90-1

Printed in India

Published by B.S. Uppal, Uppal Publishing House
3, Ansari Road, Daryaganj, New Delhi-110002
Printed at Sainion Printary, Delhi - 11 00 32.

Acknowledgements

The present study examines the job reservation policy of the Government of Bihar for the other backward classes (1977-1979). The adoption of this policy led to street fighting, destruction of Government property and above all a division of the people of Bihar into two camps—one of the upper castes and the other of the backward castes. I became naturally interested in examining this socio-political issue in details.

I am profoundly grateful to my supervisor Dr (Mrs) Lila Sinha,Department of Political Science, M.M. College, Patna University for her guidance and supervision in completing my rescarch work. I am greatly indebted to Mr A.S. Hebbar of the Jawaharlal Nehru University for his suggestions and encouragement. I also offer my immense regards to Dr M.N. Jha, Head of politicai Science, Patna Uuiversity and Professor R.C. Singh of the Labour and Social Welfare, Patna University, for their constructive comments and valuable critical analysis on job reservation.

I am thankful to Late Shri Karpoori Thakur, Shri Mungeri Lal Shri Satyendra Narayan Sinha, Shri Thakur Prasad and Shri U.N. Sinha in particular and many other legislators and politicians in Bihar whom I met for sparing their valuable time and gladly replying my queries and furnishing me with valuable information. The officials of the Government of Bihar and the Ministry of Home Affairs, Government of India have helped me immensely during data collection. So did the library staff

A.N. Sinha Institute of Social Studies, Patna; Bihar Vidhan Sabha Library, G.V.P.G. College, Sangaria (Raj); Government College, Dungarpur (Raj.); Jawaharlal Nehru University, New Delhi; M.S. University, Baroda; Ministry of Home Affairs New Delhi; Nehru Memorial Museum and Library, Teen Murti House, New Delhi; Patna University Library, Patna; Parliament Library, New Delhi; Sinha, Library, Patna; Secretariat Library, Government of Bihar.

I am also thankful to my colleagues and friends who gave me friendship and understanding during my research. I am indebted to members of my family for their immense support for my academic pursuits. My wife Shashibala helped me a lot during writing this book. I am obliged to Mr Mahamaya Prasad and Mr Satayan Narayan Singh for typing it nicely.

Ajmer
18th, October 1990

Dr. SHYAMA NAND SINGH
Department of Political Science
University of Ajmer
Ajmer—355 006
(Rajasthan)

Contents

List of Tables

Table Nos.	Title of Tables	Pages

CHAPTER 1

Introduction

Importance of the Study

The policy of reservation is an important socio-political issue in India today. No other decision in the field of social welfare has been so widely debated, particularly in Andhra Pradesh, Bihar, Gujarat, Karnataka, Maharashtra, Madhya Pradesh and Uttar Pradesh. It has in fact led to much street fighting, closer of educational institutions, hampering of trade and business and destruction of Government property. Executive action on the policy of reservation is also a controversial issue susceptible to different judicial interpretations. The policy of reservation is unique to India, its object being to establish an egalitarian society and to ameliorate the traditional underprivileged position of untouchables, tribals and 'other backward classes'. The aim of the present study is to examine this issue both in the national perspective and in the context of its relevance in a particular Indian State, viz. Bihar.

India is a multi-ethnic society. There are a large number of othnic groups of varying sizes. There are highly localized caste and tribal groups as well as linguistic and religious groups. No single group is clearly dominant and the boundary between one group and another is not distinct.[1] Among these social groups, inequality is deep-rooted in the social, economic and political spheres. It is, thus, a difficult task before our statesmen to modernize a tradition-bound society.

The social environment in the developing countries is marked by a great degree of inequality. Social status, economic means and political power are concentrated in the hands of a rather small social section, and this makes it impossible for the majority of the population to gain access to positions of power and prestige.[2] Whenever the Government or social reformers take steps to eradicate social, economic and political evils, they are branded parochial.

Nationalist elites in new states tend to be deeply suspicious of tribal, linguistic, religious, regional, and caste loyalties and structures. Generally they perceive them as a threat to the incipient nations and the fragile states they govern. This frequently leads them to attempt to dispense with those structures instead of integrating them.[3] In India, with its composite culture, ethnic loyalties are inherent in the very system, and they lend themselves easily to political mobilization. If this is within limits, it can be tolerated; it may even facilitate the functioning of the political system concerned. When, however, it goes beyond limits, it creates a threat to the existence of that political system.

In the light of the aforesaid statements, it would be a good idea to examine the emergence of the backward caste conscious-

1. Paul R. Brass, *Language, Religion and Politics in North India*, (New Delhi, 1975), p. 142.
2. Ramashray Roy, "A Study of the Bihar Congress Committee, Bihar, India" (Ph.D. Thesis, University of California, Berkeley, Calif., 1966), p. 21.
3. L.I. Rudolf and S.H. Rudolph, "The Politics of Caste", in John K. Pulparampil, ed., *Indian Political System*, (New Delhi, 1976), p. 399.

ness, the backward caste politics and subsequently, the decision to follow a policy of reservation of jobs for the backward communities in Bihar. This necessitates the study of dynamics of the pro- and anti-reservation movements in the light of fast changing situation, the demand for protection of economically poor groups and necessity of changing criteria of reservation of jobs. It also becomes desirable to check the evils of reservation policy in order to save the society from undesirable development threating peace and progress. It should not lead to further unbalance of society, one overpowering the other.

The Problem

The development of inequality, the exploitation of poor and backward castes and rule of minorities over majorities are rooted in history. Social and political thinkers predicate equality of mankind and propound a number of political theories. In practice, however, it is always the aristocracy, the warlords, and the kings who ruled.[4] Karl Marx regarded the State as an instrument of exploitation in the hands of the ruling class and asked the proletariat to overthrow it. He said, and rightly, that while philosophers might interpret the world, they would not be able to change it. In the beginning of the eighteenth century, the political philosophers of the liberal school (Locke and Rousseau for example) and Utopian Socialists gave much thought to inequality and exploitation and showed different paths for the establishment of a society based on the principle of equality of mankind. Rousseau's political philosophy found expression in the French Revolution[5] of 1789 and that of Marx in the Russian Revolution (1917) and the Chinese Revolution (1949).

4. Max Weber, *Theory of Social and Economic Organisation*, (New York, 1965), p. 154.
5. The slogan of the French Revolution was "Liberty, Equality, and Fraternity"; it prepared the ground for the establishment of an egalitarian society.

The publication of the Communist Manifesto in 1848 brought about a change in the political and social thinking of the world. The democratic countries of the wertern world experimented with the concept of a Welfare State and made attempts to promote popular political participation. Later, upon realizing that people from different ethnic groups were not getting their due share in the Government services, they instituted reservation of jobs for them. During the freedom movement in India it was realized that individual freedom and equality before law could not, by themselves, confer economic and political justice on the downtrodden. Our national leaders like Mahatama Gandhi and Dr. B.R. Ambedhkar highlighted the problems of Scheduled Castes and Tribes. Certain measures were taken for the eradication of untouchability and socio-economic development of them during freedom struggle. After Independence policy of reservation became a nationally accepted programme for the upliftment of the Scheduled Castes and the Scheduled Tribes. Reservation for other backward classes (OBCs), howover, became a national controversy as the various political parties differed over it.

The research problem before us is to examine the issue by looking into the various factors affecting reservation policy such as the social, cultural, economic and political backgrounds of the legislators and the pressures brought by them individually and collectively.

It is reasonable to expect that greater exposure to mass media and other forms of communication and intimate contact with the outside world would broaden the outlook of the elites and infuse in them a tendency to make rational, scientific, modern, forward-looking decisions. In the absence of these variables, the decision-makers would make decision on the basis of the traditional norms, which create social and political problems, as evidenced by the pro- and anti-reservation agitations in Bihar and some other Indian States.

The problem in these circumstances is to examine such values of pluralism as individuality, equality, negotiation and compromise in the making of the policy of reservation. Even then the sentiment of caste plays a major role. Caste associations have emerged as associational pressure groups. In Bihar a number of caste groups, though diverse in appearance and segmented in terms of interests, have acted in tandem to further specific interests.

Existing Literature : A Review

The study of caste and class and their impact on politics in India has been a fertile field of research; so much so that a vast literature has grown up, consisting mostly of Ph.D. thesis in different universities and books and articles by social and political scientists. There are some autobiographies[6] by those involved in Bihar politics.

Rajni Kothari's book *Politics in India*[7] is a study of Indian politics from the politico-sociological angle. Kothari underlines the importance of "support structures" in the constituencies, the party preferences of voters, and local or national issues at stake as determinants of electoral victory in Indian politics. *Caste in Indian Politics*, a work edited by Kothari, gives a framework for the study of State politics in relation to the social *milieu*.[8]

The Ph.D. works relating to the Bihar scene are based upon extensive field work. W.H. Blair[9] and Ramashray Roy[10] are

6. A.N. Sinha, *Mere Sansmaran* (in Hindi) (Patna, 1961); and Sachchidananda Sinha, *Some Eminent Bihar Contemporaries* (Patna, 1944).
7. Rajni Kothari, *Poltics in India* (New Delhi, 1970).
8. Rajni Kothari, ed., *Caste in Indian Politics* (Delhi, 1970).
9. W.H. Blair, "Caste, Politics and Democracy in Bihar State, India : The Elections of 1967" (Ph.D. Thesis, unpublished, Duke University, Durham, N.C., 1969).
10. Roy, n. 2.

concerned with voting and legislative behaviour. Their work is truly path-breaking. Books by Dayadhar Jha[11] and M.P. Singh[13] and articles by Chetkar Jha and Shree Negesh Jha[14] are based upon legislative research and caste politics in Bihar.

Some American scholars have contributed valuable articles on politics and society in Bihar in their books and articles. Paul R. Brass[15] and W.H. Blair[16] deal with the present-day politics of Bihar. Inspite of their extensive field works they have failed to notice the emergence of class consciousness among the people as well as the breaking of the caste system. Paul Brass's article on the Maithili movement is an analysis of the domination of the Maithil Brahmans with their social, economic and cultural superiority.

Blair focusses on the emerging power of the *kulaks* in Bihar politics and society. On the basis of empirical data he concludes that some backward castes like the Yadavas, the Kurmis, the Koiris, and the Banias are challenging the ascendancy of the upper castes.

A number of research works and books have been published

11. Dayadhar Jha, *State Legislature in India* (New Delhi, 1977).
12. Sashishekhar Jha, *Political Elite in Bihar* (Bombay, 1974).
13. Mahendra P. Singh, *Cohesion in a Predominant Party : The Pradesh Congress and Party Politics in Bihar* (New Delhi, 1975).
14. Chetkar Jha and Shree Nagesh Jha, "Some Aspects of Bihar Politics", *India Quarterly* (New Delhi), July-September 1964, pp. 312-29; and Shree Nagesh Jha, "Caste in Bihar Politics", *Economic and Political Weekly* (Bombay). This periodical is cited hereafter as *EPW*. pp. 341-344.
15. Brass, n. 1. See also his article "Radical Policies of the Left in Bihar : A Comparison of the SSP and the CPI", in Paul R. Brass and Marcus F. Franda, eds., *Radical Politics in South Asia* (Cambridge, Mass., 1973), pp. 325-397.
16. W.H. Blair, "Rising Kulaks and Backward Castes in Bihar", *EPW*, 12 Januury 1980, pp. 65-70.

on the reservation policy adopted by some States in India. By and large these works project five viewpoints.

First of all, there is the viewpoint that merit and efficiency are the only valid criteria for admissions into educational institutions and for recruiting personnel for Government jobs. The Government service is an opportunity to serve society and it cannot be wasted by boosting a certain section of society at the cost of the whole society. Services, irrespective of employer and nature, tend to serve the people and the society. Better the services better would be the benefit. Therefore, the modern recruitment policy aims at recruitment of best available persons through most scientific recruitment and selection system. Naturally any criteria which results into recruitment of a person other than best available person would not help in maintaining efficient staff. This is their strong argument against job reservation policy. The proponents of this viewpoint like Marc Galanter[17] and Andre Beteille[18] advocated for abolition of all reservations, whether based on caste, class, occupation, sex, or region. Alok Srivastava[19] and Sanjay Sinha[20] too in their M. Phil. dissertations on the reservation poilcy in Bihar have expressed a simillar viewpoint.

17. Marc Galanter, *Competing Equalities : Law and the Backward Classes in India* (New Delhi, 1984); and "Who Are the Other Bacward Classes ? : An Introduction to a Constitutional Puzzle", *EPW*, 28 October 1978, pp. 1812-1828.
18. Andre Beteille, *Backward Classes and Their Future* (Delhi, 1981). See also his "The Problem" in *Seminar* (New Delhi), 268, December 1981, pp. 10-13.
19. Alok Srivastava, "The Emerging Patterns of Caste Conflicts in Bihar : A Study of Post-1977 Period" (M. Phil. dissertation, unpublished, Jawaharlal Nehru University, School of Social Sciences, New Delhi, 1982).
20. Sanjay Sinha, "Backward Class Movement in Bihar : A Sociological Study" (M. Phill Dissertation, Jawaharlal Nehru University, School of Social Sciences, New Delhi, 1984).

The second viewpoint, represented chiefly in the writings of I. P. Desai[21] and Upendra Baxi[22], is that all caste-based reservations should abolish. Those, who subscribe to this viewpoint, profess faith in the Directive Principles of State Policy and are committed to social change and the upliftment of the neglected sections of society. In selecting people for preferential treatment, however. they would go by their occupation or social class and not by their castes. The door of reservation would not be closed for the poor people of the upper castes as they consider that poverty is a greater hindrance to development than anything else. The Rane[23] Commission of Gujarat has in its report expressed views which by and large endorse this viewpoint. Attention may be drawn towards context Sachchidanand's book *The Harijan Elite*[24] in which he examines the development of the Harijans in the context of the reservation policy. He finds that reserved jobs, scholarships and seats in the legislatures have only helped to create and reinforce a dual society among the Harijans. The advanced Harijans do not care for their own community. Instead they only seek to improve their equation with the status and power groups in the wider society. Sachchidanand favours economic development for the mass of the Harijans which would foster national integration and promote articulation of interests on a class basis rather than on the basis of caste.

The third viewpoint, represented by Nirmal Mukherji[25] and

21. I.P. Desai, "Should Caste be the Basis for Recognising Backwardness ?" *EPW*, 14 July 1984, pp, 1106-1116.
22. Upendra Baxi, "Caste, Class, and Reservation", ibid., 9 March 1985, pp. 426-428.
23. *Gujarat : Report of the Socially and Educationally Backward Classes* (Second) *Commission* (Chairman : C.V. Rane) (Ahmedabad, 1984).
24. Sachchidanand, *The Harijan Elite* (New Delhi, 1977).
25. Nirmal Mukherji, "Perspective of a Policy", *Seminar*, 268, December 1981, pp. 14-18.

N.S. Saxena[26], is that the Scheduled Castes have suffered from poverty and humiliation for a long time. These castes are still considered untouchable. They remain neglected throughout history and have lived isolated from the mainstream of the socio-political life of the country. To assimilate them into our national life, reservation is a nationally accepted principle. The backward castes, however, have never suffered the curse of untouchability. In fact they are economically and politically dominant. They are, therefore, not entitled to get benefits similar to those provided to the Scheduled Castes and the Scheduled Tribes. Their objective conditions are quite different. Had there been any justification for a reservation policy for them, the makers of our Constitution would have certainly provided for it. Why, after so many years of independence, when a lot of improvement has taken place and the chances of upward mobility for the backward classes are brighter than ever before, should they be given preferential treatment ?

The fourth viewpoint favours extension of the benefit of reservation to certain backward classes, whose conditions of life are similar to those of the Scheduled Castes and the Scheduled Tribes. It is totally unnecessary and wrong to extend this benefit to the upper backward castes, which consist of prosperous peasants and traders. These castes have improved their economic conditions and are notorious for the atrocities they commit on Harijans in rural areas. To this school of thought belong Ghanshyam Shah,[27] D.L. Sheth,[28] and

26. N.S. Saxena, "The Reservation Issue : A Possible Basis for a Consensus", *Times of India* (New Delhi), 3 May 1985.

27. Ghanshyam Shah, "Caste, Class, and "Reservation *EPW*, 19 January 1985; pp. 132-136; and "Reservation for Backward Castes and Classes", *Economic Times* (New Delhi), 14 June 1978.

28. D.L. Sheth, "The Great Reservation Debate", *Indian Express*, 12 May 1985.

Parmanand Singh,[29] who favour evolving a scientific criteria for the purpose of preparing a list of backward classes to ensure that those, whose conditions of life are almost comparable to those of the Scheduled Castes and the Scheduled Tribes, should enjoy the benefits of reservation.

The fifth viewpoint, the chief protagonists of which are Ram Moanohar Lohia[30] and Devaraj Urs[31] favours caste-based reservation. In India's unique socio-historical context, reservation is essential for improving the lot of those who are backward not only in economic terms but also in cultural and psychological terms. The Backward Classes have had to put up with low social status on account of their humble occupations. The bureaucracy, which is an important organ of socio-economic development, is dominated by the upper castes, and it, therefore, favours only the upper castes. If the fruits of development have to be distributed equally, preferential treatment for the backword castes is a must. Such treatment would then eradicate parochial tendencies and strengthen national integration. The findings of most of the Backward Classes Commissions constituted by the Central and State Goverments by and large endorsed this viewpoint.

In the view of the present researcher only the fourth viewpoint is acceptable. The first viewpoint regards merit as the only criterion for filling up seats and posts. Such a viewpoint, however, cannot solve our age-old social inequalities. Candidates of the deprived sections of society are in no position to compete

29. Parmanand Singh, "Equal Opportunity and Compensatory Discrimination : Constitutional Policy and Judicial Control", *Journal of the Indian Law Institute* (Delhi), vol. 18, April-June 1976, pp. 302-306.
30. Ram Manohar Lohia, *The Caste System* (Hyderabad : Samata Nyaya, 1964); and, see also Ishwari Prasad, "Job Reservation for Backward Classes in Bihar", *Janata* (New Delhi), 23 April 1978.
31. Devaraj Urs, "The only Way", *Seminar*, 268, December 1981, pp. 25-26.

with the meritorious candidates of the developed castes. Some sort of protective discrimination is required to put them on a par with the advanced castes.

The second viewpoint is not against the reservation policy as such. It only emphasizes the class or occupation criterion and rules out the caste criterion. Even this viewpoint cannot be accepted as it would be difficult in practice to define certain class or occupations as backward. Again, if it is defined, the beneficiaries would be the lower or middle classes of the upper castes and not the backward classes.

The third viewponint is in favour of reservation for the Scheduled Castes and the Scheduled Tribes but opposes any such reservation for the backward classes. It is a fact that in the social ledder or in Government service some of the backward classes have suffered more than the Scheduled Castes and the Scheduled Tribes. At present the backward classes constitute 52 per cent of the population in India, but their representation in the various categories of Central services is just 12.5 per cent. This is much less than the representation given to the Scheduled Castes and the Scheduled Tribes. This shows that the backward classes deserve the benefit of reservation.

Freedom of profession has been available to citizens in all most all countries. There is no bar on it except in few countries where race had been a criteria. In India people have been enjoying freedom of occupation. And it has been utilised by Indians cleverly. The Governments jobs have failed to attract certain castes like Marwari, Suri, Teli, Sonar and Bania. The profession of trade and business in which these castes have monopolised since long has been more alluring than salaried jobs. The children of these castes receive education only with a view to manage their business and trade then to look for a job. This is most important factor for lower percentage of Government jobs held by them.

The fifth viewpoint supports a caste-based reservation policy for all the backward classes irrespective of their economic conditions. This viewpoint too has some serious drawbacks. The backward classes are not a homogeneous group; their economic and social conditions vary widely. It the reservation policy is extended to all of the backward classes, the benefits would be cornered by the advanced sections among those classes. That is why this viewpoint cannot be accepted.

The research scholar feels that fourth viewpoint is most acceptable. Preferential treatment in jobs should be given to those classes or groups of people which are backward economically, socially and politically. This would help in greater development of society without creating inter-class or inter-caste differences and struggle. Any policy based on caste would not allow national integration nor would create environment for social and economic equality. Further the job reservation policy, with preferential treatment, would affect efficiency adversely. No society can advance by sacrificing efficiency. Therefore, from all points of consideration the fourth viewpoint seems acceptable.

The Present Study

The specific aim of the present work is to analyse and understand the job reservation policy of Bihar with the help of the variables of caste and class. These two variables have greater relevance in areas where the social *milleu* is the most important factor in political activity. There have been a few researches so far into the role of non-rational factors such as caste in politics.

The Indian and foreign scholars regard caste as the basis of political alliance, reliance and voting behaviour. But that is not the only variable. Class, region, selfinterest, etc., are also important variables. They have overlooked the role of class as a political factor in Bihar. The present study is an attempt to give equal importance to these two social and economic variables : it looks upon the legislature as society in miniature. Different sections of the people are represented there and there are robust interactions of ideas.

A study of the socio-economic background of legislators helps in understanding their responses to the problems before the State, the structure of social groups and interests of the electorates.

In this study caste has been equating with *jati,* not *varna.* A *jati* is a group with hereditary membership. Each *jati* has a specific location in Bihar, which is not the case with *varna.* Even *Varna* produces confusion in Bihar—as, for example, in the context of the claim of the Bhumihars to be categorized as Brahmans. In the 1902 census they were in the same category as intermediate castes like the Yadavas, the Kurmis, the Hajams and the Kayasthas. In the 1931 census, however, in view of their progress in education and in the economic and political fields, they were placed between the Brahmans and the Rajputs. The Kayasthas were also accepted as an upper caste.

Class is an economic category related to wealth. The present study uses class as a means of stratification. It discusses urban and rural class structures in terms of legislative representation, possession of wealth, income, education, etc. It uses both subjective and objective criteria in determining the class of each legislator.

In rural areas the present study takes into consideration such criteria as possession of land, agricultural equipment, servants, and personal involvement in production. It characterizes those peasants or cultivators as self-sufficient agriculturists, who transfer some of their products (which constitute a part of the economic surplus of the village) to non-cultivating groups.

In the urban set-up the study gives importance to monthly income :

1. Those whose monthly income does not exceed Rs 500—lower lower middle class;

2. those whose monthly income is more than Rs 500 but below Rs 1,000—lower middle class;
3. those whose monthly income is between Rs 1,000 and Rs 1,500—middle middle class;
4. those whose monthly income range from Rs 1,500 to Rs 2,500—upper middle class;
5. those whose monthly income is higher than Rs 2,500 but less than Rs 5000—upper class;
6. those who earn Rs 5,000 a month and more—upper class.

Scope and Limitations

The present study focusses on a detailed examination of the emergence of backward castes consciousness and the implementation of the Mungeri Lal Backward Classes Commission Report. It goes into the problems in depth and attempts a frank analysis. It examines, not dates and events, but the social, economic and political processes. It seeks to find out which groups benefit from particular decisions and how these decisions are made.

The topic covers a period of just two years. These years witnessed a number of changes in the social and political life of Bihar. As it is important to concentrate on the main issue which interlinks all the recent social and political developments of Bihar, the present study focusses on the issue of job reservation for backward classes.

The present work starts with the formation of the Janata Party and the emergence of the politics of backward classes in Bihar. The formation and collapse of the Janata Party Ministry and its decision to implement the recommendations of the Mungeri Lal Committee illustrate the conflict for power between different social groups.

The present work is basically concerned with the politics of the Janata Party, but it also touches upon the functioning of the Congress Party. Except for a few brief years here and there Bihar has always been ruled by the Congress Party. The backwardness or development of the State is largely attributable to Congress rule.

Hypothesis

Our hypotheses are derived from the correlation of caste, class and politics in Bihar. Caste and class play a part in both the positive and negative aspects of the process. On the positive side there are secular issues, social integration and heightened political consciousness; on the negative side caste promotes the interests of the elite groups. Caste favours the rich among the backward castes and hurts the poor among the upper castes. As for the role of class, it strengthens the secular aspect of politics.

The following are our hypotheses :

1. The economic condition of a society exercises a great influence on social and political consciousness; it also leads to political development and decay.

2. The protest movement against the policy of reservation in Bihar during 1977-79 was fuelled by the growing awakeness of the lower class and the middle class of Bihar.

3. The movement was precipitated by the sidetracking of the State legislature by the Janata Party, especially in the matter of implementation.

4. The movement for job reservation was led by students, legislators and bureaucrats belonging to the higher, upper-middle, and middle classes in the backward castes because almost all the higher positions and key posts were occupied by the middle classes among the upper castes.

5. Casteism has been an obstacle in the way of proper shaping of class consciousness and all-round development of the backward State of Bihar.

6. The ritual value of caste is broken, but its political value has escalated. Caste can be said to have declined with the decline in the domination of the upper castes; it can at the same time be said to have been responsible for the polarization of the upper castes and the backward castes into two mutually hostile or adverse groupings.

7. Backwardness should not be determined on the basis of caste alone. Education and the economic condition should also be taken into account.

Methodology

The subject of our study bristles with a number of controversial issues. Even from the methodological point of view the subject presents many difficulties. The mechanism of decision-making is beyond public scrutiny. It is by no means easy to identify the real circumstances under which the decision to pursue a policy of job reservation was made. The senior bureaucrats are not willing to allow researchers to scrutinize the records relating to the Cabinet meetings in which the decision to go in for a policy of job reservation was made. Therefore, the interview method has been used for collecting information from the decision-makers—viz the Chief Minister, the Cabinet Ministers, the legislators, the bureaucrats, the Chairman and the Secretary of Backward Classes Commission of 1976, etc.

For collection of data an interview schedule including both closed and open-ended questions have been used. The aim of the open-ended question schedule is to seek opinion on certain socio-political problems,

Caste and class are two variables. It is easy enough to identify the caste of a legislator, but it is difficult to determine his class. There are two problems. First, most legislators conceal their class, the lands and other properties they possess. In our schedule there are a number of questions which are so designed as to yield fairly reliable information on the social class of the legislators. To find out the social origin, training and experience of the legislators it would be necessary to know not only individual characteristics but also the value system of the society, the basis of social stratification, etc.[32] Our questions are aimed at finding out what occupation each legislator was engaged in prior to his election, what was the extent of his father's qualifications, the ancestral occupation, etc. Attempts have been made to ascertain the views of the legislators about the reservation policy of the Janata Party Government.

Although inspite of best efforts, only 200 legislators out of 324 members in the House can be interviewed. Data have been supplemented by meeting members of the families as well as office bearers of the political parties at district level. Some of the legislators of 1977, who were deteated in the subsequent elections to the legislature were not easily available in Patna. Therefore, help of other legislators belonging to their political parties was taken in this study.

Experience of Field Work

The field work undertaken in course of study was interesting and fruitful. It enabled the researcher to meet a cross-section of the entire political world of Bihar—students, legislators, politicians, bureaucrats, etc. By and large the legislators and other elite groups were generous in sparing time, giving information and were hospitable.

32. Wester G. Seligman, "Elite Recruitment and Political Development", *Journal of Politics*, Vol. 16, no. 2, August 1964, p. 12.

Interviews were conducted in the Vidhan Sabha lobby, the offices of the different political parties in the Vidhan Sabha complex and at their residences. The legislators appeared to be more worried about their own problems than the problems of the people. They were, however, quite accessible to research scholars and pressmen.

Important political leaders interviewed included Madhu Limaye, Bhishma Narayan Singh, Jagjivan Ram, S.N. Sinha, and Karpoori Thakur. Meetings were held by appointment. Most of the leaders made inquiries at the outset about the scope of the discussion planned to have with them. They were quite frank and forthcoming on the different aspects of Bihar politics.

Outline of the Present Work

The thesis is divided into eight chapters.

Chapter one contains discussions of the importance of the study, the nature and scope of the research proble on hand. A review of the literature available was made along with examination of their positive and negative aspects. Hypotheses have been framed. An outline of the present thesis, the methodology used, and the experience gained during field work have been presented.

The second chapter discusses the theoretical aspects of caste, class and potitics. Different approaches are discussed and critically examined.

The thrid chapter is concerned with the political aspect, especially in the goings-on in the legislature. It shows how the movement was influenced by the caste and class factors. It examines the formation of the first Janata Party Ministry on the basis of empirical data concerning the caste and class composition of the Janata Party, the Congress Party and other political parties as well as the caste and class composition of the Legislative Assembly itself.

The fourth chapter presents the constitutional and legal perspectives on the reservation policy.

The reports submitted by the different Backward Classes Commissions and the criteria suggested by them for the determination of backwardness are the themes of the fifth chapter.

Backward caste politics in Bihar has been X-rayed in the sixth chapter. The chapter analyses the emergence of the backward classes in Bihar and their influence in the formulation of the policy of reservation. It also examines the political compulsions of the decision-maker in implementing decisions on job reservation and the impact thereof on the social, economic and political aspects of the lives of the people of Bihar.

The seventh chapter presents arguments advanced in favour of and against reservation. A comparative picture of reservation in the northern and the southern states has been presented.

The eighth chapter contains conclusions of the entire study and endeavours to re-evaluate the hypotheses. All the political developments in the State during the years 1977-79 are semmed up in this chapter. Suggestions have been made for helping the statemen and bureaucrates in restructuring the reservation policy.

CHAPTER II

Conceptual Formulation

Social stratification in a traditional society is based on caste, ethnic and racial groups. Priority is given to the group rather than to the individual. Insecurity in life makes the individual acknowledge his tie to his family, caste, village and others—in that (descending) order. A man classifies his fellow men in terms of his closeness to, or distance from, his family, caste, etc. Social interactions and political relationships too are dominated by the same consideration.

Caste

In India caste is the most important basis of social categorization. Though caste is believed to have originated in a division of people on the basis of their natural inclinations and occupations, it has turned out in course of time to be hereditary. It has created social groups based on kinship and ethnicity. The hereditary occupations have created vested interests in the form of socio-economic monopolies and have bred an extreme form of exploitation.[1] The caste system is overburdened with considerations of ritualistic purity, and this

1. G. Thimmaiah, "Caste and Class in Karnataka", *Social Scientist* (Trivandrum), February 1983, pp. 31-32.

in its turn has engendered inflexibility, rigidity and feelings of superiority and inferiority.

How does one define caste? Although the social scientists have done much work on the Indian caste system, they have found it difficult to define it. They also differ on meaning of caste. Some scholars hold that caste is a particularly rigid form of class and find its distribution world-wide. Others believe it to be a system peculiar to India and its environs.

Edmund R. Leach[2] considers caste a cultural or a structural phenomenon. Max Weber[3] regards it as a fundamental institution of the Hindus and of the other communities native to India. Louis Dumont[4] looks upon caste as a part of the pan-Indian civilization. Caste is ingrained in Hindu religion, culture and society so much that Dumont calls the Hindu *homo hierarchicus* on the basis of its four characters, such as :

1. hierarchy;
2. commensality;
3. restrictions on marriage; and
4. hereditary occupation.

He rejects all materialistic interpretations of caste in which social relations and norms of individual behaviour change with the economic structure. He explains caste as an ideological or cultural system based on conceptions of purity and pollution derived from the scriptures.

2. Edmund R. Leach, "Introduction : What Should We Mean by Caste ?", in E.R. Leach, ed., *Aspects of Castes in South India, Ceylon and North West Pakistan* (Cambridge England, 1960), pp. 1-6.
3. H.H. Gerth and C.W. Mills, eds., *From Max Weber : Essays in Sociology* (New York, 1958), pp. 398-404.
4. Louis Dumont, *Homo Hierarchicus* (Delhi, 1970), p. 21.

Refuting Dumont's view, Dipankar Gupta[5] argues that caste does not imply any "hierarchy". Castes are, according to him, "discreet" groups, each with an independent ideology of its own. The notion of "hierarchy" is part of the upper-caste ideology.

Risley defines caste as "a collection of families or groups of families bearing a common name, claiming a common descent from a mythical ancestor, human or divine, and professing to follow the same hereditary callinng; and regarded by those who are competent to give an opinion as forming a single homogeneous community".[6] He finds the caste name as generally associated with a specific occupation.

J.H. Hutton questions this defination on the ground that descent from a mythical ancestor is claimed rather by the *qotra*, the internal exogenous division of the endogamous caste, than by the caste as a whole.

Caste is usually defined in terms of cultural characteristics or traits. E.A.H. Blunt[7] characterizes caste in terms of heredity. endogamy and restrictions on commensality.

On the other hand G.S. Ghurye[8] says that caste is strictly

5. Sanjaya Baru, "Marx Centenary : Karl Max and Analysis of Indian Society", *Economic and Political Weekly* (Bombay), 10 December 1988, p. 2108. This periodical is hereinafter cited as *EPW*. (There is a reference in this article to Dipankar Gupta's paper "Continuous Hierarchies and Discrete Castes", which is a critique of Louis Dumont's views on the caste system).

6. J.H. Hutton, *Caste in India : Its Nature, Function, and Origins* (Bombay, 1980), edn. 4, p. 47.

7. E.A.H. Blunt, *Caste System of Northern India with Special Reference to the United Provinces of Agra and Audh* (Delhi, 1969), p. 5.

8. G.S. Ghurye, *Caste, Class and Occupation* (Bombay, 1957), edn 2, pp. 2-17.

limited to the Hindus. He gives six outstanding features of caste system :

1. Segmental division of society;
2. hierarchy;
3. restrictions of feeding and social intercourse;
4. civil and religious disparities and privileges of different sections;
5. lack of unrestricted choice of occupation; and
6. restrictions on marriage.

The caste system is one of the oldest and the most elaborate systems of social organization. The position of an individual in the ritually determined hierarchy defines the entire course of his life. Kingsley Davis gives seven features of the caste system. These are hereditary caste membership, fixed membership of caste, endogamy, commensal restrictions, caste ethnocentrism, common traditional occupation, and hierarchy.[9]

The caste system is based on a religious philosophy which supports a functional division of society. The word used in all the scriptures is "Varna". The "Purushasookta" in the Rigveda says that after the primeval sacrifice, the Brahmana came out of the face of the Purusha or the primaeval person, the Kshatriya sprang from His arms, the Vaishya arose from His thighs, and the Shudra emerged from His feet (Rigveda 10 : 90). The first three, having had their origin in the upper part of the body of the Purusha, acquired the status of "twice-born", the Shudra, having emerged from the lowest part of the Purusha, remained at the lowest rung of the hierarchy.

Castes are local endogamous groups; *Varnas* are categories of an all-India frame of division of the Hindu society. *Varna* means "colour", originally used to differentiate the Aryans

9. Kingsley Davis, *Human Society* (New York, 1967), pp. 377-8.

from the non-Aryans. Later it became popular after the coming of the Portuguese. The Portuguese word "casta" is uscd to denote breed, race and kind.

Five different theories have been propounded about the origin of the caste system. The first is the Hindus religious view of Manu and others; the second is the occupational explanation of Nesfield; the third is the tribal and religious explanation given by Ibbetson; the fourth is the family or gentile explanation offered by Senart; and the last is the racial and hypergamous explanation advanced by Risley.

The British historian H.H.Risley[10] propounds a racist theory of caste. He argues that there were basic racial and physical differences among the various castes. This theory traces the origin of the caste system to the Aryan invasion of India and links it to the process by which the invaders could subordinate the indigenous inhabitants and integrate them as peasants and slaves within a stratified society. This theory fails to explain the taboo on food and marriage. This view has been rejected by Indian intellectuals and politicians, including Dr. B.R. Ambedkar. Social reformers like Jatirao Phule and the leaders of the non-Brahman movement in Tamil Nadu also reject the Aryan theory in which social superiority has been given to the Brahmans.

Recently Morton Klass[11] explains the origin of the caste system in terms of the development of an economic surplus. The caste system, according to him, turned a tribal equalitarian society into an inequality-generating society. He considers caste a part of the social superstructure. When people started a settled life and the cultivation of rice and wheat, the

10. Herbert Risley, *The People of India*, W, Crooke, ed. (Delhi, 1969), edn 2.

11. Morton Klass, *Caste : The Emergence of the South Asian Social System* (Philadephia, Pa, 1980), p. 23.

use of iron provided them with an economic base. This ushered in a division of labour and provided the caste system with an ideological foundation.

Some Marxists attempt to assimilate the broad fourfold *Varna* division to a class system. Paul Rosas[12] explains that the caste system obscures the nature of class. According to him, the feudal forms often conceal the character of India as an Asiatic Society.

M.N. Srinivas like Dumont and Leach considers caste a cultural phenomenon. He refers to four features of caste as embodied in *Varna* :

1. There is a single all-India hierarchy without any variations between one region and another.
2. There are only four *Varnas*. The Harijans, who are literally "beyond the pale", constitute a fifth category—*panchama*.
3. The hierarch is clear.
4. And it is immutable.

He further observes that "caste is unboubtedly an all-India phenomenon in the sense that there are everywhere hereditary, endogamous groups which form a hierarchy, and that each of these groups has a traditional association with one or two occupations".[13]

In the Hindu religious texts, the Brahmans have a superior position. However, in many parts of the country they do not enjoy social superiority; it is the dominant caste which has power, if not social prestige. In the words of M.N. Srinivas :

"For a caste to be 'dominant', it should own a sizeable amount of the arable land locally available, have strength of

12. Paul Rosas, *Caste and Class in India* (Delhi, 1943), p. 159.
13. M.N. Srinivas, *Social Change in Modern India* (New Delhi, 1982), p. 3.

numbers, and occupy a high place in the local hierarchy. When a caste has all the attributes of dominance, it may be said to enjoy decisive dominance."[14]

He further observes that factors affecting dominance such as western education, jobs in the administration and urban sources of income significantly contribute to the prestige and power of a caste group in a village.

Ghanshyam Shah[15] uses the term "caste" as a social group based on dominance and distinguished by economic and educational conditions. To him the caste system has become week and its traditional structure has been eroded. He feels that "caste consciousness" consists in the sense of "we-ness" among the members of a particular caste still persist. He does not consider it a "false consciousness". Upendra Baxi[16] considers caste consciousness as the "we-they" feeling within the same caste group between its "upper" or "dominant" stratum and its "lower" or "subject" stratum.

F.G. Bailey[17] in his study of an Orissa village identifies the warrior caste (Rajput) as the dominant caste. The Rajputs are superior in large areas of Bihar, Rajasthan and Uttar Pradesh. The Nayars are the leading caste on the Malabar coast and the Okkaligas and the Lingayats are the commanding castes in different parts of Karnataka.

14. Ibid., p. 11.
15. (a) Ghanshyam Shah, "Caste, Class and Reservation", *EPW*, 19 January 1985, p. 132 and
    (b) "Caste In Contemporary India" in *Caste, Caste-Conflict and Reservation*, (New Delhi, 1985), p. 1.
16. Upendra Baxi, "Caste, Class and Reservation", *EPW* 9 March 1985, p. 426.
17. F.G. Bailey, *Tribe, Caste, and Nation : A Study of Political Activity and Political Change in Highland Orissa* (Manchester, 1960) pp. 257-63.

The Marxists do not consider caste a primordial reality of Indian society, The caste system is said to conceal the contradictions between the various classes in society and to provide a rationale for exploitation. It justifies the exploitation of an inferior caste by the superior classes on the basis of the myth of natural superiority.[18] The Marxist approach does not deny the relevance of caste. However, as it seeks the origin of the caste system in material history,[19] it believes that the ideology of the caste system is rooted in a sort of ruling class myth. The caste system is by no means an infrastructure; nor does it separate power from status.

To sum up, the caste system is a segmental division of society into endogamous, hereditary descent groups. These groups constitute a hierarchy in which the Brahmans occupy the top position and the Shudras the bottom. Conceptions of purity and impurity are the basis of the hierarchy. Secondly, the different castes all over India have their place in the *Varna* system as well. The hierarchical ranking of castes, however, depends upon the region also. Thirdly, the origin, development, and the present status of castes are related to occupations also. Now the various occupations are open to all castes, and yet mobilization of upper castes towards inferior occupations is limited only in highly paid jobs. The caste and occupational relationship has gone underchange with advent of industrial revolution, spread of education, scarcity of job and change in social value. In shoe making industry people of other than *Chamar* caste also work. So is the case of tailoring, metal industry, trade and business. The traditional caste barrier has gradually become loose. Lastly there are the marriage restrictions among different castes. Even in some castes marriage is strictly limited to the sub-castes. The structural distance

18. Dipankar Gupta, "Caste, Infrastructure and Super-structure : A Critique", *EPW*, 19 December 1981, p. 2093.

19. Gail Omvedt, "Class Struggle or Caste War", *Frontier* (Calcutta), Vol. 11, 30 September 1978, p. 10.

between the various castes is defined in terms of pollution and purity. It is generally believed that a higher caste is always "pure" in relation to a lower caste. In order to retain their higher status the higher caste abstains from certain forms of contact with those belonging to lower castes.[20] All these more or less support the superior position of the upper castes. That is why the protagonists of a reservation policy advocate Caste as a criterion.

Caste and Politics

Caste as a social institution has deep roots in our society. An individual is born, lives and dies within the limits of his caste. Other professional organizations are not strong enough to given him a sense of security, identity, participation and self-interest. He, therefore, stays within the caste system.

According to L.P. Rudolph and S.H. Rubolph[21] the relation of caste to social and political change and to the conduct of Government and politics varies. They feel that seven factors affect the rule of caste :

1. the number and size of other caste actors;
2. regional differences and their effect on the caste profile of particular states;
3. differences in the land and characteristics of relevant political systems;
4. the relative significance of dominant and subject castes and the related propensities towards vertical and horizontal mobilization;
5. changes over time in the social and political environment in which particular castes operate;

20. Srinivas, n. 13, p. 120.
21. L.P. Rudolph and S.H. Rudolph, *The Modernity of Tradition : Political Development in India* (New Delhi, 1969), p. 70.

6. the degree ot self-consciousness and cohesion that characterize particular castes; and
7. the countervailing power of other castes, interest groups and integrative forces, particularly political parties.

V.M. Sirsikar[22] observes that caste plays four roles—personal, social, economic and political. The personal role of caste means, in general, one's sense of belonging to a particular caste, one's belief in the traditional structure, and one's preference for marriage relationships within one's caste. The social role of caste is very important. It operates in a subtle manner through educational, social and charitable institutions. The economic role of caste lies in occupational exclusiveness. It is, however, getting blurred owing to development af education, industrialization and urbanization. The political role of caste is important in a democracy.

Politics is a competitive enterprise. Its purpose is the acquisition of power for the realization of certain goals. Politicians seek to identify and manipulate the various existing and emerging allegiances in order to mobilize support and consolidate their position.[23] In India they have in caste a ready-made instrument for political mobilization.

The caste system provides an institutional basis for tolerance. A caste-based society is a pluralistic cultural universe, with each caste having its own occupation, customs, rituals, traditions, etc. The involvement of castes in politics is a process of mobilization of different sections of society for political purposes.

All political parties reinforce the caste sentiment. In each constituency, during election, they put up candidates belonging

22. V.M. Sirsikar, "Caste and Politics", *Seminar* (New Delhi), June 1965, p. 27.

23. Rajani Kothari, *Politics in India* (Boston, Mass., 1970), p. 4.

to the dominant caste in that constituency. They use caste associations and persuade caste leaders to appeal to their caste fellows to vote for them. Of course people do not vote on the basis of caste alone.[24] This is borne out by the debacle of the Lok Dal and the Janata Party in the 1980 and 1984-85 elections. For political success the various castes enter into alliances and realliances. If any political party gets the support of more than one caste or community, one cannot regard it as a caste or communal party. Its politics cannot be described as caste-based. However, certain castes have dominant position in particular parties. This has become apparent more during last decade.

Caste is the unit of social organization in India. Its role in political system of India can not be denied inspite of adult franchise. To pursue casteless politics in India is, according to Kothari, to look for a sort of politics which has no base in society.[25] He observes that the politicization of caste brings about outward-looking, upward-moving orientations and this results in the phenomenon of multiple memberships and overlapping potentialities. It takes a secular form for organizational purposes through associations, institutions, conferences and federations of castes. Caste is now a variable along with other variables in power politics. It is no longer confined to ritual and religious activity. In this context reference can be made from the objectives of the Kurmi Sabha (an important backward caste in Bihar). The aims of the All India Kurmi Sabha as indicated on the draft constitution in 1909 were as under.[26].

24. The Lok Dal is basically a political party of intermediate castes like Yadava, Jat, Kurmi, Koiri, and others in Bihar, Haryana, Rajasthan, and Uttar Pradesh. It supports the cause of the rural people. It also espouses a policy of reservation for the backward classes. Of course the Jats do not claim to be a backward community.

25. Rajni Kothari, *Caste in Indian Politics* (New Delhi, 1970), p. 20.

26. K.K. Verma, *Changing Role of Caste Associations* (New Delhi, 1981), pp. 48-49.

(i) To foster unity and promote solidarity among the different sections of the community.

(ii) To promote social, material and general welfare of the community.

(iii) To make available educational facilities to Kurmi children by opening schools, hostels and libraries.

(iv) To educate people in new agricultural practices.

(v) To publish periodicals and newspapers to keep the people in touch with the movement.

(vi) To raise funds by subscription, donation, and other means for above objectives.

The aims of the Sabha are by and large secular. It works for the education and social development of the Kurmis. In 1960 they revised the constitution but aims remained the same. The other caste associations' aims and objectives were similarly designed for the welfare of their caste fellow.

Rudolph and Rudolph observe that national associations based on religion, language, ethnicity and locality have not been assimilated or dissolved in modern nations. They point out how such associations play important, even decisive, roles in society.[27] Indeed, the forces that cut across caste in modern pluralist societies have not prevented the formally voluntary structures of such associations from taking on ascriptive features. Bureaucratic organizations can and often do assume familial qualities in ways that approximate the experiences of those living within transformed primary groups. Rudolph and Rudolph are, therefore, convinced that the institution of caste has not hindered the development of democracy based on adult franchise in India. But their observation is far from truth. The selection of candidate, pattern of convassing and voting are based on caste-politics. In a reserve constituency

27. Rudolph and Rudolph, n. 21, pp. 64-65.

such caste sentiment is strong. The distribution of ticket by political parties also gives caste-consideration. Thus, in India democracy bears caste-colour. Naturally the caste-politics generates caste rigidity. Politics in this country has only resulted in making the bond or caste more rigid.

The social basis of a political party can be built on the basis of its ideology and organization. Political parties in India. except the Communist parties, are not clear as to their ideologies. The Socialist parties and the Congress have from time to time short-term goals, policies and tactics to win elections. When they are not able to win their voters through ideological and problem-oriented politics, they adopt caste politics.

Sachchidanand observes that Political behaviour, like any other aspect of human behaviour, takes place in a particular socio-cultural *milieu.* It is affected by social structure, economic development and historical factors. Family, kinship and neighbourhood still determine the choice of an alternative in most aspects of life.[28] He further observes that primordial loyalties like caste, tribe, region, religion, etc. play a vital role in elections. They satisfy the aspiration of the people for special mobility and also meet their demand for political participation. He regards political behaviour in India as determined by the traditional social order, which is characterized, among other things, by the caste system.[29]

The main motive of Indian politics is not to change the existing exploitative social and political structures but to capture political power anyhow. This is the motive of Indian political parties from left to right. Power politics in India is limited only in the hands of dominant social groups of higher

28. Sachchidanand, *The Harijan Elite* (New Delhi, 1977), pp. 163-164.
29. D.L. Sheth, "Caste and Politics ', in Rasheeduddin Khan and others, eds., *Political Dynamics* (New Delhi, 1976), p. 5.

echelon and they are not allowing implementation of any progressive measures on social or economic reforms. The objective in forming a political party is to capture power. But then no political party can overlook its responsibility towards programmes for betterment of the socio-politico-economic conditions of the country. Political parties must declare its commitments and its ideological orientation, towards facing socio-economic problem in true sense. This is what we lack in India. The role of caste has been on an increase since 1967. Paul Brass[30] and Rudolph and Rudolph speak of a politics of vertical mobilization, faction and personalism by the upper castes which leads to the horizontal mobilization of the lower castes, which numerically pose a threat to the power elites of the upper castes. However, in recent decades with strengthening of political consciousness amongst Scheduled Castes, Scheduled Tribes and backward castes the political picture has changed. Formation of Lok Dal and regional political parties, the political pressure and dominance have put on new look. These caste-groups have become strong enough to demand and snatch due share. Indian politics can no longer ignore emerging lower castes political strengh.

Although castes have been playing an important role in the Indian political system, they have not demanded separate political identities.[31] As parts of a larger society, they are symbolically related to one another and are participants in Hindu culture. This relationship is integrated and legitimized when they come to mobilize themselves politically. They are concerned with the distribution of values, status and resources within a political system, not with their realization.[32] They affect Indian political life more at the State and local levels than at the national level.

30. Paul R. Brass, *Language, Religion and Politics in North India* (New Delhi, 1975), p. 142.
31. Rudolph and Rudolph, n, 21, p. 68,
32. Ibid., p. 69,

In early 1960s some social scientists had observed

1. that caste was only one of several factors at work in politics;
2. that caste was gradually losing its influence from the village level to the constituency, state, and national levels of politics; and
3. that politics was using caste as a means of articulation and even changing it in the process.[33] They also emphasized on integrative and democratic role of caste.

Indian politics took a turn in general election of 1967. Caste-based politics established its grip in North India with the emergence of politicians belonging to the intermediate castes. Long back in South India—as, for example in Tamil Nadu—caste politics had taken deep root.

Political participation in India earlier was only limited to a few upper castes. The Britishers introduced Western education, established speedier means of communication, and extended franchise to cover ever-increasing number of people in India. The leadership provided by lower castes during national movement was the proof of increasing participation by these castes in politics. The rate of participation increased by manyfold after independence. After independence the inter. mediate castes started competing for political power. This increased the number of participants. Earlier power politics was limited to a few upper castes; now the intermediate castes are also in the picture. The caste system is today responding to the processes of representational politics. The caste structures have grown stronger under the impact of adult franchise.

The introduction of adult franchise and *panchayati raj* (local self-government at the village, tehsil, and districal levels)

33. Kothari, n. 23, pp. 234-235.

has, since independence, resulted in the development of a new sense of self-respect and power among the lower castes, particularly the Harijans, who have seats reserved for them in all elected bodies from the village to the Union Parliament. Further, power has passed in many parts of rural India into the hands of the numerically large land-owning peasant castes; it is likely to remain there for some time except in villages where Harijans are numerically strong and are also taking advantage of the new educational and other opportunities recently made available to them.[34] To conclude, they are getting the benefits of the politicization of caste which in return has helped in their upward mobility.

Social Structure in Bihar

Bihar is a multi-ethnic society. It consists of Hindus, Muslims, Christians and others. Caste system is basically a phenomena of Hindu social system. The exact number of castes and sub-castes is not known. Bihar has four major caste categories among Hindus :

1. upper castes—4;
2. intermediate or backward castes—128;
3. Scheduled Castes (Harijans)—140; and
4. Scheduled Tribes—29.

Bihar's Muslims are also divided into different castes. They follow the rule of caste endogamy. Rules regarding commensality vary. But this does not have the same implications as in the case of the Hindus. The concept of pollution is not in vogue among them. Important among the Muslim castes are Pathans, Sheiks, Saiyyads, Ansaris and Kunjaras. These asstes are classified in three main groups, viz Ashraf, Ajlaf, and Arzal.[35]

34. Srinivas, no. 13, p. 11.
35. R.R. Diwakar, ed., *Bihar Through The Ages* (Bombay, 1959), p. 696.

Among the upper castes, the Brahmans, the Rajputs, the Bhumihars and the Kayasthas are equally important in politics. Members of all these four upper castes possess landed property. The new avenues of job and education are also mostly in the hands of these upper castes.

TABLE 1

Major Caste Groups in Bihar

(1931 for Upper and Backward Castes and 1981 for S.C., S.T. and Muslim)

	Caste	*Percentage of Total Population*	
Upper Castes	Brahman	4.7	
	Bhumihar	2.9	
	Rajput	4.2	
	Kayastha	1.2	
		Sub-Total—	13.0
Upper Backwards	Bania	0.6	
	Yadev	11.0	
	Kurmi	3.6	
	Koeri	4.1	
		Sub-Total—	19.3
Lower Backwards	Barhi	1.0	
	Dhannk	1.8	
	Hajjam	1.4	
	Kahar	1.7	
	Kandu	1.6	
	Kumhar	1.3	

Lohar	1.3	
Mullah	1.5	
Tatwa	1.6	
Teli	2.8	
Others	16.0	
Sub-Total		32.0
Scheduled Castes		14.4
Scheduled Tribes		9.1
Muslims		12.5
Grand Total :		100.0

Source : Harry W. Blair, "Rising Kulaks and Backward Classes in Bihar", *EPW*., 12 January 1980, p. 64; and 1981 Census Series 4.

The upper castes are approximately 13 per cent of the total population of Bihar. They are, however, dominant in all walks of life. Now they are moving towards urban areas, in search of better opportunities.

In rural area the upper castes place is being taken by some of the newly prosperous backward castes like Yadava, Kurmi, and Koiri. They were clean castes and earlier assigned a service relationship with the upper castes. Along with Bania they constitute 19.3 per cant population of the Bihar. The Banias are forward in respect of all variables of social and political development, they claim themselves to be backward. Previously they were money-lenders and even now they are in control of trade and commerce in Bihar.

The population of the more backward castes is 32 per ccnt in Bihar. Their share in land, commerce and Government employment is negligible. In context of ritual status they are clean castes and distinguished from untouchables, but in the field of education and government job are far behind them.

A large number of Harijans in Bihar belong to the old professional castes. Among them the Chamars, the Dushadhs, and the Dhobis have made perceptible progress in educational and other fields. The political privilege given to them is mostly enjoyed by the first two—viz the Chamars and the Dushadhs. Their problem is basically economic and cultural. They are mostly landless labourers in rural areas.

In this study tribes have been mentioned as a caste category although they are not so. There are about 29 tribal groups in Bihar. The Santhals, the Mundas, the Uraons and the Hoes have been benefited somewhat from Government-sponsored measures and the work of Christian missionaries. They are concentrated in the Chotanagpur Plateau, which contains abundant mineral resources and extensive forests. The soil, however, is not fertile. Although a large number of heavy industries have been set up in the area, the beneficiaries are mostly outsiders. The tribes had once demanded a separate State for themselves under the banner of the Jharkhand Party. In 1963, however, the Jharkhand Party merged in the Congress Party. Discontentment still persists among them as they are among the most backward people. However, the fast industrialisation of Chotanagpur areas has changed the situation. The job opportunities have increased. Income level has gone up. Education has changed their outlook and quality of life. The backwardness is gradually decreasing.

As for the backward castes, they have improved their position during the last thirty-five years. They were once just tenants; now they are small or middle farmers, thanks to the abolition of the *zamindari* system. Forty percent of the Yadavas, the Kurmis and the Koiris are supposed to be landless labourers or artisans; 25 per cent of them are small peasants; another

25 per cent of them are medium peasants; and the rest are rich peasants and landlords.[36]

Bihar's social structure is in a state of flux. The privileged position of the upper castes has been challenged by the emerging backward castes. These backward castes have overtaken the upper castes in a few districts of Bihar and are progressing further by means of hard work. A few backward castes like Yadavas, Kurmis and Koiris have been rich from the beginning. They are living in districts of Patna, Nalanda, Madhepura and Monghyr. They are educated and well placed in services. The economic conditions of the more backward classes, as well as the Scheduled Castes and the Scheduled Tribes, are, however, pitiable.

Economic Structure in Bihar

Physiographically, Bihar is divided into two distinct units :

1. the vast alluvial breadth of the Middle Ganga Plain; and
2. the plateau of Bhotanagpur, which is rich in mineral resources.

Political Geography

The Ganga Plain is divided by the River Ganga into two parts—the North Bihar Plain and the South Bihar Plain. The North Bihar Plain covers an area of 56,320 square kilometres; and the South Bihar Plain, an area of 33,280 square kilometres. The Chotanagpur Plateau covers about 46 per cent of the total area but only 25 cent of the total population of the State. North Bihar is chronically affected by floods. It does not

36. Arun Sinha, "The Caste Factor in Bihar", *Indian Express* (New Delhi), 12 January 1979.

have proper irrigation facilities. South Bihar is free from flood devastation and has good irrigation works.

The State is not self-sufficient in foodgrains. The main drawback is lack of adequate irrigational facilities, besides infertile soil and occasional droughts and floods. This has led to agricultural stagnation. The absence of food and an agricultural raw material surplus are also an important barrier to rapid industrial growth. That is why about 80 per cent of the people are engaged in agricultural activity. Only 20 per cent are engaged in household industries and other works.

TABLE 2

Occupational Pattern in Bihar, 1981

(In Terms of Percentage)

Category	*Persons*	*Men*	*Women*
Cultivators	43.47	46.71	25.54
Agricultural labourers	35.50	30.65	63.33
Household industries	02.38	02.32	02.76
Other wokers	18.55	20.32	08.37

Source : *Census of India*, 1981, Series 4, Bihar. p. xii.

Density of Population

The population of Bihar in March 1981 was 69,823,154 (which was 10.21 per cent of the national population).[37] The density of population was 402 persons per square kilometre. Bihar ranks third among the States after Kerala and West Bengal in respect of density of population. The vast alluvial belt of the Middle Ganga Plain is very densely populated. The

37. *Census of India*, 1981, Series 4, Bihar, p. 30.

highest density is to be found in Patna 947 per square kilometre; the lowest density is in Palamu with 150 per square kilometre. The hilly region of the Chotanagpur Plateau is, with the exception of Dhanbad, an area of low population density. The density of population in Dhanbad is 702 persons per square kilometre.

Literacy in Bihar

By literacy one means the ability to read and write with understanding in any language. According to the 1981 Census, the all-India literacy average was 34.8 per cent (excluding Jammu and Kashmir and Assam); the average for Bihar was 26.01 per cent. This reflects low level of educational development in the State.

Political Economy

Bihar is basically an agrarian society, where 85 percent of the people depend for their livelihood on land.[38] Agriculture is not mechanized. Even after the Green Revolution capitalist farming has not improved. In industrial development North Bihar has a few sick sugar and jute factories and the industrial complex of Barauni; South Bihar is in the slow process of industrial development. Only the Chotanagpur belt, which accounts for 40 per cent of the mineral resources of India, has an industrial complex. That is not sufficient for a big and backward State like Bihar. Indeed it has had little impact on the overall economy of the State.

There was very little industrialization in Bihar during British rule. There are several reasons why Bihar was industrially backward during the British days. First, Bihar has no coastline and hence no port or harbour for transporting the raw

38. Kedarnath Prasad, *The Economics of a Backward Region in a Backward Economy : A Case Study of Bihar in Relation to Other States of India*, Vol. I (Calcutta, 1967), pp. 146-216.

materials that the British needed for their industries. It was but an appendage of the Bengal Presidency with its capital in Calcutta. Second, Bihar was foremost in the rebellion against British rule in 1857. The Biharis fought against the Birtish under the leadership of Kunwar Singh, a *Zamindar* of Jagdishpur. The Britishers, therefore, took a vindictive line towards Bihar and favourald Bengal at the expense of Bihar. The Bengalis were preferred for appointment in all Government-owned establishments. People of Bihar origin were cold-shouldered. Third, Bihar had no indigenous capitalist class. Some of the old *zamindars*, who were inclined to invest in industry, were not able to compete with the big *bourgeoisie*.

Bihar witnessed the worst of the exploitative aspect of imperialism. It was from the beginning kept insulated from the industrial benefits of contact with the West.[39] In contrast Bengal, Maharashtra and Tamil Nadu were fortunate enough to receive the benefits of modern scientific education and the growth of a metropolitan culture to some extent, and this led to a ferment socially and culturally.

Accumulation of wealth is very important for capitalist development. The feudal set-up in Bihar denied the needed surplus to farmers.[40] Even the petty *bourgeoisie* in Bihar belonged to other provinces. Naturally they were disinclined to invest their profits in Bihar. Besides, people spent lavishly on marriages and other ceremonies. They squandered all the liquid cash they had on unproductive activities and enterprises. No wonder that the accumulation of wealth needed for industrialization and capitalist development never occurred.

Bihar, North Bihar in particular, is one of the poorest, most backward and most feudal regions in India. In terms of social

39. Arvind N. Das, "Bihar Under the Raj : Roots of Under-Development", *Times of India* (New Delhi), 30 October 1985.
40. Pradhan H. Prasad, "Dynamics of Growth in Rural Bihar", *Times of India*, 17 March, 1981.

indices like per capita income, literacy, infant mortality, employment, agricultural productivity, status of women, etc., Bihar ranks almost at the bottom of the scale from the all-India point of view. In North Bihar 94.8 per cent of the people live in rural areas. And yet there is landlordism, exploitative share-cropping and oral leases in 40 per cent of the cultivated area. Semi-feudal relations in the countryside are a bar to agricultural development. The landlords and the rich peasants have found ways of circumventing the laws relating to land-ceiling, share-cropping and agricultural wages. This has compelled a large umber of landless workers to look for work as manual labourers in Bengal, Assam, Punjab, Haryana and other parts of the country.

Bihar's economic backwardness is all the more regrettable when one knows that it has the potential to become the Ruhr of India. It has most of the copper deposits of the country. It has 98 per cent of the bauxite and 24 per cent of the iron-ore deposits. It is one of the main producers of coal. Besides Manganese, uranium, sulphur, phosphorus and lead are found in abundant quantities. Even then only 6 per cent of the people of Bihar are industrially employed.[41] The figure for the other States is 20 per cent.

Caste and Politics in Bihar

Caste politics has deep roots in Bihar. It began with the movement for the partition of Bihar from Bengal. When the English-educated Kayasthas became leaders of the freedom movement in the 1920s,[42] they were challenged by the land-owning, numerically stronger Bhumihars in different spheres. Subsequently, the Brahmans and the Rajputs also joined the

41. B.G. Verghese, "Kusi Kranti—I : Land Reforms in Bihar", *The Statesman* (New Delhi), 18 September 1977.
42. R.C. Prasad, "Educational Development (in Bihar)", *Seminar*, July 1968, pp. 27-29.

race. Till 1967 these four castes dominated the political scene. In 1967 a number of backward castes or *kulaks* emerged. These castes included the Yadava, Kurmi, Koiri and Bania castes. The Dushadh and Chamar castes among the Harijans are also politically conscious and are in the race for political power.

The emergence of the backward castes on the political scene in Bihar was due to three reasons. First, the leaders of the upper castes felt impelled to align themselves with the politicians of the backward castes because of the intense rivalry among them. For example, there was keen political rivalry between the land-owning dominant castes, the Rajputs and the Bhumihars. Both had played an active role in the freedom movement. In fact, till the 1950s they were both in the limelight of State politics. However, owing to their mutual rivalry, the Brahmans and the Kayasthas found it possible to wrest the leadership from them.

Second, the leaders of the Brahman and Kayastha castes, whenever weak, sought to use the backward castes to counterbalance the dominance of the Rajputs and the Bhumihars.

Third, the economic and educational development of certain backward castes like the Yadava, Kurmi, Koiri, and Bania castes made them conscious of their rights and of their numerical superiority.

Bihar is a highly cleavaged society with multiple lines of linguistic, religious and caste divisions. The upper castes and some of the other castes like the Yadava, Kurmi and Koiri castes are politically well mobilized. They have been well represented in the Legislative Assembly over the years. (See Table 3)

The politics of Bihar during 1967-72 centred round the political domination of the backward castes. During this period the State had four Chief Ministers (Satish kumar Singh, B. P.

Mandal, Daroga Rai and Karpoori Thakur) from the backward castes. The victory of the Congress Party in 1972 arrested this trend. The political domination of the upper castes under the leadership of the Brahmans returned. The Chief Minister and the Speaker of the Vidhan Sabha were both Brahmans. This frustrated the backward castes and even some of the upper castes.

The political domination of the Kayasthas started declining with the emergence of the Bhumihars and the Rajputs during the early 1930s. Some Kayasthas like Dr. Rajendra Prasad and Jayaprakash Narayan were leaders of national fame. At the State level K.B. Sahay was a striking success. The Coalition Government of five opposition parties in 1967 was led by Mahamaya Prasad Sinha, a Kayastha leader, who had newly formed a political party called the Jana Kranti Dal. Since then no Kayastha politician has achieved political eminence worth mentioning in Bihar. Even the number of legislators from this caste has declined. (See Table 3).

Some political scientists, who have written on caste politics in Bihar during the 1960s, say that during the Chief Ministership of S.K. Sinha, the backward castes forged an alliance with the Bhumihars. They observed that when B.N. Jha was Chief Minister, the same castes entered into an understanding with the Brahmans. At the time of forming a government however, the leaders neglected these castes.

Political power in Bihar was for long the of the privilege of the upper castes. They gained from their superior ritual status and their economic prosperity. The Chief Ministers of Bihar, with the exception of Bhola Prasad Shastri, Karpoori Thakur and Ram Sundar Das, were all from zamindar families. The two Harijan Chief Ministers, viz Bhola Prasad Shastri and Ram Sundar Das, were never able to control the Government independently. They were just playthings in the hands of the upper-caste politicians, only Karpoori Thakur, who belonged

TABLE 3

Caste Composition of the Bihar Legislative Assembly
(General Seats), 1962-1980

(In Terms of Percentage)

Caste	*1962*	*1967*	*1969*	*1975*	*1977*	*1980*	*General population (Non-Scheduled Castes and Tribes population)*
1	2	3	4	5	6	7	8
Brahman	17.20	13.20	12.30	18.30	07.60	14.80	06.00
Bhumihar	12.60	14.80	14.80	14.70	14.80	12.00	03.60
Rajput	23.38	22.20	23.50	19.80	21.70	16.80	05.30
Kayastha	05.40	04.90	03.30	02.00	04.40	02.80	01.60
Total Upper Castes	59.00	55.10	53.90	54.80	48.60	46.42	16.50

1	2	3	4	5	6	7	8
Bania	03.30	05.50	06.20	04.60	03.20	06.00	00.80
Yadava	11.70	15.20	18.50	11.70	20.50	18.40	13.80
Kurmi	07.10	05.30	03.30	05.60	04.80	07.20	04.50
Koiri	06.70	05.80	04.10	05.60	06.40	06.00	05.20
Total upper backward castes	28.80	31.60	32.10	27.50	34.90	37.60	24.30
Lower backward castes	01.70	02.90	02.50	02.00	03.60	02.00	40.30
Total backward castes	30.50	34.50	34.60	29.50	38.50	39.60	64.60
Muslims	08.80	07.40	07.80	13.20	10.00	11.50	15.80
Bengalis	01.07	02.90	03.70	02.50	02.80	02.40	03.10

Contd.

1	2	3	4	5	6	7	8
Total	100.00	100.00	100.00	100.00	100.00	100.00	100.00
	242	243	242	197	242	243	

Note : Members of the Scheduled Castes and the Scheduled Tribes are excluded as they are represented in proportion to their population through reserved seats.

Source : W.H. Blair, "Rising Kulak and Backward Castes in Bihar, Social Change in the late 1970s", *Economic and Political Weekly* (Bombay), 12 January 1980, p. 67. Additional data were collected by means of interviews with legislators.

to a backward caste (viz the Hajam caste), was able to lead the Government in a real sense. Even he was sometimes exploited by the leaders of the backward castes on account of his dependence upon them.

Of all backward castes, the Yadavas were well entrenched both in the Congress and in the opposition parties, particularly in the Samyukta Socialist Party (SSP). The powerful Yadava Congressman, Ram Lakhan Singh Yadav, was a ring leader in deciding the leadership of the Congress Party in the 1960s. The Yadavas have given two Chief Ministers of Bihar, B. P. Mandal and Daroga Rai. They headed coalition Governments in Bihar during 1968-70. Chief Ministers belonging to the upper castes used to depend upon them for support. Their support was crucial for the coalition Government headed by Karpoori Thakur in 1970-71.

The caste composition of population and legislators in Bihar shows that no single caste has been in majority. The upper castes in legislature had been on marginal line and the backward castes in population. The inter-caste differences between upper castes rarely allowed them to form the Government and rule the state without support of others. The support of other castes was a must for stable Government. Under such political situation the exchange of support between upper and lower castes was a necessary corolary. This. is also necessary for justifying democracy. In democracy proper representation of different groups/classes/castes has been accepted. This too establishes mutual support of castes whichever the political party may form the Government.

The upper backward castes have always had the lion's share of the seats in the State Legislative Assembly. Although the combined population of these castes in Bihar is only 18.8 per cent of the total population, the legislators belonging to them accounted for about 25 per cent of the seats in the Legislative Assemble during the period 1962-80. The backward castes emerged as a political force first in 1967. Their percentage in the Legislative Assembly increased to 25.9 per cent. High party posts in the different political parties went to them. Political conflict in Bihar is now between the traditional forward castes (the Brahmans, the Rajputs, the Bhumihars, and the Kayasthas) and the neo-forward castes (upper backward castes).[43]

The lower backward castes are the most neglected among the social groups of Bihar. They are next only to the Scheduled Castes and the Scheduled Tribes in terms of education, income and social status. Poverty and poor social status make it easy for the powerful upper backward castes to dominate. Thus, even among the backward castes the power and resources are not properly distributed.

It may be noted here that although the backward castes were numerically stronger than all the upper castes put together, yet they were not able to make any headway earlier owing to a consensus among the upper castes with regard to keeping the political leadership confined to themselves and the wide illiteracy and ignorance amongst the backward classes.

Social Class

The division of society into classes ranged in a hierarchy on the basis of wealth, prestige and power is an almost universal feature of social structure and has attracted the attention of social theorists and philosophers everywhere. Different interpre-

43. The term "neo-forward" is used for the upper backward castes. In Bihar they are grouped together as Yadava, Kurmi, Koiri and Bania. The term "forward" in popular parlance applies to the four so-called upper castes. They are forward in point of social status, education, economic means, political domination, and control over the bureaucracy. The upper backward castes are moving fast in this direction. That is why the term "neo-forward" is used for them.

tation of this social feature have been advanced. Marx[44] takes the economic determinist view. Max Weber[45] emphasizes human behaviour and values, attitudes and beliefs in relation to class.

The concept of class is to a large extent a contribution of Karl Marx. He speaks of the "capitalist class" and the working class", not on the basis of any occupational division of the people but on the basis of control of means of production and production relations. He also mentions a number of other classes like landlords, the petty bourgeoisie, etc. The basis of his whole stratification is ownership of property.

A class (the economically constituted class) in itself does not lead automatically to the class-for-itself (a self-conscious class). Marx does not define class-in-itself and class-for-itself. He stresses that the formation of a class depends considerably on class struggle. A class-in-itself becomes a class-for-itself only when economic differentiation leads to the emergence of antagonistic interests.

Bipan Chandra[46] argues that while the bourgeoisie in India has made the transition from being a class-in-itself to being a "class-for-itself", the working class has not made such a transition. He quotes the instance of several working-class areas in the country voting for parties of the ruling class rather than for a working-class party.

In the Marxian view, there is class division in all forms of society. It is only in a tribal society, where there is no surplus production and no private property, that class is not to be found.

44. Ralf Dahrendorf, *Class and Class Conflict in Industrial Society* (Berkeley, Calif., 1959), pp. 3ff.
45. Max Weber, "Class, Status and Party", in C.S. Helles, ed., *Structural Social Inequality : Readers in Comparative Social Stratification* (New York, 1969), p. 25.
46. Baru, n. 5, p. 2104.

Surplus production generates the class which lives on the produce of others' labours.

Indian society is not only divided into classes but also stratified into hierarchically ordered castes. Marx does recognize the role of caste in Indian society, but he believes that it would wither away with the development of industries.

Those, who are able to gain control of the means of production which is generally land in pre-capitalist societies, constitute the dominant or ruling class both economically and politically. Class relations for Marx are, thus, necessarily exploitative and imply division of interests between the ruling and subordinate classes.[47] In short, all Marxist treatments of class revolve round concepts like exploitation, social relations of production, mode of production, property relations and so on.[48]

Weber suggests a "multidimensional" model. He acknowledges the importance of economic factors in any system of stratification, but claims that political power is another, independent determinant which produces its own hierarchical order. A third determinant is "social prestige" or "honour", which consists in the ranking of a man according to the amount of "esteem" in which is held as member of a traditional aristocracy, or in terms of occupation, education, and living standards.[49]

Weber's notion of status refers to the way people are ranked in terms of the esteem in which society holds them. Status

47. Anthony Giddens and David Held, eds, *Classes, Power and Conflict : Classical and Contemporary Debates* (London, 1982), p. 4.
48. Erik Odin Wright, "The American Class Structure", *American Sociological Review* (Bloomington, Ind.), December 1982, p. 710.
49. Raja Jayaraman, *Caste and Class Dynamics of Inequality in Indian Society* (Delhi, 1981), p. 20,

may be achieved through improvements in education, occupation and income or ascribed as in the caste system through birth.

Inter-class conflict, however, is often superimposed on the traditional social hierarchy so that castes with a high social status may be found in control of economic resources, and those with a low social status may be victims of economic deprivation.

Class Structure in Bihar

Bihar is predominantly a rural society. It has 67,546 villages and 220 towns.[50] The growth of cities has been slow.

Just about 15 per cent of the people live in the cities. Most of these cities are of administrative, religious, and educational importance. It is only in South Bihar that there are a few cities of industrial importance.

The Rural Picture

When one talks about the class structure in Bihar, he has to study it differently for rural and urban areas. In rural Bihar land is still the basic source of livelihood. One finds different types of classes with different characteristics in rural and urban areas. Andre Beteille divides the rural population of India into four or five main socio-economic groups according to their position in the system of production.[51] In Bengal these are the

50. In a town, by definition :
    (1) the population is not less than 5.000;
    (2) density of population is not less than 1,000 persons per square mile; and
    (3) at least three-fourths of the adult male population is engaged in non-agricultural pursuits. See *Census of India*, 1971, Series-4, Bihar, Part VI-A, p. 28.
51. Andre Beitelle, *Studies in Agrarian Social Structure* (Delhi, 1974), p. 126.

zamindars, the *jotedars* (most often big tenants), the *bargadars* (share-croppers), and the *khetimajdurs*. Then, of course, there are the merchants and artisans. In rural Bihar, Max Harcourt distinguishes *ashraf* (landlords), *bakal* (village shopkeepers), *pawania* (artisans), *jatiya* (small peasants directly cultivating their land), and a class of low castes at the local level.[52]

S.C. Gupta[53] classifies farmers into three groups on the basis of the types of labour employed, use of modern agro-technology, surplus production and land-holdings. The first group consists of capitalist farmers, who employ wage labour, invest capital, and use technical skill so as to maximize production and generate a large surplus for the market. The second consists of market-oriented, large-family farmers who depend mostly on family labour and who also employ hired labourers. They also use technical skill for maximum productivity and surplus production. They have ten to twenty acres of land. The last group in the hierarchy of farmers is comprised of small holders of land with a small surplus production. They depend basically on family labour and make a small profit out of agricultural production.

The actual effect of social class varies from one culture to another. What constitute a class in one place may not do so in another. Are Indian farmers, for example, a class distinct from business men and workers ? Or are farmers and business men together members of a class distinct from workers ? In this context many problems are judged, not in terms of class, but in terms of interests.

Let us take, for instance, the small and marginal farmers in Bihar. There are also agricultural labourers who possess

52. Max Harcourt, "Kisan Populism and Revolution in Rural India, in D.A. Low, ed., *Congress and the Raj* (Colombia, South Asia Books, 1977), p. 324.

53. S.C. Gupta, "Structural Causes of the Economic Crisis", *EPW*, 18 January 1975, p. 84.

little or no land. Besides, there are unskilled manual labourers. Most of these are poor and socially and educationally backward. And yet, they all have specific roles, functions and positions within the system as casual, unskilled labourers, as tenants, as share-croppers, as artisans, etc. Any attempt to organize them on a class basis would affect not only the rural poor but also the rural rich, who are their landlords, their money-lenders, their employers, etc. It would threaten the established patterns of privilege and exploitation.[54]

If one starts right from the bottom, he finds that there is a class of landless workers. They sell their labour to landlords and village headmen just to ensure their own survival. Some of them are bonded labourers. Most of them are from the Scheduled Castes and the Scheduled Tribes and the backward castes. The number of those belonging to the upper castes among them is negligible. They engage in their respective skilled or unskilled occupation. They have not added to their land-holdings. They are today where they have always been.

Above the class of landless labourers, there is the class of share-croppers. They possess some land, some capital and instruments of production such as fertilizer, ploughs, cattle, seed, etc. They sometimes work as labourers in fields belonging to others also.

There is a third category of people in rural Bihar, viz marginal farmers. They usually possess not more than five acres of land. They have sufficient surplus labour and tools of production. They also work as share-croppers. They mainly employ what is called family labour on their own farms. They are essentially self-producers without hired labour. Occasionally they hire labour to work on their behalf. They

54. P.C. Joshi, "Organising Rural Poor : Some Basic Issues", *Mainstream* (New Delhi), 12 August 1978, p. 7.

have considerable control over labour power as occasional employers of hired labour. Because they have a little land, they are regarded as land-owners, and because they cultivate others' lands they are regarded as tenants. Economically they depend upon the assistance of the rich and middle farmers. They are self-sufficient around the bare subsistence level.

And then there are farmers, who possess between five to ten acres of land and the instruments of production. As they cannot themselves cultivate all the land they possess they employ labourers in their fields. However, they take part in agricultural activities. They do not cullivate lands belonging to others. They secure income from agricultural activities. They cooperate with the rich peasants and do not perceive their interests and the interests of the rich peasants as antagonistic.

The rich peasants are an emerging prosperous class with substantial political and social influence. They get most of the necessary developmental resources from the Government. They have about twenty acres of land. They carry on mechanized farming and are, therefore, able to produce a large surplus for the market. They usually rent out some land. Although they heavily depend upon hired labourers they do supervisory work on their farms. They are the neo-rich. The emergence of the rich peasants has been rather slow in Bihar owing to lack of a large urban market for rural produce.

The landlords are a class by themselves in rural areas. They no longer have their old glamour and are fast losing to the rich peasants. They have more than twenty acres of land. They are getting great surplus production solely by hired labour. Large number of them are shifting to urban areas as bureaucrats, technocrats, and professional people. Middle-class tenants, who were cultivating their land on their behalf in other years, have bought their lands from them. They were once the worst exploiters of the rural masses.

The rural areas have other classes as well. The artisan class or the old *jajamani* system is one of them. The rural artisan class is identifiable in terms of skill. Members of this class pursue their occupations as village artisans and are governed by the *jajamani* relationship. Large numbers of them have shifted to urban areas—as barbars, cobblers, goldsmiths, sweepers, etc.

The oldest *jajamani* system in rural areas is of Brahamans. They have certain families or village or area—the main souace of income. This syatem is still strong.

The *jajamani* system for barbars, goldsmith, cobblers and sweepers has been weakened. The barbars have set up *Saloons* and have stopped serving from house to house. Cobblers have set up small stalls or shifted to urban areas or they sit on road side. The movement to stop man carrying night-soil and construction of latrines of modern designs have changed their job. The goldsmiths are still in rural areas but fast changing tastes has shifted the demand to urban markets—breaking the *jajamani* system. Thus, the *jajamani* system has been weakened, if not completely broken.

Another class is that of money-lenders. They are generally rich peasants or village shopkeepers. Woman belonging to the families of the rich peasants also use their small savings to lend money. Village shopkeepers work as intermediaries between the village people and the big businessmen of the cities or of suburban areas at the time of the harvesting of crops. Some of them play a dual role. For example, the village goldsmith is an artisan by occupation, but he also works as a money-lender.

In rural areas a class conflict is developing between the rich peasants and the landless laburers over such questions as wages and land distribution.[55] It is held that the frequent

55. Arun Sinha, "Class War in Bhojpur", *EPW*, 7 January 1978, p. 10.

atrocities on the Harijans are nothing but a manifestation of the class conflict between the rich peasants and the lendless workers.

The Urban Picture

In urban areas there is a large working class. In the industrial sectors of society there has emerged a new class which may be termed as an urban working class. This class includes unskilled industrial workers, fourth-grade employees in Government and semi-Government offices, and employees in private establishments. They are participating in the production process and by and large doing manual labour. They receive very low salaries and live in slums in misery.

The urban situation is much more complex than the rural. Fast changing life has led them to form organizations. They are grouped as organized and unorganized or informal sector. The relationship between urban workers and their employers is impersonal and also contractual. If and when a man gets employment, his activity is contractual and a bit constant. One thing that is common to all urban workers is that they live by selling their labour. The chief difference is that those in the unorganized or informal sectors are unprotceted unlike those in the organized sector.[56]

And then, a little above them, there is the lower middle class consisting of clerks, skilled, and primary school teachers. They are occupying lower and middle level position in their place of work. The middle-middle class consists of the supervisory staff in Government and semi-Government offices and industrial units. They are well educated and have comparatively low sources of income. Next above is the upper middle

56. I.P. Desai, "Should 'Caste' be the Basis for Recognising Backwardness ?", *EPW*, 14 July 1984, p. 1111.

class which is made up of technocrats, bureaucrats, professors, lawyers, and other intermediate white-collared gentry. They are well-to-do; they earn comparatively good salaries. They have considerable influence over the administrative, judicial, academic and political fields of the State. They are also known as intelligentsia due to high education and administrative capabilities. They are doing mental intellectual work along with supervising functions.

The upper and upper upper classes in Bihar are comparatively small. The upper class includes big businessmen and senior bureaucrats; the upper-upper class is made up of big industralists and the *zamindars*. The *zamindars* are certainly Bihari in origin, but most of the industrial *bourgeoisie* are from Gujarat, Rajasthan and the Punjab. The industrial *bourgeoisie* are not active in State politics. Their interests are protected by the various political parties. The occupants of the highest position in bureaucracy, a few Members of Parliament and State Legislative Assembly are part of ruling class and also considered as *bourgeoisie.*

A new class has recently emerged in Bihar. It is a class composed of Government contractors and senior bureaucrats and technocrats. Some landlords and rich peasants may also be included in this class. They have given up their old feudal ways and have invested their income in small-scale industries, buses and cinema houses. They enjoy economic and political dominance. They may be considered as ruling class of Bihar.

The *bourgeoisie* own and control the means of production. They are big landlords and entrepreneurs. They exploit the working class and influence their cultural and intellectual life in subtle ways. The word "exploited" has been used because the working class is paid less than the value it produces. However, this has gradually been changed by adopting policy of bonus, a share in production. It creates surplus value for the benefit of the capitalist class. Some workers are engaged in distribution or commerce. Their scales of remuneration are settled by haggling. Such workers too are petty *bourgeoisie* in Marxist terminology.[57] They are the small merchants of urban areas and shopkeepers of the rural areas. The Marxists consider even the middle classes to be petty *bourgeoisie*. The *bourgeoisie* and *kulak* members of the various castes make use of their caste identity and line up members of their own castes behind them and break the solidarity of the farming class.

Caste and Class

Indian society, as has been already noted elsewhere is based on birth status. It has not been like western society, moved appreciably in the direction of acquired status for want of industrialization, education and income. Along with the caste categories, there have emerged classes which cut across the traditional caste stratification.

The working class in the cities is basically a product of the urban *milieu* and is made up of individuals, who have migrated to cities to better their economic status. With the pace of industrialisation, the spread of education and the attraction of cities life with deterioration of rural life—the rural people have been pulled towards urban areas. The establishment of new industries like Bokaro Steel Plant, the HEC at Ranchi, Oil Refinery and Fertilizer Factory at Barauni, Fertilizer Factory at Sindri and many new industries opening new employment avenues has mobilised rural people. Before that coal fields, Jamshedpur industrial complex and Dalmianagar had provided jobs and high income. The establishment of D.V.C., Road Transport Corporation, Electricity Board and many other trades and businesses have too provided new avenues. In this process they have changed their traditional occupations and become members of a new class.

57. G.D.H. Cole, *Studies in Class Structure* (London, 1955), p. 12.

Shah suspects that what has happened within many castes is economic stratification, not class formation.[58] Economic stratification does influence the life-style and values of the individuals concerned. The life-style of highly paid industrial workers differs from that of the low-paid workers in the same factory. Such differences, however, do not necessarily lead to the emergence of antagonistic class interests. Needless to say that economic differentiations are yet to go beyond caste boundaries and result in the formation of classes.

However, industrialisation has given birth of new class weakening the traditional caste system. In industrial establishments one type of job is done by people of different castes, for example, the Bata India Co. So is the case of textile industry where not only *julahas* work. In iron and steel industry—not only *lohar* works. In ready-made garment industry—people of all castes are engaged. In business and trades occupations have been adopted by other caste people. Thus, the present picture of society does not exist on traditional line.

The owner-cultivators and the rich tenants, who are almost all from castes traditionally engaged in farming, have emerged as exploiters of wage labour and different forms of other labour belonging to the lower castes. Now the sharpest conflict is no longer between the middle and low-caste peasants on the one side and high-caste landlords on the other. It is between the rich farmers and the agricultural labourers and the poor peasants. This signifies that the caste structure of rural Bihar has changed although one cannot say that a class-based society has emerged in a caste-ridden society.

The *zamindars*, the tenant landlords, and the big peasants are mostly upper-caste Hindus. The poor-middle peasantry and

58. Shah, n. 15a, p. 134.

the middle peasantry are drawn mainly from the middle castes. Their caste consciousness is a major obstacle to the growth of class consciousness. There are many rich people in backward castes like Yadavas, Kurmis, Koiri, baniya, Marwari, Suri, Teli and Goldsmith. They like to be called as Backward castes in order to enjoy privileges—but they identify themselves with upper castes for all other purposes. They too exploit people of their own castes.

On the other hand there are large number of people in upper castes, who are economically poor. Brahmans are mostly poor—who work as cook. Kayasthas do not possess much land—their main source of livelihood is service. Rejputs are also not much rich, except a small percentage. They work in police, military, night-guards services. Though they belong to upper castes—but economically they have poor standard of life lower than many Yadavas, Kurmis, Marwari etc.

The changes that have occurred in Independent India have generally increased the power and prestige of the peasant castes, usually at the expense of such higher castes as the Rajputs and the Brahmans.[59] In the opinion of E.M.S. Namboodiripad, caste associations were "the first forms in which the peasant masses rose in struggle against feudalism".

> "At present these caste organizations are not the class organizations of the peasantry; they do, on the contrary, consolidate the caste separatism of the people in general and of the peasantry in particular, so that the grip of these organizations on the peasantry has to be broken if they are to be organized as a class."[60]

59. Srinivas, n. 13, p. 21.
60. E.M.S. Namboodiripad, *The National Question in Kerala* (Bombay, 1952), pp. 102-6.

Owing to their rural connection the working class cannot even in urban areas behave like a class. In industry they are members of a class according to their occupation, but in the villages they behave like members of their respective castes. Even in trade-unionism caste is a potent factor. So in India in general and in Bihar in particular, the emergence of an industrial culture is only a distant possibility. The Indian Conference of Social Work in a Seminar on Casteism and Removal of Untouchability in Delhi held during September 26th-2nd October, 1955 had observed.

> "Caste is one of the biggest things in India today, if not the biggest, and this has been recognised during elections. Most of the big cities are the strongholds of casteism. But while caste is so powerful and pervasive and every one wants it to go, actions are more or less at complete variance with professed beliefs. Caste performs several useful functions for its members and people are keenly aware of this fact. Till the time comes when there are other agencies to take over these functions, caste will not disappear."[61]

Caste and class, thus, go together. They cannot be separated each from the other. In these circumstances the class as a criterion for the determination of beneficiaries under any social policy cannot be used.

Gail Omvedt too observes that caste and class continue to be heavily interlinked.[62] The educated *elite* are over-whelmingly drawn from the higher castes, who have a literary tradition – viz the Brahmans, the Kayasthas, and others. Men from the peasant and artisan castes of Shudra status constitute the large majority of factory workers. Members of the Scheduled Castes

61. *Report of the Commissioner for Scheduled Castes & Scheduled Tribes*, 1955 (New Delhi : Government of India), p. 213.
62. Gail Omvedt., ed,, *Land, Caste and Politics in Indian States* (Delhi, 1982), p. 20.

have been able to find openings in the factories and in the transport industry (including the Railways).

Shah concludes that there is no perfect co-relation between caste and class. A majority of a few upper castes do not belong to the upper class. Rajputs (upper caste) of Gujarat are a case in point. Almost 50 per cent of them are small and marginal farmers or landless farm labourers.[63] If lower strata in both upper and lower castes become more distinct and class consciousness emerge only then caste factor might become less effective.

The present social picture is in the stage of fermentation. Traditional caste and religious customs are giving ways to modern thinkings. Relationships between castes and occupations have put on new colour-breaking customary relationship. Changing economic opportunities, spread of education, changing consciousness towards new ways of life have changed the rural and urban social picture. The grant of democratic right has arouse political consciousness -which in return has changed social life. The caste sentiment, though slowly, has changed with inter-caste marriages. The traditional rigidity maintaining untouchability, restrictions in religious places and other narrow sentiments have become loose. Thus, the fast changing economic-social and political environment has helped in changing traditional relationships between castes, class, occupation and social and political status. Any one of any caste can require status by getting modern education and economic means. Through there are many constraints in the way—but one has to work hard if he wants to rise in terms of social status and economic means.

63. Ghanshyam Shah 1985, n. 15 b, p. 7.

CHAPTER III

Legal and Constitutional Aspects of Reservation Policy

Special Provisions for Backward Castes in Pre-independence Period

In the last quarter of the nineteenth century the Government of India initiated certain measures to help those sections of the society which were socially and economically at the lowest rungs of the ladder. In 1885 the Government of Madras made financial grants to educational institutions providing educational facilities to students of the Depressed Classes.[1] In 1918 the then Maharaja of Mysore acceded to the demand of certain aggrieved communities for special consideration. He appointed a commission under the chairmanship of Sir L.C. Milton, the then Chief Justice of Mysore, to recommend steps to ensure adequate representation for non-Brahmans in the services of the State. Later, in 1921, special facilities were extended to the backward communities in the fields of education and employment.

1. *Report of The Backward Classes Commission.* (Chairman, B.P. Mandal), Parts I-II (New Delhi, 1981), p. 5 (Hereinafter cited as Mandal Commission, Report).

All Parties Conference in 1928 examined the problem faced by the non-Brahmans and the depressed classes. It was concluded that they need protection and their grievances against Brahmans are all traceable to the ascendency gained by the latter in the political and social life of the country. It further observed in context of the "depressed" classes that they should be raised socially and economically so that they may take proper place in the community.[2]

A Backward Classes Commission appointed by the Government of Bombay in 1930 placed that various backward classes into three categories :

1. Depressed Classes
2. Aboriginal and hill tribes; and
3. Other backward classes.

It recommended that all these three categories be given special facilities in the fields of education and employment.

The Montagu-Chelmsford Reforms of 1919 provided separate electorates to the Depressed Classes in the form of a few nominated seats for the first time in provincial legislative councils. The Scheduled Castes and the Scheduled Tribes were granted reserved represenatation under the Government of India Act, 1935, in the Federal and provincial legislatures. They were not granted separate electorates as in the case of the Sikhs and the Muslims in consequence of the Poona Pact between Mahatma Gandhi and Dr. Bhimrao Ramji Ambedkar in 1932. No reservation was, however, made for the other backward classes. It renamed the Depressed Classes as Scheduled Castes and backward tribes. Prior to this both these communities were known as "Depressed Classes."

2. *Report of the All Parties Conference Proceeding* (Chairman, Motilal Nehru) Allahabad : AICC, 1929, pp. 58-59.

Constituent Assembly and the OBCs

As leader of the Congress Party in the Constituent Assembly of India in 1946, Pt. Jawaharlal Nehru moved a resolution for providing adequate safeguards to the "minorities, backward and tribal areas, and depressed and other backward classes."[3] The Constituent Assembly was opposed to reservation on the basis of religion. It was also opposed to the according of preferential treatment of the other backward classes. It, however, accepted the claim of the Scheduled Castes and the Scheduted Tribes for safeguards. The term "backward classes" was then in vogue. Members from North India thought that it signified the Scheduled Castes Members from South India, including those from Bombay, thought it to mean not only the Sched uled Castes but also tribal societies and those classes of people who were distinctly and perceptibly backward economically, educationally, and socially in relation to other classes of people in India.

A member from Bihar, Chandrika Ram, defined the term "backward classes" as a section of society between the highest castes and the Scheduled Castes.[4] In India there are some communities, besides the Scheduled Castes and tribes, who give a definite impression of social and educational backwardness and inferiority compared to the traditional upper castes. The Sub-committee on Fundamental Rights has discussed the question of other backward classes in detail. It, however, failed to provide any reservation to them. It left it for the State Governments to identify the backward classes in their respective territorise and to assist them.

3. Anil Chandra Banerjee, *The Making of the Indian Constitution, 1939-1947*, vol. I (Calcutta, 1948), p. 313.

4. India, Constitutional Assembly, *Debates*, vol. VII, p. 687.

Indian Constitution and the other Backward Classes

The framers of the Indian Constitution were aware of the discrimination being practised in society. The institution of caste was a dominant feature of the Indian social system. A large section of the people were being regarded as "untouchables". In view of this, the Constitution of India imposed certain restrictions on fundamental rights :

> In the Constitution, the compensatory theme appears juxtaposed with the theme of formal equality. The provisions for compensatory preference appear as exceptions within a framework of enforceable fundamental rights which attempt to curtail the significance of ascriptive groups and to guarantee equal treatment to the individual.[5]

The Constitution of India contains a number of Articles which deal with compensatory preference for the backward classes. The backward classes have been divided into three main groups, viz.:

(*i*) Scheduled Castes,

(*ii*) Scheduled Tribes, and

(*iii*) Other Backward Classes.

The most important among them are Articles 15 (4) and 16 (4). Articles 46, 335, 338, 340, 341, 342, 366 (24), and 366 (25) also have a bearing on the subject.[6] Article 15 (1) says[7] :

5. Marc Galanter, *Competing Equalities : Law and the Backward Classes in India* (New Delhi, 1984), p. 364.
6. D. Narasimha Rao and M. Ramchander, "Reservation to Backward Classes : In Search of Criteria", in B.A.V. Sharma and K.M. Reddy, eds, *Reservation Policy in India* (New Delhi, 1982), p. 136.
7. *The Constitution of India* (New Delhi : Government of India, 1980), p. 8.

"The State shall not discriminate against any citizen on grounds only of religion, race, caste, sex, place of birth or any of them."

Article 16 (2) prohibits discrimination in regard to State employment. It lays down[8] :

> No citizen shall, on grounds only of religion, race, caste, sex, descent, place of birth, residence or any of them, be ineligible for, or discriminated against, in respect of any employment or office under the State.

The Constitution of India, for providing protective discrimination used criteria of socially and educationally backwardness. Backwardness is not related just to these two variables. It may be economic or in terms of wealth and openings available to new avenues of life. It may be measured with reference to low levels of income, the degree of illiteracy and a low standard of life as demonstrated by living conditions.[9] It is the responsibility of the Government of India to improve the conditions of the backward classes.

According to K.M. Munshi, one of the legal luminaries associated with the drafting of the Constitution of India,

> ......the word "backward" signifies that class of people—it does not matter whether you call them untouchables, belonging to this community or that—a class of people who are so backward that special protection is required for them in the services.[10]

The Constitution uses a different terminology for the backward classes. For example. Articles 15 (4) and 340 use the

8. Ibid., p. 9
9. *The First Five-Year Plan : A Draft Outline* (New Delhi : Government of India, Planning Commission, 1951), p. 634.
10. India, Constitutional Assembly, *Debates*, vol. VII, pp. 696-7.

words "socially and educationally backward classes", Article 16 (4) speaks of just "backward classes"; and Article 46 is concerned with the "weaker sections of the people". Even now the term "backward classes" is differently defined in the reports of the different backward classes commissions and the judgements of the High Courts and the Supreme Court of India. Discrimination is prohibited in regard to admission into educational institutions in Article 29 (2) :

> "No citizen shall be denied admission into any educational institution maintained by the State or receiving aid out of State funds on grounds only of religion, race, caste, language, or any of them."

The Constitution is against any type of discrimination, public or private. It directs the Government at the same time to undertake special measures for the upliftment of the backward classes. Article 15 (4), which was incorporated into the Constitution under the Constitution (First Amendment) Act, 1951, declares :

> "Nothing in Article 15 or in Clause (2) of Article 29 shall prevent the State from making any special provision for the advancement of any socially and educationally backward classes of citizens or for the Scheduled Castes and the Scheduled Tribes."

Article 15(4) enables the State to make special provisions for the backward classes in all the areas within its jurisdiction. The expression "class"[11] in Article 15(4) implies a homogeneous section of the people grouped together on account of certain likenesses or common traits and by being identifiable by some common attributes such as status, rank, occupation, residence in a locality, race, religion, and the like. In defining whether a

11. D.V. Chitaley, *AIR Commentaries* : *The Constitution of India*, Vol. I (Nagpur, 1970), p. 1277.

particular section forms a class, caste cannot be excluded altogether. At the same time a test solely based upon caste or community cannot be accepted.

Article 16 (4), which relates to Government jobs, says[12] :

> Nothing in this Article shall prevent the State from making any provision for the reservation of appointments or posts in favour of any backward class of citizens which, in the opinion of the State, is not adequately represented in the services under the State.

Other Articles of the Constitution too make references to the backward classes. The Directive Principles of State Policy enjoin the Government to undertake special measures for the advancement of the backward classes. In 1950 the Government was in no position to provide reservation to other backward classes in the field of education, Government employment and legislative representation. Article 46 declares[13] :

> The State shall promote with special care the educationl and economic interests of the weaker sections of the people, and, in particular, of the Scheduled Castes and the Scheduled Tribes, and shall protect them from social injustice and all forms of exploitation.

The policy of reservation subequently adopted in many States in India is linked to the need for the maintenance of efficiency in administration. This is clear from Article 335[14] :

> The claims of the members of the Scheduled Castes and the Scheduled Tribes shall be taken into consideration, consistently with the maintenance of efficiency of administration,

12. *The Constitution of India*, n. 7, p. 9.
13. Ibid., p. 27.
14. Ibid., p. 214.

in the making of appointments to services and posts in connection with the affairs of the Union or a State.

This Article, thus, makes it clear that in order to get the benefit of reservation a candidate for a post in the Government or in a public undertaking would have to fulfiil the minimum educational and other qualifications prescribed for that post in consonance with the nature and requirement of that post.

The Constitution talks only about reservation of jobs. It does not fix any particular percentage of jobs. In 1950 the Government of India reserved 12½ per cent of posts for the Scheduled Castes and 5 per cent for the Scheduled Tribes, in the all-India services to be recruited on the basis of open competition.

It also extended the age limit in their case by three years. In 1952 it raised the age limit to five years more than the maximum presecribed for others. Now in the Central and State rervices seats and posts are reserved in proportion to population In 1970 the Central Government raised the reservation for the Scheduled Castes to 15 per cent; and for the Scheduled Tribes to 7½ per cent.

Reservation of seats in the legislatures was originally only for ten years. It was subsequently extended for more years through a series of amendments of the Constitution. The latest amendment extends reservation up to 1990.

As for reservation of jobs, the Constitution mentions no fixed period. Naturally, the State is expected to continue such preferential treatment until the Scheduled Castes and the Scheduled Tribes make substantial progress educationally and economically and reach a level of equality with the rest of Indian society.[15]

15. M.V. Pylee, *Constitutional Government in India*, (New Delhi, 1984), p, 609.

Articles 335, 338, 341, 342, 366 (24), and 366 (25) are related to reservation for the Scheduled Castes and the Scheduled Tribes. Article 338 provides for a Commissioner of Scheduled Castes and Scheduled Tribes and defines his duties and responsibilities. Article 340 is related to the Commission for the investigation of the Socio-Economic Conditions of Scheduled Castes, Scheduled Tribes, and other Backward Classes. Article 340 makes provision for the appointment of two commissions by the President, one to investigate and report on the administration of the Scheduled Areas and the welfare of the Scheduled Tribes and the other to investigate the conditions of socially and educationally backward classes and to make recommendations as to the steps that should be taken by the Union or by a State Government to ameliorate those conditions.[16]

The leaders of the other Backward Classes have been striving to get for their people benefits similar to those granted to the Scheduled Castes and the Scheduled Tribes. It is possible that our national leaders presumed that the "backward classes" are sufficiently potent politically to look after their own interests at the local level and that unlike in the case of the Scheduled Castes and the Scheduled Tribes, there is no need for any Central control to ensure the inclusion of all deprived classes of people in the category of backward classes. The Constitution, however, made it obligatory for the Government to appoint a Backward Classes Commission within ten years of the commencement of the Constitution. And Article 340 (3) declares[17] :

> "The President shall cause a copy of the report so presented together with a memorandum explaining the action taken thereon to be laid before each House of Parliament."

Although the Government of India appointed two Backward Classes Commissions Kaka Katelkar Commissim in 1953 and

16. Ibid., p. 610.
17. *The Constitution of India*, n. 7, p. 218.

Mandal Commissim in 1978, it has so far failed to implement the recommendations of 26 per cent reserved seats and posts for them.

The special clauses of the Constitution[18] providing for reservation are based on two premises—viz.,

1. An egalitarian society is a worthy ideal and
2. Reservation is an efficient means to achieve an eqalitarian society.

It is also presumed that this policy will in course of time raise the deprived classes to a reasonable level of equality with the rest of Indian society. Articles 15(4) and 16(4) express the Constitutional values of compensatory or protective discrimination for the levelling up of the lonely, the deprived and the oppressed.[19]

Judiciary and the Backward Classes

The Fundamental Rights and the D irective Principles of State Policy have been matters of controversy between the judiciary on the one hand and the Indian Parliament and the State legislatures on the other. The policy of reservation of jobs in Government services and of seats in educational institutions followed by some State Governments has been challenged a number of times in the High Courts and in the Supreme Court of India. The main problem is : What should be the criteria for determining backwardness ca ste or economy ? When some Governments sought to reserve more than 50 per cent of the posts for the backward classes, they were again challenged in the courts.

18. P.C. Chatterji, "In Defence of Reservation", *Patriot* (New Delhi), 23 April 1985.
19. Paramanand Singh, "Equal Opportunity and Compensatory Discrimination : Constitutional Policy and Judicial Control", *Journal of the Indian Law Institute* (New Delhi), vol. 18, April-June 1976, p. 302.

The Supreme Court in 1951 handed down its first judicial pronouncement on the policy of reservation in the case of *State of Madras* V. Smt. *Champakam Dorairajan.*[20] It upheld the judgement of the Madras High Court that the Communal Government Order of the Government of Madras fixing the proportion of students of each community that could be admitted into the educational institutions aided or maintained by the State was ultra-vires under Article 29(2) and that Article 46 of the Constitution could not be cited in support of that order. This judgement provoked public protests in many South Indian States so much so that the Government of India enacted a Constitutional amendment to check judicial intervention in the reservation policy and incorporated Clause 15(4) into the Constitution in 1951.

In *Balaji* v. *Mysore State* (1963) the Government policy of reservation of jobs for the backward classes in Mysore was challenged in the Supreme Court, with the plea that the list of backward classes had been prepared only on the basis of caste and that, therefore, it was unconstitutional.

In 1962 the Government of Mysore (now Karnataka) had reserved 50 per cent of the posts/seats for the backward classes (28 per cent for backward classes and 22 per cent for the most backward classes). Besides, reserved 15 per cent for the Scheduled Castes and 3 per cent for the Scheduled Tribes. Thus, as a whole, 68 per cent of the posts/seats were reserved. This order was challenged under Article 15 (4) in the Supreme Court. The following issues were raised by the petitioner :

1. What are the criteria for identifying social and educational backwardness ?
2. What is the role of caste in determining social backwardness ?

20. See Chitaley, n. 11, p. 1269.

3. Is the sub-classification of backward classes into categories valid ?

4. In the quantum of reservation excessive ?[21]

The Court, therefore, went into the criteria used for preparing the list of backward classes. It was up to the Government to show that the criteria used in the determination of backwardness was not based only on caste. In the judgement, Justice P.B. Gajendragadkar observed that the procedure for determining social backwardness on the basis of caste did not have universal application although it might have relevance to the Hindu castes. He remarked that social backwardness was itself a product of economic backwardness in as much as an economically backward section meekly accepted its inferior position in society.[22] It struckdown the sub-classification of the backward classes.

On the basis of the *Balaji* case the Patna Hight Court in *Nanda Kishore Sharma* v. *State of Bihar* delivered a judgement in 1964, said that the classification of backward classes on the basis of caste alone would be legally invalid.[23] It also rejected the validity of the Government's action in dividing backward classes into backward and more backward. The Court declared the list of backward classes prepared by the Bihar Government exclusively on the basis of caste as unconstitutional. It also struckdown the 10 per cent reservation for the backward classes in medical colleges.

In 1967 the Government of Jammu & Kashmir appointed a Commission of Inquiry to go into the question of backward classes in the State. Justice P.B. Gajenderagadkar, who had; as the Chief Justice of India, pronounced judgement in the *Balaji*

21. *Mandal Commission Report,* n. 1, p, 10.

22, Supreme Court, *Balaji* v. *State of Mysore,* AIR 1963, p. 649.

23. Patna High Court, AIR 1965, p. 372.

case four years earlier, was nominated to head this Commission of Inquiry. He then said that in the case of the Hindus, caste was a valid criterion for determining social backwardness.[24] The Commission went into the case, *Triloki Nath* v. *State of Jammu & Kashmir* (A.I.R. 1967 S.C. 1283, 1286) in which the petitioner had challenged the action of the State Government in treating the entire Muslim community as backward. By its policy of reservation, the Government had reserved 50 per cent of the jobs for the Muslims, 30 per cent for the Hindu Dogras and others, and the rest 20 per cent for the Kashmiri Pandits. The Kashmiri Pandits considered this to be unjust, for, prior to the adoption of the reservation policy, they had been enjoying 90 per cent of the Gorvernment jobs in the State. The Government order was held invalid as it failed to produce sufficient data before the Court.

In *K.S. Jaysree* v. *State of Kerala*[25] the Supreme Court agreed with the Kerala High Court that economie backwardness played a part in social and educational backwardness and that poverty or economic deprivation was a relevant factor in determining backwardness. It held that caste could not be made the sole or even the dominent criterion although it might not be irrelevant. It was of the view that social backwardness was in the ultimate analysis the result of poverty although membership of a low caste might aggravate the sense of backwardness.

The decision of the Allahabad High Court in *Chhote Lal Pandey and others* v. *State of Uttar Pradesh* case is quite important in the context of discussions on the policy of reservation. The petitioners had alleged that several of the so-called backward castes like the Ahirs and the Kurmis were not economically and socially backward. Many people belonging to these castes

24. G.P. Verma, *Caste Reservation in India : Law and the Constitution* (Allahabad, 1980), p. 17,

25. Ibid., p. 49.

were rich, prosperous farmers; others were highly educated; and a few even occupied high offices. The petitioner asked for the test applied for the determination of backward classes of citizens. The Court agreeing with the view had observed that to regard caste alone as a criterion was a "fraud on constitutional power".[26] It pronounced the appointments made in 1977 to the judicial services by the Government of Uttar Pradesh as invalid.

The Allahabad High Court's position may be summed up as under :

1. The bracketing of socially and educationally backward classes with the Scheduled Castes and the Scheduled Tribes in Article 15 (4) and the provision in Article 338 (3) that references to the Scheduled Castes and the Scheduled Tribes were to be construed as including such backward classes as the President might by order specify on receipt of the Report of the Commission appointed under Article 340 (1), showed that in the matter of backwardness these backward classes were comparable to the Scheduled Castes and the Scheduled Tribes.
2. The concept of backwardness was relative. In other words, a class which might be considered to be backward in relation to the most advanced class in society need not necessarily be included in the list of backward castes.
3. Backwardness should be both social *and* educational, not social *or* educational.
4. The reference in Article 15 (4) was to "backward classes", not to "backward castes". Indeed the criterion of caste would be rendered meaningless in the context of the existence of communities which had no castes among them.

26. Allahabad High Court, AIR 1979, p. 135,

5. Caste was a relevant factor in determining social backwardness, but it could not be the sole or dominant factor.

6. In the ultimate analysis social backwardness was largely the result of poverty. The social backwardness arising from poverty was likely to be aggravated by considerations of caste. This, however, only went to show the relevance of *both* caste *and* poverty in determining backwardness.

7. A classification based only on caste without regard to other relevant factors was not permissible under Article 15 (4) even if some castes, considered in their entirety, might be socially and educationally backward.

8. The occupations followed by certain classes (which were looked upon as inferior) might contribute to social backwardness. And so might the habitation of people for, in a sense, the problem of social backwardness was the problem of rural India.

9. The division of the backward classes into backward and more backward classes was in substance a division of the population into the most advanced and the rest being divided into backward and more backward classes. This was not warranted by Article 15 (4).

10. Article 16 (4) did not confer any right on a person to require that a reservation be made. It conferred a discretionary power on the State to make such reservation if, in its opinion, a backward class of citizens was not adequately represented in the services of the State. More inadequacy of representation of a caste or class in the services was, however, not sufficient to attract Article 16 (4) unless that caste (as a whole) or class was also socially and educationally backward.

11. The object of reservation would be defeated if, on the inclusion of a class in a list of backward classes, that class was to be treated as backward for all time to come. Hence the State should keep under constant periodical review the list of backward classes and the quantum of reservation of seats for the classes determined to be backward at any given point of time.

12. The aggregate reservation for various categories (including the backward classes) should be less than 50 per cent.

13. The Court's jurisdiction was limited to deciding whether the tests applied by the State in determining the backwardness were valid or not. Even if the relevant tests had not been applied, it was not open to the Court either to modify the list of backward classes prepared by the State or to modify the extent of reservation. It must, however, strike down the operative part, leaving it to the State to take a fresh proper decision after applying the correct criteria.[27]

In the case of *K.C. Vasanth Kumar* v. *State of Karnataka*, Supreme Court (AIR 1985, p. 1499) Chief Justice Y.V. Chandrachud accepted the policy of reservation in principle. But it suggested two tests for identifying OBC's for the purpose of reservation in employment and education :

"One, that they should be comparable to the Scheduled Castes and Schedueld Tribes in the matter of their backwardness; and two, that they should satisfy the means test as a State Government may lay down in the context of prevailing economic conditions."

As a whole judiciary in India accepted policy of reservation for certain deprived social sections. For giving its benefit, its

27. Ibid., pp. 151-2.

emphasis were on the proper fact finding Commission, suitable criteria not exclusively caste and reservation in any circumstances not more than 50 per cent of the seats and posts. Most of the State Governments are using caste-cum-means test.

Backward Class Commission (Kaka Kalelkar Commission) 1953

Most States have enacted legislations aimed at eliminating the worst concentrations of rural economic and political power. *Zamindars*, *jagirdars*, *watandars* and *talukdars* have all been deprived of their major land-holdings and their places have been taken by the middle peasants castes. These castes started demanding reservation of seats for their children in educational institutions and jobs in Government service. The Backward Castes Federation[28] has played an important role in this matter. Ultimately, realising the numerical stength and political importance of these castes, the Central Government set up the first Backward Classes Commission on 29 January 1953 under Article 340 of the Indian Constitution. Kaka Kalelkar, a wellknown Gandhian, was nominted Chairman of the Commission along with ten members.

The Commission was assigned the task to find out the criteria for determining whether any section, other than the Scheduled Castes and the Scheduled Tribes, need to be treated as socially and educationally backward, to prepare a list of such classes, and to recommend steps to remove their difficulties and improve their conditions.[29] It realized soon enough that the problems of the backward classes were essentially the problems of rural India. Accordingly, it decided that the relevant factors to consider in classifying the backward classes would be their

28. The Bihar Backward Classes Federation was founded in September 1947. The All-India Backward Classes Federation was founded in 1950 to highlight the problems faced by other Backward Classes.
29. K.K. Katyal, "Exercise to Perfect Old Reasoning", *The Hindu* (Madras), 12 January 1981.

traditional occupations or professions and the percentage of literacy or the general level of education attained by them.[30] It also decided that the social position which a community occupied in the caste hierarchy, would have to be considered as well as its representation in Government service and in the industrial sphere.[31]

The Commission used the term "classes" as if it was synonymous with "castes" and communities" and prepared a list of backward classes on the basis of caste. It used the following four criteria to determine backwardness ;

1. Low position in the traditional caste hierarchy of Hindu society.
2. Lack of general educational advancement in a caste or community taken as a whole.
3. Inadequate or no representation in Government service ; and
4. Indequate representation in the fields of trade, commerce and industry.[32]

The Commission listed 2,399 castes as backward classes. It chose 837 castes treating as "more backward castes" for purposes of development and upliftment. It also made the following recommendations :

1. The Goverment of India should undertake a caste-wise enumeration of the population in the Census of 1961.
2. It should seek to relate the social backwardness of a class to its low position in the traditionl caste hierarchy of Hindu society,

30. Verma, n. 24, p. 27.
31. *Backward Classes Commission Report*, (*Chairman* : Kaka Kalekar), Parts I-II (New Delhi, 1955), p. 38.
32. Ibid., p. 46.

3. All women should be treated as backward.
4. Seventy per cent of the seats in all technical and professional intitutions should be reserved for qulified students of the backward classes and
5. A certain minimum number of vacanies should be reserved for the backward classes in Government service and in the service of local bodies on the following scales:

Class I	...	25 per cent
Class II	...	33⅓ per cent
Class III and IV	...	40 per cent[33]

There of the members (Anup Singh, Arunangahu De and P.G. Shah) were opposed to one of the most crucial recommendstions of the commission, viz the acceptance of caste as a criterion for determining social backwardeness and the reservation of posts in Government service on that basis.[34] Kaka Kalelkar too seemed to have second thoughts for he stated almost at the end of his investigations that it would have been better if the criteria for backwardness had been fixed on the basis of principles other than caste. Advocates or reservation blamed Kalelkar for destroying the very edifice he had built.[35]

The report of the Commission was placed before both Houses of Parliament on 3 September 1956 along with a memorandum explaining the action taken on it. It was explained in the memorandum that if the bulk of the country's millions were to be regarded as backward classes, no useful purpose would be served by a separate enumeration of such classes.[36]

Govind Ballabh Pant, the then Home Minister of the

33. *The Mandal Commission, Report*, n. 1, p. 1.
34. Ibid., p. 1.
35. Katyal, n. 23.
36. *The Commissioner for Scheduled Castes and Scheduled Tribes, Report*, 1979-81 (Delhi, 1981), p. 44.

Government of India, was totally against caste-based reservation. He observed[37] :

> "It cannot be denied that the caste system is the greatest hindrance in the way of our progress towards an egalitarian society, and recognition of the specified castes as backward may serve to maintain and even perpetuate the existing distinctions on the basis of caste."

He asked the State Government to prepare lists of backward classes on the basis of their own criteria. The Central Government's effort to evolve practica criteria for the determintion of backwardness thus did not lead to any clear or generally acceptable result.

The Deputy Registrar-General of India tried to prepare a list of backward occupations—i.e. occupations which made those engaged in them socially and educationally backward. He however, failed to develop such a list. He felt that it would be batter to choose the economic criterion than the criterion of caste. Some states favoured the economic criterion.

The determination of criteria of backwardness has been a debatable issue. There had been sharp differences between our statesmen, members of various commissions, academicians and common people. Failure of the Central Government in adopting a rational basis of bakwardness has been exposed by the fact that it left the State Governments to adopt own criteria. Caste as the sole basis of backwardness is not correct. There is no direct relationship between caste and backwardness. Many people belonging to so-called backward castes as Scheduled Caste and Scheduled Tribe are econmically well-to-do. On the other hand so-called upper castes have poor people. Really speaking backwardness is the result of many factors which have to be

37. *Memorandum on the Report of the Backward Classes Commission*, (Delhi : Ministry of Home Affairs, Government of India, 1956), p. 2.

taken into account if any society proposes to adopt measures for upliftment of backward people. Adoption of policy based on caste would generate differences in due course which would be injurious for the society. A rational view has to develop—set-a-siding the narrowness of the policy makers.

Meanwhile the Governments of Andhra Pradesh, Assam Bihar, Delhi, Gujarat, Haryana, Himachal, Pradesh, Jammu & Kashmir, Karnataka and Pondicherry identified certain classes as backward in their respective territories and started providing special facilities to those classes. Delhi and Orissa subsequently withdrew their respective lists.[38]

Mandal Commission, 1978

The economic problems that the country was confronted with in the early 1970s in the wake of the crisis in Bangladesh and the Indo-Pakistani War, the students unrest in Bihar and Gujarat, the emergency and the excesses committed by the police and petty bureaucrats during that period, and the unity forged by the opposition parties ended the 30-year rule of the Congress Party in 1977. For the first time, the Lok Sabha withnessed a change in the social composition of the Members of Parliament. The Brahmans, who used to constitute 35 to 47 per cent of the total membership of the Lok Sabha, now found that they were no longer so predominant. They were barely 25 per cent of the new Lok Sabha in 1977.[39] The backward castes increased their strength at the expense of the Brahmans. This emboldened them to demand the implementation of the recommendations of the Kaka Kalelkar Commission as promise in the Janata Party election manifesto of 1977.[40] The Government

38. *The Commissioner of Scheduled Castes and Scheduled Tribes,* n. 36, p. 45.
39. Charan Singh, *who is Casteist ? : An Analysis* (Delhi, 1982), p. 41.
40. *Election Manifesto of the Janata Party, 1977* (New Delhi, 1977), p. 34.

of India, however, thaught it expedient to order a fresh investigation into the conditions of the backward classes and appointed a Backward Classes Commission under the Chairmanship of B .P. Mandal on 20 December 1978. The terms of reference of the Commission were as follows :

1. To determine the criteria for defining socially and educationally backward classes.
2. To recommend steps to be taken for the advancement of the socially and educationally beckward classes.
3. To examine the desirability or otherwise of making provision for the reservation of appointments or posts in favour of such backward classes which are not adequately represented in public services and posts in connection with the affairs of the Union or of any State.
4. Present to the President a report setting out the facts as found by them and making such recommendations as they think proper.[41]

The Mandal Comisson also settled upon the rough-and-ready tool of caste with which to identify backward classes. The Research Team, appointed by the Commission to conduct a village-level survey, chose family as a unit of observation. The team found caste as a horizontal segmental divsion of society spread over a district or a region or the whole State and even beyond. In each village a section of a caste exists largely in vertical relationship with other castes. The suvrvey, thus, ignored the community aspect of caste.[42] It is because of this caste criterion that the Commissions' recommendations have not so far been implemented.

41. *Mandal Commission, Report*, n. 1, p. vii.
42. I.P. Desai, "Should 'Caste' Be the Basis for Recognition of Backwardness ?", *Economic and Political Weekly*, (Bombay), 14 July 1984, p. 1108.

The Commission prepaed one consolidated list of backward clsses. L.R.Naiku, a member of the Commission, suggested that a separate list be prepared for each State and that each list should be in two parts—one part detailing the intermediate backward classes and the other enumerating the depressed backward classes.[43] The Commission did not accept this suggestion. It even cited the judgement of the Supeme Court of India in *Balaji* v. *State of Mysore*, which had, *inter alia*, stated :

> In introducing two categories of Backward Classes, what the impugned order, in substance, purports to do is to devise measures for all the classes of citizens who are less advanced as compared to the most advanced classess in the State, is not the scope of Article 15(4).

The Commission found that the representation of the backward classes other than the Scheduled Castes and the Scheduled Tribes) in the Central service in different categories is less than that of the Scheduled Castes and the Scheduled Tribes. (See Table No.1). Although the population of these backward classes in more than double of the Scheduled Castes and the Scheduled Tribes. The better representation of the Scheduled Castes and the Scheduled Tribes due entrely to the reservation policy.

The Commission indentified 3943 castes covering 52 per cent of the total population of India as Other Backward Classes. It, therefore, recommended reservation for these backward classes in proportion to their population. However, in view of the legal constraint that total reservation should not exceed 50 per cent for all categories, it limited this reservation to 27 per cent in Government service and in educational institiutions. It proposed the following overall scheme of reservation for the other Backward Classes :

1. Candidates belonging to these classes recruited on the basis of merit in an open competition should not be adjusted against their reservation quota of 27 per cent.

43. *Mandal Commission, Report*, n. 1, p. IV.

TABLE 1

Representation of Backward Classes, the Scheduled Castes and the Scheduled Tribes in the Service of the Central Government, 1979

	Class I			*Class II*		
	Total	*SC/ST*	*O.B.C.*	*Total*	*SC/ST*	*O.B.C.*
1	2	3	4	5	6	7
Ministry/Department	11,707	840 (7.18)	303 (2.59)	43,803	5,985 (13.66)	1,742 (3.98)
Autonomous Institutions	81,325	5,399 (6.64)	4,147 (5.09)	503,337	91,431 (18.16)	59,079 (11.74)
Public Corporation	80,994	3,652 (4.51)	3,719 (4.59)	365,785	68,566 (18.74)	36,242 (9.91)
Total	174,026	9,891 (5.68)	8,169 (4.69)	912,925	165,982 (18.18)	97,063 (10.63)

(Contd.)

(*Continued Table 1*)

Classes III & IV			*All Classes (consolidated)*		
Total	*SC/ST*	*O.B.C.*	*Total*	*SC/ST*	*O.B.C.*
8	9	10	11	12	13
17,829	5,518 (30.95)	1,500 (8.41)	73,339	12,343 (16.83)	3,545 (4.83)
322,948	67,118 (20.78)	67.786 (20.98)	907,610	163,948 (18.06)	131,0 (14.4)
143,910	45,646 (31.72)	22,689 (15.77)	590,689	117,864 (19.95)	62,6 (10.6)
484,687	118,282 (24.10)	91,975 (18.98)	1,571,638	294,155 (18.72)	197,2 (12.5)

Note : Percentage figures are given within brakets. SC/Scheduled Castes; ST=Scheduled Tribes; and OBC=Other Backward Classes.

Source : Report of the *Backward Classes Commission*, (New Delhi, 1980), Parts I and II, p. 88.

2. Reservation should also be made applicable to promotions at all levels.
3. Reserved quota remaining unfilled should be carried forward for a period of three years and de-reserved thereafter.
4. Relaxation in the upper age limit for direct recruitment should be extended to candidates of the backward classes as in the case of the Scheduled Castes and the Scheduled Tribes.
5. A roster system for each category of posts should be adopted by the authorities concerned as in the case of the Scheduled Castes and the Scheduled Tribes.[44]

The Report of the Commission was placed before Parliament in 1982 for debate. The whole house supported the report. They did not oppose the caste criterion test as it should affect their standing with the electorate. The Ministry of Home Affairs, Government of India then created a Backward Classes Cell. This cell, which consists of five officers, is concerned, not with the implementation of the recommendations to the report, but with the preparation of replies to questions raised in Parliament. The decision to implement the recommendations is a political decision which the Prime Minister takes up as and when he deems it expedient to do so. Now the Prime Minister is advocating a national consensus on the issue. It means he is not in favour of caste criteria for identifying OBCs'. He has taken note of anti-reservation agitation in the different parts of the country and trying to avoid agitations with the help of national consensus. This means that the recommendations will not be implemented for a long time.

There is a general consensus that the economic factor should also be one of the criteria besides social and educational factors.

44. *Mandal Commission Report*, n. 1, p. 58.

On the other hand our society cannot be stratified on the basis of class alone; for caste and religion are too deeprooted. It is, therefore, necessary to consider all aspects of backwardness—economic, social, and educational. It would be wrong or unjust to accept just one or two aspects and totally ignore the other aspects.

Any reservation policy must be accepted with due considerations. The appointment and promotion of persons must be done carefully keeping in view the expected impacts on efficiency and productivity. No economy, company and establishment can maintain high efficiency and better productivity by ignoring efficiency of individual persons. We have to seek a balance between upliftment of backward classes and maintenance of efficiency.[45] Recruitment policy must be based on worldwide accepted principle "right man for the right job." Does the policy of reservation manitain high efficiency? Is the policy of reservation in tune with the well accepted scientific recruitment policy? Those are some of the questions that haunt the minds of academicians and statesmen.

45. Shriful Hussain, "Prefential Admission in Medical & Technical Course. A Critique *Cochin*, University of Law Review, (1982), p. 6.

CHAPTER IV

Reservation for the other Backward Classes : A National Perspective

The present chapter presents a comparative assessment of the reservation policy as formulated and implemented in the various States of India and to evolve a national perspective on the problem. Each State has adopted a reservation policy in the light of its own special conditions. The Central Government has failed so far to fulfil the long-cherished demand of the backward classes for reservation. It has not acted on the recommendations of the Kaka Kalelkar and Mandal Commissions for the caste based reservation policy. It has left the matter of reservation entirly to the States. That is to say, it wants each State Government to prepare its own list of backward classes on the basis of its own criteria. It favoured the economic criteria rather than the casteism in context of OBCs.

General Outline

The Constitution of India envisages both social and educational backwardness, not just social *or* economic backwardness. Before the judgement in the *Balaji* case, caste, was the sole criterion used for determining backwardness. When the judiciary struck down the reservation policies of a number of State

Governments, the latter undertook an effort to evolve more scientific criteria. The criteria used at present in most States in India are caste, socio-economic backwardness, occupation, education and income. Some States like Andhra Pradesh and Karnataka added a few more castes in OBCs and have even failed to eliminate the advanced backward classes from their lists.

There are differences between the States of South and North India not only in the criteria chosen for determining backwardness, but also in the procedures of implementation. The backward classes are getting the benefits of reservation policy in twelve States (See Table No. 1) In the recommendations of most of the Backward Classes Commission Reports and implementation by the State Governments, caste with income limit are in practice. It varies between 2,400 to Rs 12,00 per annum. In some States (like Andhra Pradesh and Tamil Nadu) they are treated even on a par with the Scheduled Castes and the Scheduled Tribes as regards to age limit, payment of fees and the number of attempts allowed in taking competitive examinations. They have been given additional facilities in the matter of hostel accommodation and other welfare measures.

The Backward Classes Commission headed by B.P.Mandal identified more castes as other backward classes in each State than the Backward Classes Commission headed by Kaka Kalelkar. The Backward Classes Commissions appointed by the various States added yet many more castes to their respective lists of backward classes. For example, in Punjab[1] the number of castes identified as backward was 14 in 1953, it was raised to 25 in 1958 and to 63 in 1959. In Bihar it was 109 in 1951, and it went up to 128 by 1976. The Kaka Kalelkar Commission had identified 126 backward castes in Bihar; the Mandal Commission named 168 castes as socially and educationally

1. Government of the Punjab, *Report of the Evaluation Committee on Welfare of Scheduled Castes, Backward Classes and Denotified Tribes in Punjab, 1947-1966*, (Chandigarh, 1966), p. 112,

TABLE 1

Number of Other Backward Classes and Reservation Quotas for Them in Different Indian States

S.N.	State	State Government list of OBC's	Kaka Kalelkar Commission 1955 list of OBC's	Mandal Commission 1980 list of OBC's	Percentage of Reservation	
					in Government services	in educational institutions
1		2	3	4	5	6
1.	Andhra Pradesh	146	124	292	44	44
2.	Bihar	128	126	168	20	20
3.	Gujarat	82		105	10 (extended to 28 and with drawn)	10 (extended to 28 and with drwn)
4.	Haryana	64	88	76	5	2
5.	Himachal Pradesh	48	27	57	5	2
6.	Jammu & Kashmir	19		63	42	42
7.	Karnataka	221	64	333	35	33

1		2	3	4	5	6
8.	Kerala	76	48	208	40	40
9.	Madhya Pradesh	254	110	279	25 (struck down by High Court)	25 (Struck down by High Court)
10.	Maharashtra	196	360	272	10	10
11.	Punjab	63	88	83	5	5
12.	Tamil Nadu	124	156	288	32	32
13.	Uttar Pradesh	58	120	116	15	15

backward. This does not mean that a number of castes became socially and educationally backward in the interval. It only reflects the anxiety of the different social groups to enjoy the benefits of perferential treatment. The variations in the number of castes identified as backward by different commissions reflect the absence of uniform basis of backwardness. The two Central Commissions had different outlook. The State Government's Commissions had different considerations. Wide differenecs between these commissions on various issues, in some cases irrational, have not only shown absence of uniform policy rather it has become source of constant bittering between two groups of people. Some, though better well-off are enjoying privileges of backwardness, others who really deserve privileges, suffer because they belong to castes outside the jurisdiction of backwards.

Different pictures in different states call for presentation, even in brief, the existing situation and approaches towards this.

Andhra Pradesh

In the composite State of Madras several castes had been identified as backward and were getting preferential treatment in the matter of admission into educational instutions, appointment to posts in Government service, award of scholarships, etc. When the Telugu-speaking districts were detached and constituted a separate State, the new State inherited the list maintained by the Madras State, albeit with some modifications. In the Hyderabad State too some castes and communities had been identified as backward and granted preferential treatment. When the Telugu-speaking districts of the State known as Telangana were separated and added on to the Telugu-speaking districts of the former Madras State, the new State of Andhra Pradesh found that it had two lists of backward classcs—one for the Andhra region (eighty-six communities) and the other for the Telangana (sixty communities).[2]

The Government of Andhra Pradesh passed an Executive Order in 1963 declaring 139 castes as backward and reserve for them 25 per cent of the seats in educational institutions. This order was struck down by the High Court of Andhra Pradesh on the ground that it was based solely on caste. The Court specifically noted that the Government had not adopted any valid standards for determining backwardness.[3]

The State Gsvernment thereupon decided that the criterion for determining backwardness should only be the economic one and this criterion should apply to the individual family rather than to an entire caste. Scrapping the then existing lists of backward classes effective from 1 April 1964 on 3 February 1964 the Government ordered to provide financial assistance to the economically poorer sections of the population. It defined "economically poorer sections" as those whose family having income below Rs 1,500 a year.

Later a Cabinet subcommeittee was constituted in 1964 to draw up a list of backward classes. After obtaining information from different States as to the criteria for determining backwardness, the subcommittee adopted the following criteria for determining backwardness :

1. Poverty.
2. Low standard of education.
3. Low standard of living.
4. Place of habitation.

2. Government of Andhra Pradesh, *Report of the Backward Classes Commission*, (Chairman : Manohar Prasad), Hyderabad, 1970, p. 4.

3. G.P. Verma, *Caste Reservation in India : Law and the Constitution* (Allahabad, 1980), pp. 40-41.

5. Inferiority of occupation ; and
6. Low status of caste.[4]

On the basis of the above criteria it drew up a list of 112 backward communities and recommended 20 per cent of the total seats and posts be reserved for them. The Government accepted the recommendation.

This was challenged in the High Court of Andhra Pradesh in *Sukhdev* v. *Government of Andhra Pradesh, 1966*, on the ground that the list had been prepared only on the basis of caste and that it violated the constitutional provisions and the fundamental rights guaranteed to citizens. The High Court struck down the reservation made for admission into professional colleges for the backward classes with observation that the material placed before the court did not show that the Government had applied the criteria laid down by the Supreme Court in the *Balaji* case in preparing the list of backward classes.[5] The Supreme Court upheld the decision of the Andhra Pradesh High Court on 27 March 1968.

Manohar Prasad Commission, 1968

Thereafter, on 12 April 1968, the Government appointed a Backward Classes Commission, headed by Manohar Prasad, for preparinge a list of all the backward classes which were not adequately represented in the service of the State and to make recommendations as to ;

1. the reservation of Government posts in favour of such backward classes ; and
2. the percentag or proportion of such reservation and the period during which such reservation might be made ;

4. *The Manohar Prasad Commission Report*, n. 2, p. 8.
5. Ibid., p. 9.

The Commission carried out an exhaustive survey of the trades and occupations being pursued by the various classes of people and other matters relavant to the determination of social bacwkwardness. It indicated that only castes or communities, which had traditionally followed unclean and undignified occupations, could be called backward classes. Representatives of such castes demanded reservation up to 40 to 50 per cent. Some of them demanded percentage of reservation in proportion to the population in accordance with the principle adopted by the Government of India in the case of Scheduled Castes and the Scheduled Tribes.[6]

The Manohar Prasad Commission submitted its report on 20 June 1970 to the Government. It listed 92 classes a backward classes. It suggested that caste-wise enumeration be made during the next censuse to determine the progress made by the different classes and communities. Further it recommended reservation of 30 per cent of the vacancies in Government service and educational institutions for candidates belonging to the backward classes. This would be in addition to the seats the backward-class candidates might obtain in the open competition.[7] The Commission distributed the reserved vacancies among four categories of backward classes, as shown in Table No. 2 and its acceptance by the Government.

Even this was struck down by the Andhra Pradesh High Court on ground that the list of backward classes had been prepared on the basis of caste alone. The Supreme Court, however, in *State of Andhra Pradesh* v. *U.S.V. Balaram* did not accept the judgement of the High Court. It observed that "even on the assumption that the list is based exclusively on caste, it is clear from the materials before the Commission and the reasons given by it in its report that the entire caste was socially and

6. Ibid., p. 100.

7. Ibid., p. 103.

TABLE 2

Proposed Reservation for Backward Classes other than the Scheduled Castes and the Scheduled Tribes in Andhra Pradesh : By Manohar Prasad Commission, 1668

	Reservation as recommended by the Commission	*As accepted by the State Government*
	(In terms of percentage)	
Aboriginal tribes	7	7
Nimukta *jatis* and nomadic and seminomadic tribes etc.	13	10
Harijan converts	1	1
Other classes	9	7
Total	30	25

Source : Cited in the *Mandal Commission*, *Report*, Vol. I-II, p. 6.

educationally backward".[8] It accepted the view that a caste was also a class and that reservation in favour of an entire caste was acceptable if the entire caste was socially and educationally backward.

A new Department of Backward Classes Welfare started functioning on 1 September 1975. The Fifth Vidhan Sabha of Andhra Pradesh appointed a committee of the legislature headed by Agiram Veerappa to recommend welfare measures for the benefit of the backward classes. This committee, submitting its report in 1977, had recommended the following measures :

1. award of scholarships from Class I onwards in place of the then practice, i.e. from Class VI onwards ;

8. *State of Andhra Pradesh* v. *Balaram* (AIR, 1972, S.C. 1375).

2 an increase in the amount of the scholarship, and

3. a lowering of the mainimum marks needed for students belonging to backward classes to qualify for scholarahips from 40 per cent to 35 per cent.[9]

Along with reservation of posts and the seats, the backward classes in Andhra Pradesh get an age concession of five years as in the case of the Scheduled Castes and the Scheduled Tribes. They also get housing facilities, lands, scholarahips, hostels, and dress materials.

Murlidhar Rao Commission, 1982

The Congress Party Government of the Andhra Pradesh, to satisfy the backward classes for the time being constituted the Third Backward Classes Commission in February 1982 headed by Murlidhar Rao. The commission in its report of September 1982, recommended 44 per cent reservation of seats and posts for 52 per cent state population of OBC's.[10] The Commission included 10 more castes and sub-castes in the list of OBC's and list went to 102. The recommendations could not be implemented as the Congress Party was defeated in the state assembly election in 1983 and the ruling Telgu Desam failed to take any action till July 1986.

In July 1986, to win back the sympathy of backward classes in coming *Panchayat* election the Congress Party raised the issus. N.T.Rama Rao, who banked on the support of backward classes, announced a fresh reservation policy on 5 July, 1986 for OBC's to maintain control over their support. The State Government added 44 castes to the list prepared by Rao

9. *India, Report of the Backward Classes Commission* (Chairman : B.P. Mandal), (New Delhi, 1980), p. 5.

10. T.N. Ninam and Amarnath Menon, "Andhra Pradesh Reservation Ruckm Sparking off an Anti Reservation Agitation", *India Today* (New Delhi), 31 August, 1986, p. 99.

Commission making it total of 146 OBC's. The new addition of castes was motivated to acquire support of more OBC's.

NTR Reservation Policy, 1986

The NTR reservation policy was designed to benefit the most backward sections of the OBC's. The 44 per cent reservation was divided among the fiive categories of the OBC's according of their backwardness and population. Again the reservation quota was only open to those with family incomes of less than Rs 12,000 a year. The large number of Government employees dependent were not able to enjoy the benefit due to low income limit. In contrast, the students belonging to the agriculturist and trade background might had been benefited with fake income certificates easily available.

Protest Movement

The emerging anti-reservation agitation in Andhra Pradesh was getting strength from *Brahmana Sangham* and even from the Andhra Pradesh Backward Classes Sangham, dominated by prosperous and advanced backward classes. The upper castes were demanding withdrawal of reservation policy and Backward Classes Sangham was raising voice for enhancing income limit from Rs 12,000 to Rs 24,000 per annum. Even pro-reservationists were organized to fight back the anti-reservationists.[11] They formed Andhara Pradesh Sama Sangrama Parished to take cudgels for other backward classes.

The non-beneficiary group of the NTR reservation policy had formed the Andhra Pradesh Nava Sanghurshana Samiti in July 1986. It had arranged a series of *bandhs* in Andhra Pradesh and registered their protest with the State Government. They were calling themselves as merit victimes. They are being denied

11. K. Balagopal, "Andhra Pradesh, Anti-Reservation, Yet Once More", *Economic and Political Weekly*, 6 September, 1986, p. 1573.

admission in medical and engineering colleges with 80 per cent of marks, whereas students from reserved categories are admitted only with 35 per cent of marks. On such valid argument, the Government further released 20 per cent more seats for the meritorious students. Still being unsatisfied, and planning strong protest on the path of Bihar and Gujarat anti-reservation agitations. In the mean time, the High Court of Andhra Pradesh In its judgement of 5th September 1986, has struck down the decision of the Government's reserving 71 per cent seats and and posts calling it unconstitution with the plea that the total reservation cannot exceed 50 per cent.[12]

Gujarat

The Government of Gujarat has appointed two Backward Classes Commissions so far.

Bakshi Commission, 1972

The first Commission was appointed in August 1972 under the Chairmanship of A.R. Bakshi, a retired High Court Judge and Chirman of the Law Commission. The terms of reference of the Commission were as under ;

1. The Commission shall inquire into social, educational, and other relevant conditions of the people, castes, races, or parts of or groups within castes or races or tribes in the State and report what section/sections of them (other than the Scheduled Castes and the Scheduled Tribes) should be treated as socially and educationally and in any other way backward and, therefore, deserving of special treatment and grants of special concessions similar to those being granted to the Scheduled Castes and the Scheduled Tribes in the State in pursuance

12. "Andhra Pradesh Caste Row" *India Today*, 30 September, 1986, p. 54.

of provisions of the various articles of the Constitution of India.

2. The Commission should also recommend what should be the quantum and extent of such concessions and assistance to them and the period during which they should remain in force.[13]

This Commission submitted its report to the Government in February 1976. It listed eighty-two castes and communities as socially and educationally backward and recommended the following measures for their advancement.[14] :

1. Reservation of 10 per cent of the seats in medical, engineering, and other professional institutions ;
2. Reservation of 10 per cent of the Class III and Class IV posts in all Government services ;
3. Reservation of 5 per cent of all Class I and Class II vacancies in all Government services, local bodies, State or public undertakings, etc.
4. reservation of 10 per cent of the seats in training-cum-production centres ; and
5. award of scholarships and other educational facilities, provided the parental income (of the students concerned) did not exceed Rs 4,800 per year. (This income-limit was raised to Rs 7, 200 in the case of nomadic tribes and denotified tribes).

The Congress Government failed to implement these recommendntions. The Janata Government, however, accepted all

13. Government of Gujarat, *Report of the Socially and Educationally Backward Classes (Second) Commission* (Chairman : G.V. Rane) (Ahmedabad, 1984), p. xv.
14. *Mandal Commission, Report*, n. 9, p. 7.

recommendations of the Commission in April 1978 and implemented them.

Some castes, which the Commission did not consider to be socially and educationally backward, made representations to the Government requesting reconsideration of their cases. Representations were also made by members of those castes which had for some reasons failed to make representations to the Bakshi Commission, requesting to treat them socially and educationally backward.

Rane Commission, 1981

The Government, therefore, appointed a second Commission in April 1981 to consider whether there were any other castes/communities/classes which could be placed in the category of socially and educationally backward classes.[15] This second Backward Classes Commission was headed by C.V. Rane, a retired Judge of the High Court of Gujarat. The terms of reference of the Commission[16] were as under :

1. To make suitable recommendations after inquiring into the representations for being considered as belonging to socially and educationally backward classes received from the members of such of the castes, other than the eighty-two castes which are accepted by the Government as belonging to socially and educationally backward classes on the basis of the recommendations of the Bakshi Commission, who had made representations to the Bakshi Commission for being considered as socially and educationally backward, and whose representations were not accepted by the Bakshi Commission; and also from the members of those castes or classes which had either failed to make any representation to the Bakshi

15. Rane, n. 18, p. xvi.
16. Ibid., pp. xvi-xvii.

Commission for considering them as socially and educationally backward or had made such representations after the publication of the Report of the Bakshi Commission.

2. To make necessary inquiry and recommendations in regard to such of the subcastes as are not included in the list of socially and educationally backward classes or in regard to which there is any ambiquity because of prevailing names of subcastes.

3. To make suitable recommendations after necessary inquiry into the question whether a certain number of seats/posts should be reserved for socially and educationally backward classes in educational institutions and public services in proportion to their population in the manner in which they are reserved for the Scheduled Castes and the Scheduled Tribes in educational institutions and public services in proportion to their population or whether some other standard or basis should be adopted in the matter.

4. Relaxation of age limit for backward classes, in what manner ?

5. The Commission may make such other recommendations jermane to the main terms of reference or may be deemed necessary by it.

The Commission undertook an extensive tour of all the districts except the district of Dangs in the State for collecting information from various sources and recording evidence.[17] It submitted its report to the Government in October 1983.

The Commission opined that the social backwardness should be determined without reference to caste. It would facilitate promotion of welfare and educational and economic interests

17. Ibid., p. xvii.

of the weaker sections of the people and accelerate the process of establishing an egalitarian society.[18] It thought that to enumerate castes for determining socially and educationally backward classes was to perpetuate casteism. Thus the Rane Commission was the first Backward Classes Commission to reject the caste yardstick for determining social backwardness.

The point raised by Rane Commission needs careful thinking. Any State decision on caste line would jeopardise the smooth progress of the society. It is well accepted facts that there are facilities rich and poor in both backward classes and forward castes. More to extend facilities to backward classes even though some are rich, prosperous and advanced educationally, culturally, economically and politically, and to deny some of the forward castes though depressed, weak and backward would create tension, turmoil and jealousy. The reservation stirs in different states and casualty. They were not against extending facilities—but based it on secular broad base for avoiding caste-war.

The Commission also held that identification of socially and educationally backward classes in terms of caste was not possible in the case of non-Hindu communities. It pointed out how some groups of people, who were socially and educationally backward, would be left out if socially and educationally back ward classes were identified in terms of caste. In reality only the lower income groups were socially and educationally... backward. In the name of caste the benefits of reservation were appropriated by the top layers of the so-called backward castes. The Commission emphatically stated that there was no backwardness in the case of well-to-do sections or families.[19]

The Commission took occupation in place of caste for identifying backward classes. It felt that there would be no

18. Ibid., p. 99.
19. Ibid., p. 100.

difficulty in ascertaining citizens belonging to socially and educationally backward classes on the basis of occupation. It declared that occupations considered to be inferior with low incomes were the main causes of social and educational backwardness. It identified sixty-three occupations as socially and educationally backward. Thus, the classes it identifled as socially and educationally backward included agricultural labourers, small farmers, marginal farmers, share-croppers, etc., as well as rural and urban artisans. It recommend that only those employed in 63 occupations and receiving less than Rupees one-thousand yearly be treated as backward and enjoy benefits.

The Rane Commission had recommended reservation of seats/posts in educational institutions and in Government service for the socially and educationally backward classes in proportion to their population, as well as a relaxation in the upper age limit in their case for entry into service.[20] The population of the socially and educationally backward classes identified by the Commission was 35.16 per cent of the total population of the State. The Commission, however, recommended reservation of only 28 per cent of the posts and seats for them. This meant even then 18 per cent increase over the quantum of reservatiyn recommended by the Bakshi Commission. In January 1985 the Government of Gujarat reserved 28 per cent of seats and posts for the other backward classes. It did not accept the occupational criteria as suggested by the Rane Commission but went with caste criteria. It witnessed anti-reservation agitation in Gujarat and ultimately Government withdrawn the increased reservation quota. At last even Chief Minister Madho Singh Solanki had to releanquish Chief Ministership.

20. Ibid., p. 103; and see also I.P. Desai, "Anti-Reservation Agitation and Structure of Gujarat Society" in I.P. Desai (eds), Caste, *Caste-conflict and Reservation*, (New Delhi 1985), pp. 124-136.

Haryana

The Government published in 1969 a list of backward classes without a formal inquiry into their economic backwardness and social status. It announced for 10 per cent reservation in Government service and 2 per cent in professional and technical institutions.[21] The facilities and concessions granted were :

1. All members of the backward classes are eligible for the reserved posts at the time of initial appointment, whatever their income.
2. Reservation covers promotions as well in the case of Class III and Class IV posts.
3. Income ceiling for students of the backward classes to be eligible for scholarships has been raised from Rs 1,800 to Rs 4,200 a year.[22]

Himachal Pradesh

The Government has not appointed any Commission so far to identify the other backward classes living on its territory. The Government officials had prepared a list on the basis of economic backwardness and social status. They identified the following categories of people as backward :

1. All the residents of Himachal Fradesh whose annual income is less than Rs 6,000 are backward whatever their caste or community and whatever their professions or occupations.

21. *Mandal Commission Report*, n. 9, p. 11.
22. Discussed in Government of Jammu & Kashmir, *Report of the Backward Classes Commission* (Chairman : Adarsh Sein Anand) (Srinagar, 1977), pp. 55-56.

2. Persons belonging to certain communities are backward if their annual family income is not more than Rs 6,000.[23]

The list of other backward classes is based on both caste and income. The quantum of reservation is 5 per cent of the vacancies in Government service and in educational institutions.[24] Students of the backward classes also get scholarships, interest-free loans. and the tuition fees paid by them are reimbursed. Besides, they have reservation in promotions to selection posts in Class III and Class IV under the Government.

Jammu and Kashmir

The policy of reservation in Jammu & Kashmir has been a controversial issue between the Government and the Judiciary. Judicial intervation compelled the State Government to appoint a Backward Classes Commission.

In 1956 the Government passed Civil Service Rules, which provided for reservention for the backward classes in Government service without specifying any class of people as backward.

Gajendragadkar Commission, 1967

In November 1967 the Government set up a Backwar d classes Commission under the Chairmanship of P.B. Gajendragadkar, who had by then retired as Chief Justice of India, and charged it to examine the recruitment policies of the Government and recommend measures to ensure an equitable share in Government employment to various regions and communities, having special regard to the claims of the Scheduled Castes and other economically, educationally and socially backward communities

23. Ibid., p. 56.
24. *Mandal Commission, Report* n. 9, p. 11.

consistent with the maintenance of efficiency of the administration.[25]

In December 1968 the Gajendragadkar Commission recommended that a high-power committee should be appointed to make a list of backward classes on the basis of the following criteria :

1. Economic backwardness (based on a suitable *ad hoc* figure of annual income)
2. The occupation or occupations pursued
3. Region of permanent residence
4. Number of students per thousand of the population
5. Caste in the case of the Hindus.

Wazir Commission, 1969

Accepting the suggestion of the Gajendragadkar Commission the Government appointed a Committee headed by J.N. Wazir in February 1969. On the basis of the recommendations of the Wazir Committee, submitted in November 1969, the Government passing the Jammu & Kashmir Scheduled Castes and Backward Classes (Reservation) Rules, 1970 reserved vacancies for Scheduled Castes and Backward Classes in each service, class, category and grade in the State service[26] in accordance with the following ratio :

1. Scheduled Castes—8 per cent; and
2. Backward Classes-42 per cent (including 2 per cent for the permanent residents of Ladakh).

This reservation policy was Challenged in the Supreme Court, which found certain defects in the rules in *Janki Prasad*

25. *Anand Commission Report* n. 22, p. 1.
26. Ibid., p. 3.

Parimoo and others v. *State of Jammu & Kashmir and others* (AIR 1973, S.C. 930) and *Triloki Nath and other* v. *State of Jammu & Kashmir and others* (AIR 1967, S.C. 1283).

After pointing out the various defects in the *Janki Prasad Parimoo* case, the Supreme Court observed :

> "We have shown above defects in the rules which purport to identify certain residents of the State as backward. Till the defects are cured, the rules are not capable of being given efiect to."[27]

Anand Commissian, 1976

In August 1976 the Government appointed a Backward Classes Committee headed by Justice Adarsh Sein Anand to advise on the removal of the various anomalies in the Act of 1970 as detected by the Supreme Court. It asked the Committee to make recommendations with regard to the follwing issues :

1. To determine the criteria to be followed in determining backardness.
2. To identify and prepare a list of backward classes.
3. To castegorize backward classes and suggest safeguards for giving benefits to the desrving only ; and
4. To examine the question of reservation in Government service at every stage.[28]

The Anand Committee noted the desire of the Government to remove the backwardness of certain classes of people of the State so as to enable all sections of the population to live as equals and enjoy equality of opportunity in all spheres of life.[29] It supported preferential representation for the backward

27. Ibid., p. 4.
28. Ibid., p. i.
29. Ibid., p. ii.

classes in Government service with due regard being paid to administrative efficiency.[30] It drew up a list of two categories of backward classes :

1. Weak and underprivileged sections ; and
2. Residents of backward areas, i.e. of
   (*a*) bad pockets ; and
   (*b*) areas within eight kilometers of the line of actual control.

On the basis of these recommendations, 42 per cent Government jobs and seats in professional and technical institutions and in other institutions of higher learning were reserved for the backward classes.

Karnataka

Even in the second decade of the present century it was brought to the notice of the Maharaja of Mysore that there was an unemployment problem among the backward classes. Earlier in 1916, seeing that there was a preponderance of Brahmans in the public service, the Maharaja ordered that steps be taken to ensure that all important communities in the State were adequately represented in the service of the State.

Miller Committee, 1918

In August 1918 the Government of Mysore appointed a Committee under the Chairmanship of Sir Weslie C. Miller to investigate and report on the poblem. The questions referred to this Committee were the following :

1. Changes needed in the then rules of recruitment to the public services.

30. Ibid., p. iii.

2. Special facilities needed to encourage higher and professional education among the members of the backward classes ; and

3. any other special measures needed to increase the representation of the backward communities in the public service without materially affecting the efficiency, due regard being paid also to the general good accruing to the State by a wider diffusion of education and a feeling of increased status which would thereby be produced in the backward communities.[31]

The Miller Committee submitted its report in July 1919. The Government accepted its recommendations that the term "backward communities" should be understood to include all communities in the State other than Brahmans, Anglo-Indians, and Christians. This was the position more or less till the Reorganization of States in November 1956.[32]

When a new State of Mysore was created on 1 November 1956 in accordance with recommendations of the States Reorganization Commission it was found that in the five areas that had been brought together to create the new State there were five different lists of backward classes. These were allowed to stand for some time. In 1959 a small commitee was set up to prepare a consolidated list of backward communities. 57 per cent of the posts were reserved for the backward classes in the State.

The validity of this consolidated list of backward classes was challenged in the High Court of Mysore. The High Court in *Ramakrishna Singh* v. *State of Mysore, 1959*, held that the Government orders listing the backward classes in the State and

31. Government of Mysore, *Report of the Mysore Backward Classes Committee* (Chairman : R. Naganna Gowda) (Bangalore : Government Press, 1961), p. 4,

32. Ibid., p. 2,

grouping them for the purposes of reservation of state in technical institutions were not in accordance with Article 15 (4) of the Constitution.

Gowda Committee, 1960

In January 1960 the Government constituted a committee headed by R. Naganna Gowda to advise on the criteria for the classification of backward classes in the State. The terms of reference of the committee were :

1. To suggest the criteria to be adopted in determining which sections of the people in the State should be treated as socially and educationally backward ; and
2. to suggest the exact manner in which the criteria thus indicated should be followed to enable the State Government to determine the persons who should secure such preference, as may be determined by the Government in respect of admission to technical institutions and appointments to Government services.[33]

The Committee collected information through a questionnaire, received representations from various organizations and individuals and toured the State extensively. It, however, failed to collect correct statistical information with regard to the percentage of literacy among them.

The Committee opined that the problem of backwardness among the Hindus had been created by a defective social system. Economic backwardness was the result, not the cause, of the numerous social evils that were to be found among the people.[34] However, in the conditions the Committee felt that :

"It was not possible for it to adopt any other basis except caste and community for classifying the backward classes.

33. Ibid., pp. 5-6.
34. Ibid., p. 10.

It was not possible to disassociate caste from social backwardness; nor was it possible to group people in terms of occupations. A Brahman taking to shoe-making did not become a cobbler by caste and his social status was not lowered. Social backwardness did not, therefore, go with the profession."[35]

The Committee recommended that the following criteria be adopted for classifying backward classes :

1. Social backwardness of a community should be judged by the status accorded to the community in society in general (apart from individuals).
2. Its general educational backwardness should be judged on the basis of some fixed standard of education.
3. The representation a community has in Government service should also be taken into account.

It recommended reservation up to 50 per cent for the Backward and more backward classes in educational institutions and Government jobs. In July 1962 the Government accepted the recommendations and the Supreme Court withheld the validity of the classification in the *Balaji* case.

Havanur Commission, 1972

The Government appointed a second Backward Classes Commission in August 1972 under the Chairmanship of L.G. Havanur, a champion of the backward classes. The Commission produced an extensive report in November 1975. It surveyed 193 villages and 185 urban blocks covering 1.18 per cent of the State population. It used the economic, educational and social standing of each community and group but found that the economic and educational conditions were far more appropriate for determining backwardness than social conditions. The caste

35. Ibid., p. 11.

and the subcaste became units for inclusion in other backward classes. Thus, one unit of a large caste was included among the backward classes while another was not. For example, the Bunts of Dakshina Kannada were excluded from the list of backward classes while the other units of the Okkaligas/Gowdas were included.[36]

The Commisson divided the backward classes into three categories to prevent the benefits of backwardness being monopolized by any dominant subcategory or group.

TABLE 3

Recommendations of the Havanur Commission

Name of backward classes	*Percentage of population*	*Percentage of reservation*
Backward communities	19.20	16.00
Backward castes	14.47	10.00
Backward tribes	8.00	6.00
Total	41.67	32.00

Source : Government of Karnataka, *Report of the Karnataka Backward Classes Commission* (Chairman : L.G. Havanur), (Bangalore : Government Press, 1975), p. 310.

The Government under Chief Minister Devaraj Urs, accepted most of the recommendations. Urs included muslims (11 per cent of the State population) in the list of backward classes. Recognising poor people in every-caste, reservation of 5 per cent seats and jobs for them was recommended. Later on reservation

36. M.N. Srinivas and M.N. Panini, "Politics and Society in Karnataka", *Economic and Political Weekly* (Bombay), 14 January 1984, p. 70. This periodical is cited hereinafter as *EPW*.

quota was raised to 15 per cent for the poor people of the non-backward classes.

TABLE 4

Implementation of Reservation in 1977

Sl.No.	Backward classes	Educational Institutions	Government jobs
		(In terms of percentage)	
1.	Scheduled castes	15.00	15.00
2.	Scheduled tribes	3.00	3.00
3.	Backward communities	20.00	18.00
4.	Backward castes	10.00	10.00
5.	Backward tribes	5.00	5.00
6.	Special groups	15.00	15.00

Source : *K.C. Vasanth Kumar* v. *State of Karnatak*, AIR 1985 S.C., p.1540.

The new formula included 185 communities but excluded dominant social groups like the Lingayats and a few others.

Urs's formula of reservation applied the income test in the matter of appointments. As regards categories 3, 4, and 5, a candidate, whose family income from all sources was Rs 8,000 a year or less, would be eligible for the vacancies reserved for the backward classes. The special groups entitled to reservation comprised the following :

1. Actual cultivators.
2. Artisans.
3. Petty business men.

4. Those holding appointments in Government service or in private employment ; and
5. Those engaged in occupations involving manual labour or self-employment.[37]

Within these categories anyone, whose family income was Rs 4,800 a year or less, would be treated as belonging to the special groups.

Venkataswamy Commission 1985

In the judgement of *K.C. Vasanth Kumar* v. *State of Karnataka, 1985* Supreme Court asked the Karnataka Government to re-determine the whole reservation of seats and posts. Thereafter in 1985. Karnataka Government cons tituted second Backward Classes Commission headed by a retired judge T. Venkataswamy to find out the OBCs in Karnataka and suggested measures for their upliftment. It went into the problem in depth and conducted extensive Survey of Secondary School living certificate students for identifying educational backwardness. It identified 33 per cent of the State population as OBCs, de-recognising many castes and suggested 27 per cent reservation for them in place of continuing 49 per cent. It divided OBCs, in four groups ('A' 'B' and 'D') in place of prevailing three (backward communities, backward castes and backward tribes). A new 'Backward special group' was also formed. Numerically strong, politically influencial and economically better Okkalingas and 35 other castes were excluded from the list of OBC's by the Commission. It was found that these castes were well off to progress without any preferential treatment.

Okkalinga and other excluded castes organised a number of *bandh* and pressurised the ruling Janata Party Government

37. B. Sivaramayya, "Equality and Inequality : The Legal Framework", in Andre Betaiile, ed. *Equality and Inequality : Theory and Practice* (Delhi, 1983), p. 48, and AIR, 1985, S.C., p. 1540.

for rejecting the Commission's report. The Janata Legislators belonging to Okkalingas threatened to quit the Party if the report would be implemented. Ultimately Karnataka Government rejected[38] the report on 7th October, 1986, and in place of it introduced a new policy which benefits 88 per cent of the State population by reservation of 68 per cent of jobs for them. In the new policy the income limit is Rs 10,000 per annum, except in case of backward tribes. This is also applicable to the most backward category.

The benefit is extended to Brahmans, Lingayats and other advanced castes for three years. The Government desired to constitute a new Backward Classes Commission for fresh fact findings. Presently the Government's decision is politically calculated to maintain power and win over the coming *Panchayat* election, but it has failed to exclude the advanced social sections from the beneficiary groups of the reservation policy.

Kerala

In Kerala State, reservation policy became the subject of an acute judicial controversy so much so that the Government appointed three Backward Classes Commissions.

Shivanathan Commission, 1961

The first Commission appointed in June 1961, was headed by B.K. Shivanathan. The Commission was asked to identify the backward classes and suggest measures for the improvement of their conditions of life and work. The Commission submitted its report in October 1963. Its main recommendations were as follows :

1. Forty per cent of the seats in technical and professional colleges should be reserved for students belonging to the backward classes and 10 per cent of the seats for

38. *Times of India* (New Delhi), 9 October 1986.

TABLE 5

Implementation of Reservation in 1986

No.	*Backward Classes*	*Per cent of Population*	*Per cent of reservation*	*Income limit per annum in rupees*
1.	Special Backward groups (Foreward castes in inferior occupations-artisan, cultivators, petty businessmen, casual labourers of class IV Government servant	8.00	5	8,000
2.	Group 'A', 62 backward tribes	4.73	5	No
3.	Group 'B' from 128 most backward castes	19.34	15	10,000
4.	Group 'C' backward communities	20.62	16	10,000
5.	Group 'D' advanced backward castes	20.79	9	10,000
	Total	73.48	50	

Source : S. Rajappa, "Something for Everyone in Reservation Policy", *The Statement* (Calcutta), 16 October 1986; Murthy, Sachidananda, "Everyone Wants Backward Tag", *The Week* (Kottayam), 19-25 October, 1986.

students belonging to the Scheduled Castes and the Scheduled Tribes.

2. The above reservation should be made applicable to all fresh appointments to posts under the State Government also.[39]

The Government reserved 25 per cent of the seats for the backward classes. This was challenged in the Kerala High Court in the case *Jacob Mathev* v. *State of Kerala.*[40] The single judge found fault with the assessment of the social backwardness of the populous Ezhava caste. The Division Bench supported reservation for Muslims, Ezhavas and Roman Catholics on the ground that they constituted socially and educationally backward classes. At the same time it said that a fact-finding commission be appointed to evolve objective criteria for making educationa benefits available to the backward classes. It added that suchal fact finding commission should inquire into the social and educational conditions of people other than the Scheduled Castes and the Scheduled Tribes with a view to determine whether they were deserving special treatment by way of reservation of seats in educational institutions.

Pillai Commission, 1964

The Second Commission, under the Chairmanship of G. Kumara Pillai in its report of December 1965 was of the view that the prosperous sections of the backward communities were not suffering from social discrimination. It viewed the then system of reservation based solely on caste or community was, to a considerable extent, being enjoyed by the wealthy sections to the prejudice of the poorer sections.[41] For the benefit of the poorer sections from reservation it recommended the adoption of a means-cum-caste/community policy.

39. *Mandal Commission, Report*, n. 9, pp. 8-9.

40. *Jacob Mathew* v. *State of Kerala* (AIR 1964, Kerala), p. 39.

41. Verma, n. 3, pp. 47-48.

The Commission rejected occupation as a criterion of backwardness on the ground that the stigma attached to certain occupations was the low income of the communities which had traditionally followed those occupations and that those communities were already covered by the "caste" criterion.[42] It recommended an income ceiling of Rs. 4,200, but the State Government raised it to Rs. 6,000 while giving effect to the recommendations. The main recommendation of the Commission was related to reservation in educational institutions. It listed ninety-one castes as backward and recommended 25 per per cent reservation for them in technical and professional institutions.

The State Government accepted most of the recommendations of the Commission in the context of reservation of seats in educational institutions, but left the previous 40 per cent of reservation of posts in Government service for the backward classes untouched as the Kerala High Court had asked the State Government to have a fresh inquiry conducted only in the context of reservation in educational institutions.

Damodaran Commission, 1967

Later in 1967, the Kerala High Court suggested the appointment of yet another Backward Classes Commission. The State Government then appointed third Backward Classes Commission headed by M.P. Damodaran in October 1967. This Commission submitted its report in June 1970.

The Damodaran Commission found the following factors responsible for social backwardness for the purposes of Article 16 (4) :

1. Lack of requisite educational attainments (test of education).

42. Report of the Kerala Commission for Reservation of *Seats in Educational Institutions* (Chairman : G. Kumara Pillai) (Trivandrum : Government Press, 1966), pp. 37ff.

2. Lack of money or wealth (economic test).
3. Lack of ability to appropriate an adequate number of appointments (test of appropriation of appointments); and
4. Caste disability, occupational stigma, and social taboos acting as depressants in the field of education.[43]

Social backwardness continued to be a matter of controversy. Some of the populous and advanced castes like the Ezhavas exerted pressure to retain their privileged status as a backward community. The Administrative Reforms Committee appointed by the Government of Kerala, realising the evils and drawbacks of caste as the basis of backwardness, recommended the economic criterion. This resulted in a prolonged and bitter conflict between the Ezhavas and the Nairs. Further, the dominant castes, irrespective of the fact whether they were really economically, educationally and socially backward, managed to enjoy the concessions accorded to the backward classes because of their political power. Owing to political pressure all the backward communities of Kerala accepted the Ezhavas as backward.

The Communities which met four tests (education, economic participation in Government service and social backwardness for historical reasons), together with families with incomes below Rs 8,000 a year, were recommended for treating backward for the purposes of Article 16 (4). It included such factors as stigmatized occupations, vestiges of caste discrimination, the custom of *purdah*, and aversion to education in English. It recommended 40 per cent reservation in Government posts for the backward classes for eight groups of backward classes as shown in Table No. 6.

43. *Report of the Kerala Backward Classes Reservation Commission* (Chairman : Nettur P. Damodaran) (Trivandurm : Government Press, 1966), p. 42.

TABLE 6

Reservation for the Backward Classes (other than the Scheduled Castes and the Scheduled Tribes) in Kerala

	Reservation in respect of	
	Class IV posts (Percentage)	*Other than Class VI (Percentage)*
Ezhavas	11	14
Muslims	10	12
Roman Catholics and Anglo-Indians	4	4
Nadars	1	1
Scheduled Castes converted to Christianity	2	1
Communities like Asaris, Kammalas, Viswakarmas, etc.	2	3
Dheevara community	2	1
Other backward classes	8	4
Total	40	40

Source : *Mandal Commission Report*, Vol. I-II, p. 9.

Madhya Pradesh

Madhya Pradesh was among the Indian States which did not prepare any list of backward classes nor took any specific action for their upliftment till 1984. In 1985 it reserved 35 per cent seats and posts for the other backward classes, which was withheld by the Madhya Pradesh High Court. Now again OBCs are not getting any preferential treatment.

Mahajan Com mission, 1980

The Government of Madhya Pradesh appointed a Backward Classes Commission under Chairmanship of Ramjee Mahajan and nine members in November 1980 for preparing a list of backward classes and suggest measures for their upliftment.[44] The Commission, identifying 254 castes and subcastes as backward classes, recommended reservation of 35 per cent of the seats for them in educational institutions. It also wanted the same percentage of Government and semi-Government jobs to be reserved for them.

Although the Commission used the caste criterion for identifying backward classes, it suggested the exclusion of prosperous groups from the benefits of reservation. For this purpose, it suggested that the benefits of reservation should be extended only to the children of those who were not income-tax payees or who owned less than ten acres of irrigated and non-irrigated land. Along with the benefits of reservation it recommended the grant of scholarships and the provision of hostel facilities.

In November 1984 the Government announced reservation of 25 per cent of the jobs for the backward classes instead of 35 per cent as recommended by the Commission. It was apparently an election gimmick on the eve of the Lok Sabha elections of 1984. The Congress (I) was able to capture the support of the backward classes by this gimmick. However, the anti-reservationists prepared a plan to oppose the Government policy. In the beginning they did not get much support due to death of Mr. Indira Gandhi and the Bhopal Gas tragedy but by January and February 1985 the movement gathered momentum.

The anti-reservationists took the matter to the streets. They also appealied to the Judiciary. The Bhopal High Court asked

44. *Report of the Madhya Pradesh Backward Classes* (Chairman : Ramjee Mahajan) Bhopal : Government Press, 1984).

the Government to refrain from implementing the reservation policy. Change of leadership in the Congress (I) (Arjun Singh, who favoured reservation for OBC's was replaced by Motilal Bora) also helped to pacify the anti-reservationists. If the Government plan for reservation is executed, it would mean 65 per cent on the basis of caste (Scheduled Castes : 22.5 per cent; Scheduled Tribes : 7.5 per cent; and the other backward classes : 35 per cent).[45] The Government also proposes to reserve 4 per cent for the economically backward; 5 per cent for ex-servicemen; 3 per cent for freedom-fighters and "technical" hands; and one per cent for miscellaneous categories. As a whole it was 78 per cent reservation of posts and seats. It was not proper and just on the part of Government to left only 22 per cent seats and posts for the open competition.

Maharashtra

The backward classes movement in India originated in Maharashtra and Tamil Nadu. Omvedt considers Maharashtra and Tamil Nadu to be States where rural impoverishment was highest. This was why they produced a cultural revolt in India.[46] The Satya Shodhak Samaj founded by Jyoti Rao Phule provided organization and leadership to backward castes like the Malis, the Telis, the Kumbis and the Satis. They fought against Brahminical dominance and created in the backward classes an awareness of their genuine rights. They prepared the social base for the leadership of Dr. Bheemrao Ramji Ambedkar in the subsequent years.

Deshmukh Committee, 1961

Other backward classes of Maharashtra whose number grew

45. A.S. Abraham, "Anti-Reservation Protest : Growing Clout of Backward Classes", *Times of India* (New Delhi), 14 March 1985.

46. Gail Omvedt, *Cultural Revolt in a Colonial Society : The Non-Brahmin Movement in Western India, 1873-1930* (Bombay, 1976).

from 125 castes in 1953 to 160 in 1967 and 198 in 1967 also mobilized themselves as social groups. The Government policy was to move from the caste to the income criterion. In November 1961 the Government appointed a Backward Classes Committee, under the Chairmanship of B.D. Deshmukh, to "report on the reservation of backward classes in services." This Committee, in its report of January 1964, grouped backward classes into four categories :

1. Scheduled Castes and neo-Buddhists.
2. Scheduled Tribes.
3. Denotified and nomadic tribes; and
4. Other backward communities.

It also recommended that reservation in Government services and in educational institutions for different categories of backward classes should be related to the percentage of their population in the State.[47]

The Government of Maharashtra accepted the recommendations on reservation in proportion to population in case of the first three groups. Scheduled Castes and Scheduled Castes convert to Buddhism, Scheduled Tribes and Denotified and Nomadic Tribes but not in the case of the other backward communities. It made reservation[48] in the service of the State and in educational institutions for the four categories of backward classes in that only 10 per cent seats and posts were provided to other backward classes.

Punjab

The Punjab is among the first North Indian States to go in for a policy of job reservation for the backward classes. It did so in 1951. It adopted a policy of reservation for the Scheduled

47. *Mandal Commission Report*, n. 9, p. 9.
48. Ibid.

Castes as early as in 1934. The Government issued instructions that duly qualified candidates belonging to the Scheduled Castes should not be deprived of a fair opportunity of securing jo s in the public services just because they were not able to compete in an open competition. In 1943 it reserved 8.5 per cent of the seats for them. Subsequently, in 1946, it raised the reservation quota to 12.5 per cent making it proportionate to the population of the Scheduled Castes in the State.[49]

In 1951 the Government appointed a Backward Classes Commission to identify the backward classes in the State. The criteria adopted for the identification of backward classes were economic educational and social backwardness. The Commision identified two percent of the population as backward and recommended the same percent age of reservation. The Government accepted the recommendation.

Brish Bhan Committee, 1965

The reservation policy was re-evaluated in 1965 by a commiittee of legislators headed by Brish Bhan. This Committee in its report of August 1963, had made following recommendations :

1. The list of backward classes should be rationalized, so that classes or castes which were no longer backward might be excluded; and
2. The reservation of two per cent of the seats in educational institutions should be raised to five per cent.[50]

The Committee was not in favour of extending the reservation policy to Government jobs, but the Government was. The

49. *Committee on Welfare of Scheduled Castes, Scheduled Tribes and Backward Classes, 1975-76*; *Fourth Report* (Chandigarh : Punjab Vidhan Sabha, 1976), p. 2; *Gurinder Pal Singh* v. *State of Punjab*, AIR 1974, Punj 125.

50. *Mandal Commission Report*, n. 9, p. 10.

Government raised reservation up to 5 per cent both in Government jobs and in educational institutions for sixty-three backward classes irrespective of their religion.

Harcharan Singh Commission, 1975

In 1975-76 the Punjab Legislative Assembly appointed a Committee on the Welfare of Scheduled Castes, the Scheduled Tribes, and the Backward Classes under the Chairmanship of Harcharan Singh. The Committee had nine members. The Committee was assigned :

1. To examine the measures taken by the Government to secure due representation for the Scheduled Castes, the Scheduled Tribes, and the backward classes in Government service (inculding appointments in public sector undertakings and in statutory and semi-Government bodies) in fulfilment of the provisions of Article 335 of the Constitution; and

2. To report to the House on the working of the welfare programmes for the Scheduled Castes, the Scheduled Tribes, and the Backward Classes.

Finding inadequate representation of the backward classes in relation to their population, it recommended 15 per cent reservation for them in Government service and educational institutions.[51] The Government, however, found it difficult to accept this recommendation as it had already provided for reservation up to 25 per cent for the Scheduled Castes and up to 20 per cent for retired army personnel. It, therefore, continued with its policy of reserving 5 per cent of the seats in educational institutions and 5 per cent of initial appointments in Government service. It also provided for 2 per cent reservation in promotions up to Class I. It, further, decided to maintain a roster of

51. *Committee on Welfare of Scheduled Castes, Scheduled Tribes, and Backward Classes, 1975-76*, n. 49, p. v.

all vacancies meant for the Scheduled Castes and backward classes[52] in the form of a running account, year by year, for each category of posts. However, it reserved its right to de-reserve vacancies at its discretion.

The backward classes are entitled to a number of facilities and concessions in Punjab. These include age concessions up to five years in non-gazetted service, up to three years in gazetted service, and fee concessions in respect of competitive examinations. There are no income limits for promotion.

Tamil Nadu

In Madras the term "backward" was used in the Department of Education in the context of payment of stipends to students coming from "illiterate" and "indigent" castes. The number of backward classes, which was 39 in 1895, rose to 133 in 1913, to 128 in 1920 and to 152 in 1950. This of course does not mean that more and more castes became backward as the years passed. It only shows that more and more castes learnt to demand and receive special educational concessions on the basis of caste rather than individual merit.[53]

The principle in 1927 was that among the qualified applicants for any job, priority should be given to those belonging to the least represented communities. For this purpose the various communities were grouped into five broad categories. The proportion of appointments to be allocated to non-Brahman Hindu 5 posts out of 12. This was revised in 1947 granting greater participation to the Scheduled Castes. Also for the first time, Backward Hindu appeared as a separate category.

Abrogating the system of communal representation in the service of the State in 1950 the benefit of preferential treatment

52. Ibid., p. 4.

53. S. Saraswati, *Minorities in Madras State : Group Interest in Modern Politics* (Delhi, 1974), p. 108,

TABLE 7

Communal Quotas in Service in Madras, 1947

Categories	*Posts to be allocated*
Non-Brahman Hindu	6 out of 14
Backward Hindu	2 out of 14
Brahman	2 out of 14
Scheduled Castes	2 out of 14
Anglo-Indians and Indian Christains	1 out of 14
Muslims	1 out of 14

Source : *Report of the Tamil Nadu Backward Classes Commission* (Chairman : A.N. Sattanathan) (Madras 1971), p. 28.

was reserved only for the Scheduled Castes, the Scheduled tribes and the backward classes. Under the new system a cycle of twenty appointments was taken as a unit. Three were reserved for the Scheduled Castes and the Scheduled Tribes, five for the backward classes and the rest were filled on the basis of merit.

On the basis of the 1951 census and in the wake of the separation of Andhra Pradesh from Tamil Nadu in 1954, the reservation was changed to 16 per cent for the Scheduled Castes and the Scheduled Tribes and 25 per cent for the backward classes.

Sattanathan Commission, 1969

In March 1969 the Government appointed a Backward Classes Commission under the Chairmanship of A.N.Sattanathan to examine the welfare measures taken by the Government to promote the welfare of the backward classes and to improve the conditions of the "most backward classes" in education and other matters. The Commission was, further, asked to make recommendations as to the steps that the State Government might take to improve the conditions of the backward classes in respect of professional and technical education, Government jobs, trade, commerce, industry and housing.

The Commission, in its report of 1970, used educational and social backwardness and the nature of the occupation pursued traditionally by a majority of the members of a caste as the main criterion of backwardness.[54] It held that to assume that there was no social and economic or educational backwardness outside the fold of the Scheduled Castes was to betray a total ignorance of Indian social conditions. As for economic backwardness, it placed most of the backward classes under the occupational categories newly listed by the Government of Mysore as socially backward, thus :

1. Actual cultivators.
2. Artisans.
3. Petty business men.
4. Those who perform inferior services, including casual labourers; and
5. Those belonging to any other occupation involving manual labour.[55]

It recommended 33 per cent reservation for the backward classes.

The Commission divided the backward classes into two parts :

1. Backward classes and
2. Most backward classes.

54. Ibid., p. 16.
55. Ibid., p. 38.

It recommended 17 per cent reservation for the backward classes and 16 per cent for the most backward classes. It was not in favour of making reservation on the basis of population as in the case of the Scheduled Castes and the Scheduled Tribes.[56] Most of the backward classes have made no progress worth the name and their position even now is worse than that of the Scheduled Castes. From this viewpoint the division of the backward classes into two parts was justifiable.

The Commission was adamant about not allowing advanced sections of the backward classes to enjöy the benefits of reservation. It, therefore, proposed the following criteria for determining the advanced sections in each backward caste :

1. Those who received salaries from the Government or from non-Governmental sources or from business undertakings and whose gross income exceeded Rs 9,000 a year:
2. Those who possessed more than ten standard acres of land.
3. Those engaged in business or industrial activity and paying income-tax.
4. Those who had income from more than one source; and
5. Those belonging to families in which both parents, earning independently, brought in a sum of Rs 12,000 or more as gross income.[57]

It held that if this upper crust in each caste was not barred from competing with the less privileged, the object of social justice, especially distributive justice, would never be achieved. It declared that benefits should not go to anybody by the sheer accident of birth in a particular caste.

56. Ibid., pp. 45.
57. Ibid., pp. 100-1.

The Government accepted the recommendations of the Sattanathan Commission but made some modifications as requird by the Suprme Court judgement in the *Balaji* case. It took the population of the Scheduled Castes and the Scheduled Tribes as found during the 1971 census, and ordered that 31 per cent of all posts in Government serivice and seats in educational institutions be reserved for the backward classes and 18 per cent for the Scheduled Castes and the Scheduled Tribcs. In November 1980 the State Government raised the reservation for the backward classes from 31 per cent to 50 per cent. This excluded the reservation (18 per cent) made for the Scheduled Castes and the Scheduled Tribes. This increase was made, not on the basis of socioecnomic and educational backwardness, but under caste and political considerations.

Students of the backward classes in Tamil Nadu get scholarships free food, free books and free school uniforms. They enjoy special educational facilities, including hostels. Such facilities are not available to students of the backward classes elsewhere in India.

The Commission found that the reservation rule was being followed generally in the case of direct recruitment only and not in the case of promotion. It noted that even in 1927 the Government had examind the matter and had come to the conclusion[58] that while the principle of reservation to redress inequalities is all right at the time of initial appointments, a Government servant should, having entered service, compete on equal terms with his colleagues and earn his promotion in the normal course by seniority or seniority-cum-merit.

A Government Order in 1980 dispensed with the ceiling of Rs 9,000 on the annual family income for eligibility for the concessions avilable to the backward classes.[59] The Government

58. Ibid., p. 102.

59. "The Clamour for the 'Backward' Label", *The Hindu* (Madras), 6 April 1985.

also scrapped the division of the backward classes into backward classes and most backward classes. This was challenged in the Supreme Court. The Supreme Court struck down the move of the Government.

Ambasankar Commision, 1980

After the Supreme Court judgement, the Government constituted a 21-member Backward Classes Commission under the Chairmanship of J.A. Ambasankar to review the classification of backward classes in the State and to reassess their reservation quota of 50 per cent.[60] The Commission recommended that the reserved quota be slashed to 32 per cent. The Finance Minister announced the Government's acceptance of the Supreme Court's ruling that the reservation for the backward classes and the Scheduled Castes and the Scheduled Tribes together should not exceed 50 per cent.

Uttar Pradesh

In the Hindu heartland Uttar Pradesh has been a stronghold of the backward class movement. Different backward castes through caste associations have been demanding job reservation since 1930. In the early twentieth century they went in for Sanskritization in the belief that it would improve their social status. Sanskritization took the edge off their hostility towards he upper castes. They also failed to forge the kind of unity that their counterparts in South India had done. Some of the prominent backward class leaders of Uttar Pradesh such as Swami Achutanand, Swami Ramchandra Mallad and S.D. Singh Chaurasia made determined efforts to forge unity.

Some agriculturist castes like the Ahirs (Yadavas), the Jats and the Gujars built a broad-based organization called "AJGAR". This organization also failed to restrict the political

60. Shariful Hasan, "Reservation Policy", *Hindustan Times*, (New Delhi), 3 May 1980.

and social dominance of the upper castes. The various backward class organizations successfully mobilized the backward classes against the Congress Party in elections of 1967 and 1977. Their leaders received due representation at the time of the formation of Governments. These leaders were in favour of a reservation policy for the benefit of the backward classes in Government service and in educational institutions.

The Jats, a predominantly agriculturist caste, though supported the demands of the backward classes, but never asked for any preferential treatment for themselves.

In 1945 the Government designated thirty-seven Hindu castes and twenty-one Muslim groupings as backward and gave them educational concessions. In 1950 it reserved 10 per cent of the vacancies in Government service and in educational institutions for the Scheduled Castes but did nothing sepecific for the backward classes. In 1955 a Cabinet Sub-committee prepared two lists of backward classes—one for the purpose of recruitment to the public services and the other for the award of educational concessions. The first consisted of fifteen backward castes and the second of fifty-nine backward castes.

In 1958 the Government prepared two lists; one containing thirty-seven Hindu castes and the second twenty-one Muslim groupings. These lists were similar to that of 1945. They were used for the award of educational concsessions. There was no move to reserve posts in Government service.

Chhedi Lal Sathi Commission, 1975

It was in October 1975 that a Most Backward Classes Commission was constituted under the Chairmaniship of Chhedi Lal Sathi to consider the conditions of the "most backward classes of citizens" as distinguished from the "backward classes" and "to suggest measures for improving their conditions."

The Commission used poverty, illiteracy, housing, occupation, caste, social inequality and representation in Government service, industry, and commerce as yardsticks for measuring backwardness. After two years' deliberations it gave its report in June 1977.[61] Classifying backward classes into three categories, it recommended separate quotas in Government service for each of the three categories, as follows :

TABLE 8

Recommendations of the Sathi Commission

	Percentage of reservation
List "A" comprising landless laboures, unskilled workers, non-artisans, and domestic servants	17
List "B", comprising marginal and small cultivators	10
List "C" Muslim Backward Classes	2½
Total	29½

Source : *Mandal Commission*, *Report*, Vol. I & II, p. 10.

The first list contained thirty-six backward castes with a little land or without land; the second had eighteen agriculturist castes like the Yadavas, the Gujars, the Kurmis, etc., and the third was exclusively for the backward classes from the Muslim community. The Commission recommended special facilities, scholarship, etc., for the castes and other groupings it had designated backward.

61. *Mandal Commission Report*, n. 9, p. 10.

The Janata Government headed by Ram Naresh Yadav largely accepted the recommendations of the Commission. It passed orders for the reservation of 15 per cent of Government jobs and seats in technical and professional institutions for candidates of the backward classes. Already 18 per cent of the jobs were reserved for the Scheduled Castes; 2 per cent for the Scheduled Tribes; 2 per cent for the handicapped; 5 per cent for the dependents of freedom fighters; and 8 per cent for retired military officers. With the reservation of 15 per cent of jobs for the backward classes, the total reservation for different social groups reached 50 per cent. This led to an anti-reservationist movement in 1977.

The reservation policy then came up before the Allahabad High Court. The petitioners alleged that many of the so-called backward castes like the Ahirs (the Yadavas) and the Kurmis were not economically and socially backward; that many of them were big farmers and were prosperous; and the quite a number were highly educated and occupied high offices.[62] It would not be right to say, therefore, that the entire Ahir, Kurmi or other castes mentioned in the Government Order were backward within the meaning of Article 16 (4) of the Consitution of India.

Further the petitioners submitted that all that the Sathi Commission had done was to enlarge the list of the "most backward classes" identified by the Kaka Kalelkar Commission.[63] They also drew the attention of the High Court to the difference between the report of the Sathi Commission and the impugned Government Order as regards the number of communities. The report had listed 120 communities, while the lists attached to the impugned Government Order contained only fifty-nine communities.

62. *Chhotey Lal* v. *State of Uttar Pradesh* (AIR 1979, Allahabad), p. 139.

63. Ibid.

The High Court observing that : "No facts have been placed before us to show that the State Government had applied the tests laid down by the Supreme Court in reaching conclusion that each of the particular castes specified constituted a backward class,[64] it struck down the reservation order.

Other States and Union Territories

Some Indian States like Assam and Union Territories like Pondicherry considering educational backwardness as the most important aspect of backwardness have reserved some seats for the educationally backward in educational institutions. They have made no such reservation in the Government services. In Delhi, Meghalaya, Orissa, and Rajasthan the backward classes are not getting any preferential treatment in the context of appointment to Government jobs and admissions in educational institutions. But they do enjoy certain concessions regarding school fees, books, midday meals, etc.[65] In 1961 Delhi and Orissa who earlier prepared the list of OBCs on the basis of caste, opted for the economic criterion in place of the caste criterion and dispensed with the lists of backward classes prepared on the basis of caste.

Some Indian States like Arunachal Pradesh, Mizoram, Nagaland, Sikkim, Tripura and West Bengal have not prepared any list of backward classes so far. None of the Union Territories has done so. States do not regard backward classes as calling for State action in respect of their socio-economic conditions. The backward classes have never emerged as a political force in these States. Not that there is no backward class lobby, but it has not acquired any perceptible influence so far.

Tripura and West Bengal have been ruled by the Communist Party of India-Marxist since 1977. This party does not have

64. Ibid., p. 154.
65. *Mandal Commission Report*, n. 9, p. 10.

faith in caste stratification of society. It considers caste a great obstacle in the process of emergence of a class consciousness.

On 1 August 1980 the Government of West Bengal set up a committee to study whether it was necessary to invoke the powers vested in the State Government under Articles 15 (4), 16 (4), and 29 (2) of the Constitution. This committee submitted its report within a month, i.e. on 30 August 1980. It recommended that—

> "poverty and low levels of living standards rather than caste should in our opinion be the most important criteria for identifying backwardness."

It favoured identification of different occupational groups as backward. It considered those below the poverty line as the most important target group for economic development and educational advancement. It set its face against[66] allotment of quotas to the various backward classes in Government service.

Summing Up

An observation of backward classes movement, the steps taken by various State Governments, the reports of commissions and committees clearly reflect many significant points. There have been common realisation that the society can not advance by backwardness of any section of the society. Economically, socially and morally the upliftment of backward families, irrespective of castes, is the demand of the time.

It is most unfortunate that till now no uniform criteria has been evolved which is acceptable to the whole society. There are differences of opinion between the States and the Centre, between the various States, between the commissions and committees and between one individual and the other. Unless a

66, Ibid.

well acceptable criteria of reservation policy is evolved – the society can not have balanced growth. Wide differences amongst commissions on criteria of backwardness, reservation policy, quota of reservation and olher concessions have become subjects of debate. This has resulted into caste-war and community-war. Reservation movement and anti-reservation movement with long term impacts have forced the whole society to move cautiously so that the society could be saved from anti-social evils. The questions : who should get protection under reservation policy ? How much posts and seats be reserved for them ? How long the present reservation policy should continue ? How the administrative efficiency could be maintained with reservation policy ? These are some basic questions which still go with Government's reservation policy.

CHAPTER V

Power Politics in Bihar : 1977-1979

The Background

Bihar and Orissa were parts of the huge Bengal Presidency till 1912. They were placed under a Lieutenant-Governor-in-Council on 1 April 1912. The province of Bihar and Orissa became a Governor's province with effect from 29 December 1920. The members of the Executive Council became ex-officio members of the Bihar and Orissa Legislative Council. It had 76 elected and 27 nominated members. Among the nominated members four seats were reserved for aborigines and depressed classes.[1] Bihar and Orissa were created separate provinces on 1 April 1936. Provincial autonomy as envisaged by the Government of India Act, 1935, came into force on 1 April 1937. The unicameral legislature of the old Government of India Act, 1919 was replaced by a bicameral legislature, consisting of a Legislative Council and a Legislative Assembly, under the new Constitution.

In 1937 the first Legislative Assembly had a strength of 152 members chosen directly by the people voting in territorial

1. Radhanandan Jha, ed., *Origin and Development of Bihar Legislature* (Patna, 1982), p. 23 and p. 19.

and special constituencies in accordance with the extended franchise qualifications embodied in the fifth and sixth schedules of the Government of India Act, 1935. It included thirty-four Muslims, fifteen members of the Scheduled Castes, seven representatives of the backward tribes and four women. There were thirteen members representing special constituencies.

The strength of the Bihar Legislative Assembly was 330 in 1952 and 318 in 1957. It increased again to 324 in 1977. The State Legislature in Bihar consists of the Governor, the Legislative Assembly and the Legislative Council. Leader of the majority party in the Legislative Assembly is appointed as the Chief Minister of the State for running the administration. Constitutionally all powers are vested in the Governor of the State. Article 166 (1) of the Constitution of India says : "All executive action of the Government of a state shall be expressed to be taken in the name of the Governor."[2]

Selection of the Janata Party Candidates, 1977

The creation of a modern Parliamentary system based on universal adult suffrage has encouraged the organisation of interests according to ethnic loyalties.[3] This, in its turn, has become the basis for the distribution of political power. That is to say, ethnic groups are organized as political parties and compete for political power. The political proceess is kept up by the interactions of contending groups and public policies[4] resulting from compromises among group leaders. The Government officials by themselves play no decisive role.

2. *The Constitution of India* (Allahabad : Law Agency, 1985), p. 47.
3. Myron Weiner, "India : Two Political Cultures", in Lucian Pye and Sidney Verba, eds, *Political Culture and Political Development* (Princeton, N.J., 1965), p. 210.
4. Earl Latham, "The Group Bases of Politics : Notes for a Theory", *American Political Science Review* (Washington N.W.), January 1952, pp. 376-97.

The political parties take into account caste, religion, tribe and other ethnic affiliations in nominating candidates for election. In the conduct of the election campaign too it is common for candidates to appeal to the loyalties of their respective communities.

The Janata Party was born in 1977. It captured power in Central Government, with the active support of Jayaprakash Narayan. The peoples apathy towards emergency and its atrocities, price-rise and number of other factors were responsible for the negative voting against the Congress Party. In Legislative Assembly election held in June 1977 it encountered problems in weighing the relative merits of the twenty thousand applicants for being chosen as the party's candidates for 324 constituencies of the Bihar Legislative Assembly.[5]

Politics in Bihar is not just party-oriented, it is caste-oriented as well. Different leaders demanded tickets for their old party (the Constituent unit of the Janata Party) and caste nominees. Jayaprakash Narayan had laid down a number of criteria for selection of candidates such as participation in the J.P. movement, suffering during the emergency, honest public life, etc. These, however, were forgotten, caste loyalties prevailed.

The Jana Sangh was the greatest beneficiary of the ticket distribution. The Jana Sangh had many active workers, who were also members of the Rashtriya Swayamsevak Sangh (RSS) and the Akhil Bharatiya Vidyarthi Parishad (ABVP). They worked heart and soul for the success of the J.P. movement. They, thus, became the largest faction within the Janata Party.[6] Other constituents were also well represented except the CFD.

The Janata list had twenty-seven Muslims and thirteen women. Not a single Muslim legislator belonging to the

5. *Indian Nation* (Patna), 20 May 1977.
6. *Indian Nation*, 21 May 1977.

TABLE 1

Distribution of Janata Party Tickets, 1977

Constitutent groups of the Janata Party	*Tickets*
Jana Sangh	70
Socialist Party	55
Bharatiya Lok Dal (BLD)	60
Congress (O)	48
Congress for Democracy	18
Chhatra Sangarsh Samiti (CSS)	45
Sarvodaya Workers and Others	25
Total	321

Source : List of Candidates of the Janata Party, Janata Party Office, Patna.

Congress (O) and the Socialist Party had resigned in 1974-75 in response to the call of Jayaprakash Narayan. On the contrary these Muslim legislators had started supporting the Congress Party. Of course a few of them continued their association with the Socialist Party and the Congress (O). Some young Muslims were given tickets to increase the number of Muslims in the Janata Party. The women, who were given the Janata ticket, were mostly near relatives of influential politicians of Bihar.

The Rajputs figured high on the Janata Party's list. The Rajputs were in the different segments of the Janata Party. Most Rajput Members of the Legislative Assembly had resigned from the legislature in response to the call issued by Jayaprakash

Narayan during the movement which bears his name. They were also better represented than others in the student's movement.[7] Those who failed to get the Janata ticket criticized the predominance of the Rajput community among the Janata candidates. They were bitter about the role played by S.N. Sinha, a Rajput leader, who was Chairman of the Election Committee of the Janata Party in Bihar.

D.N. Tiwari complained against the negligence of the CFD. Only eighteen CFD candidates had been given Janata Party tickets. They were newcomers or defectors from the Congress Party. The Chhatra Sangharsh Samiti (CSS) was against their being given Janata Party tickets. Other groups which had participated in the J.P. movement and had suffered during the Emergency were also against more representation being given to the CFD.

The Socialist leader, R.N. Tiwari, and the leader of the Congress for Democracy, D.N. Tiwari, were both members of the Election Committee of the Janata Party in Bihar. They too found that some castes had been unduly favoured and that some others had been deliberately neglected. Karpoori Thakur was not on the committee, but he had influenced the decisions of the party with the help of his lieutenants like Hukumdev N. Yadav. He too emerged as a critic. They all alleged that the Rajputs, the Yadavas and the Bhumihars had been given too large a share in the cake. Of the upper castes, the Kayasthas had gained more than the Brahman. There were a number of reasons for this. The most important among the criteria used to select candidates

7. In response to the call of Jayaprakash Narayan forty-two legislators resigned from the Legislative Assembly; twelve of them were Rajputs. Thirteen out of the twenty-seven members of the State-level Bihar Chhatra Sangharsh Samiti constituted for co-ordinating the student movement were Rajputs. Even at the social level the Rajputs were by and large with the agitation. That is why they were the largest social group among the candidates of the Janata Party.

was participation in the movement initiated and led by Jayaprakash Narayan in 1974 against the then Government of Bihar on several issues, including especially corruption. The Brahmans had generally kept out of that movement.

If one analyses ticket distribution from the angle of class, the middle-middle class and the upper-middle class were the greatest beneficiaries. The Janata candidates included the rural rich and the urban professional class (as, for example, lawyers, teachers, technocrats, etc.). Lawyers and college teachers had been active in the J.P. movement, and so they were generously accommodated, Memders of the working class on the Janata list were small in number. This was because the economic position of a candidate should be strong enough to achieve electoral victory. The Janata Party was in no position to finance every candidate. Some rich merchants too got the ticket by making heavy contributions to the party funds.

Owing to differences among the members of the Election Committee over fifty-eight candidates, the Janata Party was not able to publish its final list early enough. Aspirants were asked to file their nominations. When official candidates were announced, a number of aspirants rebelled and opposed the official candidates. This led to an increase in the number of contestants. The number of candidates, who filed their nominations, was 6,385. Of these, 3,412 candidates either withdrew from the contest later or were rejected, and 2,973 candidates were left in the field for the 324 seats of the Assembly. A large number of these candidates were either Janata rebels or independents. The threat of disciplinary action by the party leaders made little impact on the rebel candidates.

The Congress Party had suffered a defeat in the Lok Sabha elections held in March 1977. Congressmen were, therefore, unwilling to contest the elections to the Legislative Assembly in June 1977. The victory of the Janata candidates looked so certain that the Congress Party sought electoral adjustments with the Communist Party of India (CPI) as in 1972 and succeeded. It was said that the Janata Party was prepared for electoral adjustments with the Communist Party of India (Marxist) or CPI (M), but S.N. Sinha, Chairman of the Bihar Janata Party, in 1977 denied it. Other parties in the field included especially the Jharkhand Party. The main contest was between the Janata Party on the one side and the Congress-CPI alliance on the other. In spite of odds the Janata Party romped home with a two-thirds majority.

Election Manifestoes of the Political Parties

An interesting light can be brought for comparative review of policies propounded by different political parties during elections on the upliftment of backward class, Scheduled Castes and Scheduled Tribes. Attractive manifestoes are published making promises to root out injustice in economic, social and political fields. A comparative picture, based on election manifestoes, has been drawn in the following pages.

The Janata Party in its election manifesto pointed out that the choice before the electorate was "a choice between freedom and slavery; between democracy and dictatorship; between abdicating the power of the people and asserting it between the Gandhian path and the way that had led many nations down the precipice of dictatorship, instability, military adventure, and national ruin".[8]

On the reservation policy, the Manifesto said :

> The Janata Party believes that the disparities that separate these members of our society from the more educationally and economically advanced sections cannot be radically reduced without a policy of special treatment in their favour. It will accordingly provide preferential opportunities

8. Election Manifesto of the Janata Party, 1977 (Delhi, (1977), p. 34.

for education and self-employment to these sections. In this connection it will reserve between 25 and 33 per cent of all appointments to Government services for the backward classes as recommended by the Kalelkar Commission.

In the election manifestoes of the other political parties social problems were discussed. But reservation policy was not advocated in the election manifestoes of the Indian National Congress, the CPI, and the CPI (M) and others.

The Congress Party polled 23.53 per cent of the votes. This means that it polled 9.7 per cent of the votes less than it had polled in the elections held in 1972. In terms of seats it lost 110 seats. The CPI got fourteen seats less than it had in the elections held in 1972. The elections of 1977 represented the culmination of the J.P. movement. The people (and students) exposed the hollowness of the claims of the Congress Party and the CPI.

The Jana Sangh emerged as the largest constituent of the Janata Party in Bihar. Its support was vital for any faction to form a goverment.[9] After the declaration of the election results a number of controversial statements appeared in the press. Some ambitious legislators insisted on electing a leader for the Janats Legislature Party (JLP) from among members of the JLP itself. Other groups had no objection to inviting even meber of *Lok Sabha* or any other (i.e. one who was not yet a memmber of the JLP) to head the JLP and the State Government.

Contest For JLP Leadership, 1977

Article 163 of the Constitution of India lays down : "There shall be a Council of Ministers with the Chief Minister at the head to aid and advise the Governor in the exercise of his functions." The Governor usually asks the leader of the majority party in the legislature to form Government. The Council of

9. Arun Sinha, "Janata Elects a Leader" in *Economic and Political Weekly*, (Bombay), 25 June 1977, p. 1001.

TABLE 2

Elections to the Bihar Legislative Assembly, June 1977

Total number of voters	...	34,882,008
Total number of votes polled	...	17,343,402
Percentage of Valid Votes	...	49,72

Party	*Number of candidates fielded*	*Number of candidates who won*	*Nnmber of candidates who forfeited their security deposits*	*Parcentage of votes polled*
1	2	3	4	5
Congress	285	057	72	23.53
Janata	310	214	9	42.77
CPI	75	21	16	7.06
CPI (M)	16	4	9	0.91
Forward Bloc	15	1	12	0.21

Contd

1	2	3	4	5
Hul Jharkhand	2	—	2	0.01
Socialist Unity Centre	11	—	9	0.26
Hindu Shoshit Dal	32	—	27	0.83
All India Jharkhand	3	—	2	0.06
Jharkhand (Horo)	27	1	22	0.38
Independents	2197	5	2103	23.91
Total	2973	323	2283	99.93

Source : Government of Bihar, *General Election, 1977 : Bihar Legislative Assembly, Statistical Analysis* (Patna, 1977), Tables 2 and 3, p.4.

TABLE 3

Strength of the Various Constituents of the Jadata Party in the Bihar Legislature, June 1977

Janata Constituents	*Number of members (including 21 members of the Legislative Councii)*
Jana Sangh	62
Socialist	40
Congress (O)	48
Eharatya Lok Dal	50
Congress for Democracy	16
Sarvodaya (icluding Chhatra Sangharch samiti)	29
Total	235

Ministers is collectively responsible to the Legistative Assembly of the State. After the declaration of the election results every political party duly elects its leader to head its group of legislators.

In Congress culture the high command of the Party has great importance in this context.[10] Usually the legislators elect their leader themselves. Or, in the absence of unanimity, or in the face of serious differencs, they request the Central leadership to nominate a leader. During Prime Minister Mrs. Indira Gandhi's leadership of the Congress not a single Congress Party Chief Minister in Bihar was etected by the legislators themselves.

10. See Bameshwar P. Singh, "The Control of AICC Executive over Making of Congress Ministries in Bihar" (unpublished Ph.D. thesis, Bihar University, Muzaffarpur, 1978), p. 347.

The Central leadership of the Janata Party was not in a position to dictate terms to the Bihar JLP. The old constituents of the Janata Party bargained with one another over the Chief Ministerships in different North Indian States.

Madhu Limaye of the Bharatiya Lok Dal (BLD) assumed the role of mediator and came to an agreement with the Jana Sangh on behalf of the BLD on the question of leadership. Under this agreement the Chief Ministerships of Himachal Pradesh, Madhya Pradesh and Rajasthan and the position of Chief Executive Councillor in Delhi were given to the Jana Sangh as it had a good support base in these States. The Chief Ministership of Bihar, Haryana, Orissa and Uttar Pradesh went to the BLD.

In Delhi, Haryana, Madhya Pradesh, and Orissa the leaders of the Janata Legislature Party were elected unanimously. Direct contests took place in Bihar, Himachal Pradesh, Rajasthan, and Uttar Pradesh. In these four States political and personal factors comming led and operated.

After the declaration of the results of the elections to the other Legislative Assemblies, the legislators belonging to the erstwhile Jana Sangh resolutely opposed the idea of getting an outsider elected as the Chief Minister, so that there might be an elected Chief Minister in Bihar. Even some Central leaders of the Jana Sangh like Nanaji Deshmukh made statements expressing their opposition to the idea of getting an outsider installed as Chief Minister. Deshmukh himself was later appointed by the Central leadership of the Janata Party to act as an observer at the meeting of the Bihar JLP called to elect a leader.[11] The names of legislators like Kailashpati Mishra, Kapildeo Singh, Ambika Sharan Singh and Thakur Prasad were being discussed as possible candidates. The names of the members of *Lok Sabha* like S.N. Sinha, Karpoori Thakur, and R.N.

11. *Indian Nation*, 18 June 1977.

Tiwari were also being canvassed. The choice was eventually restricted to S.N. Sinha and Karpoori Thakur. Both of them were then in Delhi to work out political adjustments with the different constituents of the Janata Party. Thakur and his BLD group were able to win the support of the Jana Sangh legislators. The supporters of these two aspirants held separate meetings to further the chances of their respective leaders.[12] The supporters of Karpoori Thakur went about saying that Thakur was a champion of the cause of the backward castes and hence the most suitable man to implement the recommendations of the Mungeri Lal Commission.

When S.N. Sinha and Karpoori Thakur came back to Patna, hectic political activity started in the State capital. S.N. Sinha was expected to get the support of the Jana Sangh legislators, but Deshmukh, at a closed-door meeting with them, asked them to vote for Thakur. Thus, the balance tilted in Thakur's favour. The Socialists and the CFD were divided in their choice. Among the Socialists, supporters of R.N. Tiwari like Jai Narain Mishra and others voted for S.N. Sinha. Seven CFD legislators voted for Sumitra Devi.

The alliance between the BLD and the Jana Sangh changed the whole situation radically. As a result Karpoori Thakur, the candidate of the Jana Sangh-BLD combine, was able to defeat S.N. Sinha by an overwhelming majority at the election held on 21 June 1977. He was polled[13] 61 per cent of the votes (144 out of 235). Legislators belonging to the backward castes, almost all of them, voted for Thakur. A large number of legislators belonging to the Scheduled Castes and Scheduled Tribes, as well as most of the Muslim legislators, voted for Thakur.

Karpoori Thakur taken active part in the Socialist movement. He had been Chief Minister of Bihar in 1971 for a

12. Ibid., 21 June 1977.
13. Ibid., 22 June 1977.

few months. He was regarded as a master of the art of political adjustment and manipulation. He was also known for hard work. This time he was able to win the support of the Jana Sangh, the Socialist Party, the CFD and the CSS. He also received the backing of some legislators belonging to the upper castes and of almost all legislators of the backward castes.

Although there was political adjustment between the Jana Sangh and the BLD in different States, Karpoori Thakur's victory was the victory of the combined strength of the Jana Sangh and the BLD in Bihar. It was not just the victory of the backward castes over the upper castes. It gave the green signal for implementation of the recommendations of the Mungeri Lal Commission.

The following conclusions can be drawn :

1. Legislators belonging to the backward castes in the different constituents of the Janata Party by and large voted for Karpoori Thakur.

2. In the politics of Bihar, the Rajputs and the Kayasthas have been allies of each other. This alliance was, however, broken this time as a result of the manipulations of Sachchidanand, who was Private Secretary to Jayaprakash Narayan. About 75 per cant of the Kayasthas sided with the leader of the backward castes, viz Karpoori Thakur.

3. S.N. Sinha was not able to mobilize the upper-caste legislators in his own favour and neutralize the support that Thakur was receiving from the backward castes. The votes of the Brahmans were divided between the two rivals. The Bhumihars by and large voted for Thakur. Twenty-five per cent of even the Rajput legislators voted for Thakur. The voting pattern in fact reflected the political rivalry among the different upper castes.

TABLE 4

Leadership Contests in the Ruling Parties in Bihar 1957 and 1977 : Voting Pattern

Legislators	*Contestants, 1957*			*Contestants, 1977*		
	Congress Legislature Party	*Sri Krishna Sinha*	*Anugrah Narayan Sinha*	*Janata Legislature Party*	*Karpoori Thakur*	*Satyendra Narayan Sinha*
1	2	3	4	5	6	7
Brahmans	27	19	8	11	6	5
Bhumihars	39	37	2	26	17	9
Rajputs	42	9	33	48	12	36
Kayasthas	21	8	12	11	8	3
Backward Castes	49	28	20	65	48	14
Scheduled Castes	36	23	13	38	26	8
Scheduled Tribes	4	1	1	18	13	5

Contd.

1	2	3	4	5	6	7
Muslims	28	21	7	14	11	3
Others	10	5	4	4	3	1
Total	256	151	100	235	144	84

Source : Data for 1957, Ramashray Roy, "A Study of the Bihar Congress Committee, Bihar, India" (Ph.D. thesis, University of California, Berkeley, 1966), p. 342, Six MLAs were absent in 1957 and 7 voted for Sumitra Devi in 1977. Data for 1977 have been prepared after interviews by the present author.

4. Legislators belonging to the Scheduled Castes and the Scheduled Tribes, as well as Muslim legislators, voted for Thakur. This resulted in an impressive victory for Thakur.

5. Thakur was opposed by a few of backward-caste leaders like B.P. Mandal (who was a Member of Praliament), Baidyanath Mehta, Tej Narain Yadav, Babulal Rai, etc. They sided with S.N. Sinha as they belonged to the same class economically.

6. This trend was discernible in the middle-class back ground of some of the upper-caste legislators as well. They voted for Thakur to put a man of their own in the post in terms of social status and economic interests. These legislators included Raghubansh P. Singh, Sachchidananda Singh, Binodanand Singh, and Kapildeo Singh.

A close review of 1977 election and the pattern of voting reflect three factors—party, caste, and class. Even the social composition of the constituencies and regional considerations were also important variables.

The Rajputs (19.4 per cent) and the Yadavas (14.2 per cent) were the largest caste groups among the Janata legislators. The Bhumihars were also there in good strength (10.74 per cent). The Kayasthas improved their position in the Vidhan Sabha by 5.1 per cent. They were not represented in the other political parties.

Among the upper castes the strength of the Brahmans was just 4.2 per cent in the Janata Party. This was compensated by their being the single largest group in the Congress Party (19.4 per cent). They also accounted for 9.52 per cent of the CPI strength in the legislature.

The backward castes were 25.7 per cent in the Janata Party. This helped them in getting Thakur elected as leader. They

Sociology of the Bihar Legislative Assembly 1977-80

TABLE 5

Social Stratification of Members of the Bihar Legislative Assembly, 1977

Caste	*Janata*	*Congress*	*CPI*	*CPI (M)*	*Others**	*Ind.*
1	2	3	4	5	6	7
Scheduled Castes	18.00	05.26	09.04	—	—	04.54
Scheduled Tribes	08.06	07.00	04.76	25	33.32	13.63
Muslims	06.5	14.03	—	—	—	13.63
Brahmans	04.20	19.28	09.52	—	—	—
Bhumihars	10.74	10.52	14.28	25	—	04.54

1	2	3	4	5	6	7
Rajputs	19.40	10.52	14.28	25	—	13.63
Kayasthas	05.10	—	—	—	—	—
Total Upper Castes	39.44	40.32	38.08	50	—	18.17
Yadavas	14.20	17.54	23.80	25	—	3.63
Kurmis	02.30	03.50	04.76	—	33.32	13.63
Koiris	04.10	05.26	04.76	—	—	18.18
Banias	02.80	01.75	04.76	—	—	04.54
Total : Upper Backward Castes	23.40	28.05	38.08	25	33.02	49.98
Lower Backward Castes	2.30	—	—	—	—	—
Total Backward Castes	25.70	28.05	38.08	25	33.32	49.98
Bangalis	02.30	01.75	—	—	16.66	—

Contd.

1	2	3	4	5	6	7
Christians	—	—	—	—	16.66	—
Total Percentage	100.00	99.66	99.96	100	99.86	99.95
Total number (324)	214	57	21	04	06	22

*Other include : All-India Jharkand-2; Jharkhand-1; Socialist Samaj Dal-1; Forward Bloc-1; and nominated member-1.

Source : Personal interviews with the legislators.

TABLE 6

Classification of Membership of Vidhan Sabha, by Party and Caste, 1980

Caste	*Congress (I)*	*Janata*	*BJP*	*BLD*	*CPI*	*CPI-M*
1	2	3	4	5	6	7
Scheduled Castes	15.54	12.50	04.30	—	27.27	—
Scheduled Tribes	08.80	02.50	21.73	08.33	04.59	16.66
Muslims	09.84	10.00	—	08.33	04.54	16.66
Brahmans	15.02	05.00	13.04	—	04.54	—
Bhumihars	12.95	—	04.39	—	13.63	16.66
Rajputs	16.06	12.50	08.69	—	—	16.66
Kayasthas	01.03	07.50	04.39	—	—	—
Total : Upper Castes	45.90	25.00	30.51	—	18.17	33.32
Yadavas	08.29	27.50	13.04	66.66	22.72	—
Kurmis	02.59	07.50	13.04	08.33	—	—

Contd.

1	2	3	4	5	6	7
Koiris	01.55	07.50	04.39	08.33	13.63	16.66
Banias	05.18	05.00	08.69	—	04.54	—
Total : Upper Backward Castes	17.61	47.50	39.16	83.32	40.89	16.66
Lower Backward Castes	01.55	02.50	—	—	04.54	16.66
Total : Backward Castes	19.16	50.00	39.16	83.32	45.43	33.32
Sikhs/Bengalis/Christians	01.00	—	04.39	—	—	—
Total Percentage (100)	100.00	100.00	100.00	99.98	100.00	99.96
Total Number (298)	193	42	23	12	22	6

Source ; Personal interviews with the legislators in 1983.

Note : (26 MLA's were Independent and others).

improved their representation in the Vidhan Sabha. The upper backward castes were represented proportionately to their population in the State. However, the lower backward castes accounted for just 2.3 per cent of the JLP. Their only advantage was that the Chief Minister belonged to them.

Table 6 indicates that there was a balanced representation of all important caste groups in the Bihar Legislative Assembly in 1980. In the Congress Party all the three upper castes except the Kayasthas were better represented. Also the number of backward-caste legislators was smaller. The backward castes made it up by their representation in the Janata Party, the BLD, and other opposition parties.

In the Bihar Congress Legislature Party in 1980 the Yadavas and the Banias, both backward castes, had a fair number of legislators. Other dominant backward castes like Kurmi and Koiri suffered a setback. The Muslims on the other hand improved their position. On the whole it can be said that the Congress Party gave balanced representation to all castes, communities and interest groups. Each group got a position commensurate with its influence in the social, economic and political life of Bihar.

TABLE 7

Class Composition of the Janata Party Legislators 1977-1979

Class	*Number*	*Percentage*
Middle Class	28	13.08
Middle-Middle	66	30.84
Upper Middle	76	35.51
Upper Class	30	14.02
Upper-Upper Class	14	06.54
Total number	214	99.99

Source : Personal interviews with the legislators in 1983.

The Janata Party was basically a party of the middle class representing 79.43 per cent of the of the legislators. The upper middle class was the single largest group, a group which accounted for 35 per cent of the legislators. The middle class came next. It accounted for 31 per cent of the Janata legislators. The percentage of the lower middle-class legislators within the Janata Party was just 13.08. Although the social composition of the State is dominated by the lower classes, these were not represented in the Legislative Assembly. By and large they lack resources to contest and win expensive election. The upper and upper-upper classes with their microscopic population accounted for as much as 20 per cent of the Janata legislators in 1977.

There was a change in the ruling party. This entailed a change in the caste composition. However, the class composition remained unaffected. Whichever, political party may come to power, those who own property soon get to control it. They capture it by repeating the new slogans and mobilize it for their own benefit. That is why the Janata Party was not able to protect its own image in respect of economic and land reforms.[14] It deviated from the understanding that the real problem of the backward classes was poverty. Poverty can be eliminated by means of an equal distribution of land, creation of more job opportunities, and promotion of rural-oriented small-scale industries. But Bihar Government failed to give priority on these areas. It, however, wasted its potential by fighting the anti-reservationists. In the caste-ridden society of Bihar the upper castes favoured the Congress (I) to save their interests and honour. The policies and programmes of the Janata Party was focused towards backward castes. Its leadership in the state was in their hands. In the rural areas social harmony was disturbed and occasionally led to caste war. The Harijans and upper castes became target of their attacks. Even they did not debare children and women. All these generated favourable

14. C.P. Bhambhri, *Janata Party : A Profile* (New Delhi, 1980), p. 84.

situation for the Congress (I). This was what led to the debacle of the BLD and the Janata Party.

To conclude, the lower and middle classes did not participate in the power struggle. Only their emotion was exploited for political gain. Some of the leaders of the Scheduled Castes, the Scheduled Tribes and the backward castes belonging to these classes improved their economic and social status by getting political patronage. We have, therefore, placed them in the middle-middle class. Power politics in Bihar had so far centred round the forward and advanced backward castes and the upper and upper-middle classes. They were influencing political decisions for their own benefit.

Change in the Leadership of the Bihar JLP

The circumstances in which Karpoori Thakur became the Chief Minister showed the apex of inter-castes politics. The alliances between sub-groups of the Janata party not only exposed the hollowness of the party rather it also exposed the caste-class based groups fighting with it. The election of leadership of Janata Legislators had an all India alliance amongst constituent groups. However, in Bihar it confirmed that backward class, Scheduled Castes and Scheduled Tribes had become politically conscious and strong enough to snatch political power from upper castes and class. There had been inter-caste bickerings amongst backwards—which led the downfall of Karpoori Thakur's Government. The upper castes and class, being more politically matured, played decisive role in changing the leadership. Political maturity would come in due course but it witnessed rising political power of backwards during 1970s.

At a meeting of the JLP in April 1978 Lalmuni Choube of the Jana Sangh group posed three questions to Jayaprakash Narayan :

1. What was the party doing to promote the ideals of Total Revolution ?

2. What steps would the Government take to achieve socio-economic change ?

3 What steps had the Government and the party taken to root out corruption, which had grown by leaps and bounde ? Jayaprakash Narayan was unable to answer the questions.[15]

Thakur's political rivals in the State Janata Party—viz S.N. Sinha, R.N. Tiwari, and B.P. Mandal were constantly engaged in devising a way of removing him from his position as Chief Minister. The legislators of the Jana Sangh group were also disillusioned with Karpoori Thakur as he was criticizing the RSS and accusing the Jana Sangh of a communal bias. The CFD leaders too were unhappy with him owing to his inability to prevent the atrocities that were being committed on the Harijans. Karpoori Thakur thus lost the confidence of the JLP. At a meeting of the JLP held on 19 April 1979, 135 Janata legislators voted against him and 105 favoured. It was not Karpoori Thakur personally but the group he led, viz the BLD, that was defeated.

Ram Sundar Das, a Harijan legislator, was unanimously elected leader of the JLP even though the meeting was boycotted by the supporters of Thakur. Das was sworn in as Chief Minister of Bihar on 21 June 1976.[16] He continued till 17 February 1980.

Split in the Janata Party

The BLD was basically a party of the peasant castes belonging to the backward class. of course it had a few supporters among the upper castes also. The Chief Ministers of Bihar, Haryana and Uttar Pradesh were from the backward castes of the BLD group of the Janata party. They were

15. *Indian Nation*, 22 April 1978.
16. *Times of India* (New Delhi), 22 June 1979.

replaced in the wake of a new alliance between the Jana Sangh and Congress (O). They felt hurt, even insulted. They planned to take revenge by changing the Central leadership of the Janata Party even if this meant splitting the party. In this enterprise they did not hesitate to secure the support of their old political enemy, the Congress (I), as well as of the Congress (S). The split in the Janata Party enabled Charan Singh to become the caretaker Prime Minister of India. This development was like a balm to the lacerated egos of the backward castes and the peasantry of North India.

The split in the Janata Party at the Centre led to a split in the party apparatus in each of the different States. In Bihar, under the leadership of Karpoori Thakur, eighty-two legislators formed a party designated Janata (S), which was renamed the Lok Dal and then the Dalit Mazdoor Kisan Party. It eventually returned to its old name, the Bharatiya Lok Dal. The Janata (S) consisted of fifty legislators from the BLD, fifteen legislators from the Socialist Party, thirteen legislators from the CSS and four legislators from the Jana Sangh. Most of the supporters of Karpoori Thakur and his reservation policy joined Janata (S). Their personal contacts, the social composition of their constituencies and their ideological commitments were also important in their joining the Janata (S). The Janata (S) had a new set of caste composition.

The split in the Janata Party in Bihar was not just the separation of one constituent from it. It can only be explained with the help of the caste variable. Some of the backward caste legislators belonging to the Congress (O), the Jana Sangh, the CSS, the CFD and the Socialist Party defected to the new party. The Yadavas were in a majority. They were followed by the Kurmis, the Koiris, and the Banias. A few legislators of the upper castes, who had a BLD or a Socialist background, also joined it.

TABLE 8

Caste Composition of the Newly Created Janata (S), 1979

Caste/Group	*Number*	*Percentage*
Forward castes	18	21.95
Backward castes	48	58.54
Scheduled castes	07	08.53
Scheduled tribes	03	03.66
Muslims and others	06	07.32
Total	82	100.00

Source : Information gathered by the present author from the legislators concerned.

Table 8 shows that those who defected from the Janata Party belonged to the backward castes which had captured power at the Centre for a short while and who were determined to recapture it with the help of their superior numbers. Their mistaken caste calculations led them to split the Janata Party and ultimately to lose their new-found strength.

The class base of the BLD was different from that of the orgininal Janata Party. Upper middle-class legislators constituted the largest single group among those defecting to the BLD, They were mostly rich peasants and professionals people. Small and medium peasants and professionals of the low-income group were few. Some landlords also defected to BLD in view of the caste composition of their respective constituencies. The BID was thus, a party of the rich peasants of the intermediate castes for capturing political power under their own leadership. However, they failed of their purpose, and the Congress (I) returned to power.

TABLE 9

Class Composition of Janata (S), 1979

Class stratification	*Number*	*Percentage*
Lower middle class	10	12.19
Middle middle class	24	29.27
Upper middle class	33	40.24
Upper class	11	13.41
Upper upper class	4	4.88
Total	82	99.99

Source : Information gathered by the present author from the legislators concerned.

Return of the Congress Party

On 17 February 1980, in the wake of the Lok Sabha elections of January 1980, the State Assembly was dissolved. Fresh elections were held early in June 1980. The Congress (I) returned to power. Jagannath Mishra became the Chief Minister of Bihar.

Jagannath Mishra's Government revived the old coalition of Brahmans, Harijans, and Muslims in the politics of Bihar. The Brahman legislators in the Congress Legislature Party were divided into two factions, one led by Jagannath Mishra and the other by Kedar Pandey. Dissident activity started almost soon after to oust Mishra as Kedar Pandey was interested in becoming the Chief Minister of Bihar.

The sudden demise of Kedar Pandey weakened dissident activity for a time. Nagendra Jha, Shivchandra Jha, and other emerged later as candidates for leadership in Bihar. On 15

February 1983 eleven Ministers of Mishra's Cabinet were asked to resign. These Ministers joined hands with the dissidents, who consisted largely of Brahmans and Bhumihars. The dissidents seized on the corrupt practices of Mishra's Government and tried to demolish his image in the eyes of the public and the Central leadership.

The Central leadership eventually asked Mishra to resign from the Chief Ministership and nominated Chandrashekhar Singh for the office of Chief Minister.[17] Factional politics in Bihar then took a new turn. For the first time the Bhumihars and the Rajputs in Bihar joined hands. A number of Brahman legislators, opposing the leadership of Mishra, joined hands with the new Government.

Following elections to the Legislative Assembly in March 1985, the Congress Party formed a Government again under the leadership of Bindeshwari Dubey. Although he is still the Chief Minister of Bihar, there is much dissident activity. The faction led by Jagannath Mishra has called for a change in leadership. In Bihar politics, thus, power has shifted from one social group to another. In every change of leadership there had been new alliances between various castes and classes. Though backward classes are constituting majority of the population and are good number in legislative assembly and council, but inter-caste bickerings amongst them do not allow them to rule the State for long. A review of 1970s of Bihar politics clarify the point that gradually backwards have become politically conscious. But even amongst them the economically strong and educated persons are enjoying status and power who are less in number. The majority of backwards are still deprived of social status, economic betterment and political power. On the other hand the upper castes, who are political veterans, do not allow others to become politically strong. Even in Upper castes—a large number of them are not politically active. A fair percentage of

17. *Times of India* (New Delhi), 14 August 1983.

them are economically poor, though they enjoy high social status. But an analysis of political picture shows that in both upper and backward classes irrespective of castes, the political power is readly enjoyed by only those who are politically active. There is no direct link between caste, class and politics. Today politics is open for all. It is a profession for some and an occasional affair for others.

CHAPTER VI

Backward Classes and Protective Discrimination in Bihar

The process of emergence of the backward classes in Bihar began as a transformative social movement and became ultimately a reformative social movement.

Social Movement of the Backward Classes

A social movement means widespread, continuing and collective action in pursuit of an objective that affects and shapes the social order in some desired direction. M.S.A. Rao says that a social movement is characterized by three important features :

1. Collective mobilization.
2. Ideology; and
3. Orientation to change.[1]

The backward castes of Bihar have made a long struggle for social upliftment. In the 1920s they made attempts to get

1. M.S.A. Rao, *Social Movement in India* (New Delhi, 1979), vol. 1, p. 1.

Sanskritized by using sacred threads and calling themselves as Kshatriya, but in vain. In the 1930s politicization started among them with the formation of *Triveni Sangam*, an organization consisting largely of the Yadavas, the Kurmis and the Koiris. This organisation, however, drew a blank in the elections held in 1937.

Though *Triveni Sangam*, could not last long, however, it lit a light of awareness and consciousness amongst the backward classes. The slogan of French Revolution for "Liberty, equality and fraternity" started arousing consciousness in them. The preachings of Karl Marx for world revolution by overthowing capitalism and capitalists gave courage to them to combine strongly for their progress. The surmon of Gandhijee and call for "upliftment of Harijan women and weaker sections" has become a national call, a challenge to the society. Thus, under the national leadership of Gandhijee the backward classes began to act collectively, though slowly, for their upliftment. The proclaimation of independenee in India helped in arousing political consciousness rapidly. The political interest again brought them together. The Backward Classes Federation of Bihar was formed in 1947. This organization sought to mobilize the backward castes in Bihar for demanding reservation of seats and posts for them in the Central and State Government institutions. But it was lacking strength.

The period 1967-72 may well be regarded as an era of emergence of backward caste politics in Bihar. Their common slogan was *Pichara Jagao Desh Bachao*. They organised their youth cadre to fight upper castes and the scheduled castes. The Kurmis taken unsuccessful attempt to form a federation named "*Raghav Samaj*" with Koiri. Even attempt was made to unite other backward classes people. It became successful in 1977 when they backed behind Karpoori Thakur.

The emergence of OBCs began with Sanskritization, politicization and equalization and now it is heading towards dominance over the other castes. It stands for improvement in the social and economic status of the backward classes in order have social change.

The emerging influence, mobilization and participation of the other backward class during 1977-79 may be called a social movement and not only a pro-reservationist movement. Influencial backward castes were collectively mobilized to support reservation policy and fight back anti-reservationists. They do have ideology to change caste based exploitative social system in egalitarian social system with proper development of backward classes. They wanted to make themselves equal partners in social and political life of Bihar and not camp follower. In this context they were desiring social change in process to enhance their own position.

The leaders of the Backward Classes Federation of Bihar have taken the upper castes as their reference group and have formulated the theory that the upper castes seek invariably to subordinate the backward castes and others. This has put them in a state of confrontation with the upper castes. In the 1970s, Bihar witnessed two social movements. The first is known as the J.P. movement, and the second as the Movement of the Backward Classes.[2] In the first movement the society was not divided on the basis of caste; on the other hand the very basis of the second was caste.

The discontent of the backward classes can be explained in terms of the Marxist principle that revolution follows after progressive degradation. The benefits of economic development were appropriated by a few developed sections of society, and the others were degraded. If seen in the context of caste,

2. Pradhan H. Prasad, Caste and Class in Bihar", *Economic and Political Weekly* (Bombay), annual number, February 1979, p. 313. This periodical is cited hereinafter as *EPW*. See also Netkar Jha, "Caste Conflict in Bihar : The Competitive Elites, *Times of Iudia* (New Delhi), 5 May 1980.

some of the middle castes attained development, and the upper castes were neglected. A research scholar of the Magadh University concluded after making a comparative study of four Bhumihar and Kurmi villages that the Kurmi made rapid progress in the educational and economic fields while the Bhumihars were degraded.[3]

Independent India has been characterized by "rapid industrialization and planned development." Many social legislations have been enacted which have undermined several traditional values and have extended protection to the "weaker sections." The State is committed to socialism, secularism, and democracy.[4] In the field of education, it had opened a number of educational institutions. The educated youths are not able to get employment and that in one of the cause of rising unrest in the society. All these, however, do not apply to the backward states in a backward region like Bihar.

Unemployment is an acute problem in the State with 104 million unemployed people in 1978. Higher education has made rapid strikes (See Table 1.) In pre-independence period Bhiar education was mostly confined amongst upper castes. According to 1931 Census of Bihar 31.8 per cent of the Kayasthas, 19.5 per cent of the Brahmans, 13.6 per cent of the Bhumihas, and 12.6 per cent of the Rajputs were literate. Literacy among the backward classes was just 0.5 per cent. Since Independence the backward classes too have joined the race for higher education.

3. Kapildeo Singh, "Education and Political Change in Rural Communities" (Ph.D. thesis, Magadh University, Bodh Gaya, 1973). Quoted by R.C. Prasad, "Electoral and Political Violence", *Indian Journal of Politics* (Aligarh), vol. 15, no.3, December 1981, p.10. Singh observes a decline in the acquired power of the upper castes. The lower castes have acquired power and status, translating their skills and secular mobility into traditional terms, clamining caste status and Sanskritizing their rituals.

4. T.K. Oommen, "Sociological Issues in the Analysis of Social Movements", *Sociological Bulletin* (New Delhi), March 1977, p. 18.

TABLE 1

Education in Bihar, 1979-1980

Educational institutions	*Number of institutions*	*Number of students*
Primary/Junior basic schools	50,871	4,395,125
Secondary/Senior basic schools	10,935	2,757,250
(a) High Schools	3,100	1,029,897
(b) Higher Secondary Schools	14	13,624
General Colleges	292	339,691
Universities	8	10,510
Research Institutes	4	370
Agriculture Colleges	3	918
Engineering Colleges	54	20,547
Law Colleges	7	6,812
Medical Colleges (allopathic)	9	5,397
Ayurvedic and Unani Colleges	13	2,940
Homeopathic Colleges	24	6,480
Dental Colleges	1	67
Midwife/Nursing Colleges	1	164
Pharmacy Colleges	1	211
Public Health Training Centres	1	145
Veterinary Colleges	2	562
Educational Training Institutes	106	16,210

Source : Radhanandan Jha, ed., *Origin and Development of Bihar Legislature* Patan, 1982 p. 53.

The tough competition offered by the higher castes contributed to the social movement of the bakward classes (pro-reservation) and to a protest movement (anti-reservation) by the upper castes.

Emergence of the Political Consicousness in Backward Classes in Bihar

Caste in rural India is no longer a clear mark of status as it once was. The power and status enjoyed by a handful of *Rajas* or large landlords is a thing of the past. Education is no longer the exclusive right of any particular group of people. The middle castes were predominantly tenants in the pre-Independence days. Now, thanks the abolition of the *zamindari* system, a section of the middle castes are owners of a substantial area of land; and the upper castes have ceased to be socially and economically dominant.

In Bihar the unit of mobilization has always been caste, not village or region. There has never been a reform movement in Bihar in which the different castes of a region would have participated together.

The formation of *Triveni Sangam* or the Bihar Backward Castes Federation represented only a horizontal alliance between different castes. It did not destroy the original caste identities, nor was it able to maintain solidarity. In important matters such as diet, interdining and marriage, the various castes still follow by and large the rules prescribed for them in the traditional social order. Electioneering has reinforced caste identities and sentiments, making the horizontal caste structure a viable social entity.

According to the social pluralism model; unity arises through agreement on values and on the rules of the game.[5] Also for reasons of self-interest, group leaders[6] tend to agree

5. M.N. Srinivas, *India : Social Structure* (Delhi, 1982), p. 7.
6. D. Truman, *The Governmental Proce ss* (New York, 1951), p. 231,

to support certain rules guaranteeing group liberties in order to maximize their own group interests and to allow a peaceful competition for power to take place. After a hectic pursuation of the other backward classes leaders, in 1951 the Government of Bihar prepared a list of 109 backward classes for awarding post-matriculation scholarships[7]. It provided 10 per cent reservation from 1975 in the matter of admissions in the engineering and medical colleges.[8]

In the Samyukta Socialist Party (SSP) the backward classes had the dominant position. It also includes Muslims, the Scheduled Castes, and the Scheduled Tribes. Its manifesto in 1967 declared that "for this 90 per cent of the populace, 60 per cent of the high positions will be reserved in various sectors of life".[9] In 1967 it emerged as the single largest political part next only to the Congress Party in the Bihar Legislative Assembly with sixty-eight legislators. In terms of social composition twenty-eight of its legislators were members of the upper castes; and forty legislators belonged to the backward classes. Sixteen of these were Yadavas and seven were Koiris. The Communist Party of India (CPI) had twenty-four legislators in the Bihar Assembly; five of them were Yadavas. Thus, in 1967 the backward classes in general and the Yadavas in particular emerged as a political force. It culminated in 1977, when Karpoori Thakur captured power with the backing of the legislators of the backward classes[10] and implemented job reservation policy for their upliftment.

7. *Bihar, Report of the Backward Classes Commission* (Chairman: Mungeri Lal), Vols. III (Patna, 1976), pp. 116-117.
8. *Padmaraj Samarendra* v. *State of Bihar* (AIR 1979, Patna, 266).
9. Ram Sevak Yadav, *Samyukta Socialist Party : Election Manifesto* (Delhi : 1967), p. 11.
10. W.H. Blair, "Rising Kulak and Backward Castes in Bihar", *EPW*, 12 January 1980, p. 68.

Mungeri Lal Commission, 1971

The Indian political system in 1967 witnessed the emergence of Coalition Government and the downfall of the monolithic Congress rule at the State level in North India. The Congress Goverment under the leadership of Indira Gandhi reacted to this development and took a number of populist measures to win back the poor and backward castes. It was against this background that the Mungeri Lal Backward Classes Commission was appointed in Bihar in 1971 under the Chairmanship of Mungeri Lal. Mungeri Lal was a Congress Member of the Bihar Vidhan Parishad. Besides the Chairman the Commission Insisted of six others as members.

The appointment of the Backward Classes Commission also reflects the emergence of caste and class conflict in rural Bihar. Workers of the lower castes were becoming sympathetic to the Naxalite movement. The rich peasantry of the backward castes were voters of the SSP. The CPI also broadened its political base among the backward castes. All this led to the emergence of a class consciousness among the rural and urban masses. This went counter to the interests of the Congress and other non-Leftist parties, which were caste-oriented and heavily depended on caste vote bank.

It was the Congress-led Coalition Government of Progressive Vidhayak Dal headed by Bhola Paswan Shastri, a Harijan leader, which appointed the Mungeri Lal Commission in 1971. Shastri was not a member of any of the dominant castes of Bhiar. Through the appointment of the Backward Classes Commission the Congress Party made an attempt to win back the support of the backward classes.

Whatever the political motive behind the appointment of the Commission may be, it is certainly true that even after twenty-four years of Independence the conditions of large sections of the backward communities were pitiable in every sphere—in the spheres of education, employment and economic status. The Government, therefore, had a duty to improve the conditions of the backward classes.

The demand for job reservation reflected the realization of the middle castes that the executive had become the most powerful wing of the political system [11] These castes had already achieved predominance in the legislature and at the Ministerial level, but the upper castes with dominant in bureaucracy had been acting according to own purjudices. Reservation was an endeavour to resolve the conflict between a middle-caste-dominated legislature and a high-caste dominated bureaucracy. To consolidate their newly gained economic and political power the middle castes then tried to capture the bureaucracy, which held the key to subsidies, loans, etc.[12]

In a Parliamentary System of Government the decision-makers take a policy decision generally on the basis of the findings of a commission. Even the judiciary puts obstacles in the way of implementing a political decision if it is not based on the report of a fact-finding commission. A policy of protective discrimination entails, in the first place, the identification of the beneficiaries and formulation of valid criteria for discriminatory treatment. It was for this purpose that the Bihar Backward Classes Commission was for constituted. The Commission was asked to identify the other backward classes, prepare their list and recommend certain necessary measures for their upliftment.[13]

11. Arun Sinha, "The Caste Factor in Bihar", *Indian Express* (New Delhi), 12 January 1979.
12. Jaganath Pathy, "Politics of Reservation in India : A Case Study of Political Agitation in the States of Bihar and Gujarat", *Philosophy and Social Action* (New Delhi), vol. 8, no. 2, April-May-June 1982, p. 13.
13. *Bihar Backward Classes Commission Report*, n. 7, p. 63.

Report of the Mungeri Lal Commission, 1976

The Mungeri Lal Commission studied the conditions of the backward classes in Bihar in order to suggest measures for their upliftment. It took into account social and educational status, social and religious norms representation in Government and private services membership in elected bodies, occupation and share in trade, commerce, industry etc. It started with a list prepared in 1951 for the grant of scholarships to students of the backward and the most backward castes in Bihar. Its investigation is basically based on the other backward classes lists prepared by Kaka Kalelkar Commission.

The Commission then prepared a list of its own socially and educationally backward classes, on the basis of caste and on economic basis. This list contains 128 backward castes, including 94 castes known as "most backward classes" (Annexure I). In Bihar, it estimated 38.1 per cent population as OBCs. It had collected data and proved their soical and educational backwardness and miserable representation in Government and semi Government services. It favoured rebate of 10 per cent marks for getting admission in educational institutions, similar to Scheduled Castes and Tribes, maintenance of roster and carry forward policy for reserved quotas in any case if reserved posts for OBCs is not filled even after fresh advertisement, it should be given to Scheduled Castes and Tribes and not filled from the general category.

In its voluminous report the Commission recommended a number of welfare measures for the upliftment of the backward classes. The most important of these measures was the recommendations relating to reservation of 24 per cent of the seats in educational institutions and 26 per cent posts in Government and semi-Government jobs for the other backward classes.[14] It also opined that the backward and the most backward classes be considered separately in enforcing the reserved quotas.

14. Ibid., p. 21, 65, 67, pp. 127-128.

It based its recommendations on Articles 15(4) and 16(4) which permit the State to make reservation for the advancement of any socially and educationally backward class to ensure adequate representation for it in educational institutions and in Government service.

The educational position of backward classes can be viewed from Table No. 2. Education is key of all progress. So long educational position is poor, the class or caste can not make satisfactory advancement.

The most backward castes were far behind in the field of education. The neo-forward castes (those who are politically dominant educationally and economically advanced viz the Yadavas, Kurmis, the Koiris, and the Banias) were represented in proportion to their population. It was also witnessed in an independent research project. The Table No. 3 explains the educational advancement of advanced backward classes in comparison to the most backward classes.

In comparison to the traditionally higher castes they were very backward indeed. They were late-comers in the field of education. And the number of students of the backward classes at the college or university level was less than it was at the school level. This was due to higher drop-out rate at the school stage. Earlier they were denied access to educational institutions by the dominant castes in the villages. In 1858 the Government announced "that all schools maintained at the sole cost of Government shall be open to all classes of its subjects without distinction".[15] Since independence care has been taken to ensure their educational advancement.

The second phrase in Article 15 (4), viz "social backwardness", was not wholly true in the case of the backward castes bacause the backward castes had never suffered such humiliation as the Harijans had to suffer. In the social scale

15. Ghurya, G.S., *Caste and Class in India*, 3rd ed. (Bombay, 1957), p. 189.

TABLE 2

Educational Status of the Background Classes, 1973

Caste	*Number of schools in which students of this caste study*	*Total number of students*	*Total number of students of the backward classes*	*Nunber of students of this caste*
1	2	3	4	5
Kumhar	58	3,610	1,661	92
Koiri	86	5,053	1,950	408
Kurmi	190	14,169	4,212	815
Teli	118	6,813	2,540	381
Bania	46	2,697	1,125	161
Kamar	61	3,925	1,548	110
Hajam	196	13,141	4,613	300
Mallah	48	3,022	1,150	74

Contd.

1	2	3	4	5
Yadava	270	15,805	5,375	1,508
Ansari	6	358	150	10

Note : The total number of high schools in Bihar is 2, 800. Data collected in respect of Class **X** is 380 high schools.

Source : *Report of the Bihar Backward Classes Commissioa* (Chairman : Mungeri Lal), Part II (Patna : Government of Bihar, 1976), pp. 111-13. (Out of the forty-six castes mentioned in the table there, we have taken just ten important castes as sufficient for our purposes).

TABLE 3

Distribution of Secondary School Leaving Certificate Students in Selected School of Dhanbad District 1974

Caste	*Frequency*	
	per cent	*Number of Students*
Forward Castes	55.5	501
Advanced backward classes	19.7	178
Most backward classes	12.7	115
Scheduled Castes	7.4	67
Scheduled Tribes	4.7	42
Total	100.0	903

Sources : J.P. Meelsen, 'Class Structure, Education and Social Change in India'. Results of an Empirical Case Study in Dhanbad (Bihar) in J.P. Meelsen, ed. *Social Inequality and Political Structures* (New Delhi : Manohar, 1983), p. 70.

they were certainly below the upper castes, however, they had domination in several districts of Bihar like Nalanda, Patna, Saharsa, Madhepura and Rohtas. They are progressing rapidly and with their numerical superiority and economic advancement became the dominant caste of the area.

Yet another comment on the claim of social backwardness advanced by the leaders of the backward castes was that they had better political participation at the Central and State levels. If they had been socially backward, this would have been impossible. They had advantage of numerical superiority, for example, the Yadavas were the largest social group in Bihar having 10 per cent of the total population. All political parties were generous in giving tickets to men of this caste. They had attained a high level of political consciousness and were to be found in a wide range of political parties right from the Congress (I) to the Bharatiya Lok Dal, the Janata Party and the Communist Parties.

The educational backwardness of the backward castes in general was by no means due to their economic backwardness. Earlier they used to pursue their hereditary occupations, which did not call for a high level of academic education. They, therefore, never bothered to spend money on the education of their children. This is well brought out if one compares the educational attainments of any family of one of the backward castes with those of any family of one of the upper castes which is economically at the same level. The difference has, of course, narrowed considerably in recent times.

The Mungeri Lal Commission raised very valid grounds for reservation that would ensure "adequate representation under Article 16 (4)". It considered the volume of employment of the various backward castes in different Government departments of Bihar and compared the standing of these castes with that of the Scheduled Castes, the Scheduled Tribes, and others in the matter of Government employment.

The employment position of backward classes on various posts in Government services has been presented in Table No. 4.

In other Departments like the Forest Department, the backward classes accounted for 11.13 per cent of the jobs. Their representation in the Department of Rural Engineering and Organisation was 8.06 per cent; in the Department of Revenue and Land Reform it was 8.3 per cent and in the Department of Supply and Commerce it was 1.1 per cent. Of course, not all those who want jobs can get them. Basically, the problem of reservation is an offshot of the problem of unemployment.

TABLE 4

Representation of the Backward Classes in the Department of Education in Bihar as on 1st January 1972

Category of posts	*Total number of employees*	*Scheduled Castes*		*Scheduled Tribes*		*Backward Classes*		*Others*	
		Total	*Percentage*	*Total*	*Percentage*	*Total*	*Percentage*	*Total*	*Percentage*
Class I	114	1	0.1	1	0.1	2	1.0	110	96.7
Class II	414	3	0.8	6	1.5	4	0.9	401	96.8
Class III	9,215	259	2.8	98	1.0	742	8.1	8,121	88.1
Total	9,743					748	7.6		

Source : *Report of tha Backward Classes Commission* (Chairman : Mungeri Lal), (Patna : Government of Bihar, 1976), p. 128.

Under the present system, the Government is not able to provide jobs to all aspirants. The leaders of the backward castes, however, claimed that reservation of jobs was the best remedy, not "jobs for all."

One of the members of the Backward Classes Commission, Yamuna Prasad Singh, was a Bhumihar by caste. Not surprisingly he rejected the final list of backward classes prepared only on the basis of caste.[16] He also opposed the recommendation for reservation in the matter of promotions. In a letter to the Chairman, he remarked that the way they had gone about the question of reservation would only strengthen casteism in society. Further, he observed that backwardness would be eradicated only after economic development. He was in favour of free education, scholarships and other facilities to students of the backward classes.

One should pause for a while to review Singh's views in the context of integration and accommodation in the social and political systems. Casteism is an old phenomenon in our society. Previously only a few advanced castes used to follow casteist practices. Now the backward castes also have learnt the idiom of casteism. Of course, there can be no integration and harmony in our society unless all the segments of social systems get developed, but one must ensure with the help of scientific criteria that the perspective does not get distorted.

In his letter to the Chief Minister of Bihar, the Chairman of the Commission recommended reservation in educational institutions and in Government services. He had made caste the basis for the award of preferential treatment. Although he had done extensive field work in Bihar and elsewhere, he had ultimately come to accept the caste criterion as the only possible criterion of backwardness. The Commission had not been able to examine

16. *Bihar Backward Classes Commission, Report*, n. 7, p. च.

in detail the list of backward classes prepared in 1951 for granting scholarships to students of the backward and the most backward castes.[17]

Implementation of the Recommendations of the Mungeri Lal Commission, 1977-1978

The Mungeri Lal Commission submitted its report in February 1976, during the hey-day of the emergency. The Congress Ministry led by Dr. Jagannath Mishra. Mishra, an economist, was of the view that the main problem of the backward castes was economic backwardness and not social backwardness. Accordingly he constituted a Cabinet subcommittee-to study the full report.[18] On the basis of its recommendations he set up a Financial Corporation exclusively for the benefit of the members of the backward castes.

The Janata Party had promised, in its election manifesto in 1977, that it would eliminate the educational and economic gap between the advanced and the backward classes by giving them special facilities in education and employment. It, further pledged to implement the recommendations of the Kaka Kalelkar Commission reserving 25 to 33 per cent of the jobs for them.

However, the Janata Government at the Centre failed to implement the recommendations of the Kaka Kalelkar Commission. Kalelkar gave a second thought about caste as a criterion. He stated that it would have been better if the criteria for backwardness had been fixed as the basis of principles other than caste. The Janata Government, therefore, appointed in 1978 a commission under the Chairmanship of B.P. Mandal to look into the matter afresh.

17. Interview with Mungeri Lal, Patna, July 1982.

18. *The Searchlight* (Patna), 9 July 1976.

In the various states where the Janata Party was in power it took steps to institute reservation of jobs/seats for the backward classes. In Gujarat 10 per cent of the jobs/seats were reserved for them in 1978. There was no anti-reservationist movement as in Bihar at that time. It was only when the Government raised the reservation to 28 per cent in 1984 that a violent agitation erupted.

In Bihar Karpoori Thakur became the Chief Minister in 1977. As known to all he enjoyed the support of the backward caste legislators in becoming leader of the Janata Legislature Party. They pressurized him for implementing the Janata Party's election pledge by adopting reservation policy for the benefit of the backward classes. The Bihar Government announced on 29 June 1973 that Government in considering the recommendations of Mungeri Lal Commission Report and it will be implemented soon. It came to the news in the address of Bihar Governor to the Joint Session of Bihar Legislative Assembly and Council. It was for the reservation of 26 per cent of the jobs for the other backward classes. The reservation was made on the basis of the report of the Mungeri Lal Commission and in fulfilment of the pledge contained in the Janata Party's election manifesto.

"बिहार पिछड़ा वर्ग आयोग के प्रतिवेदनों की समीक्षा[19] करके तत्काल लागू की जाने का अनुशंसाओं को सरकार शीघ्र अमल में लायेगी।

Again on 14 March 1978, the Governor's speech in the Joint Session of Legislature mentioned the reservation policy. It declared that Bihar Government will reserve 26 per cent of jobs for the other backward classes as promised in the election manifesto of the Janata Party, with the effect from 1 April 1978.

१९. बिहार: राज्यपाल का अभिभाषण, १९४७-८२ (पटना, १९८२) पृष्ठ ३२४।

"जनता पार्टी के घोषणा-पत्र में किये गये वादों के अनुसार पिछड़े वर्ग के लोगों को राज्य सरकार की नियुक्तियों में २६ प्रतिशत आरक्षण: १ अप्रेल १९७८ से उपलब्ध होगा। यहां आरक्षण शास्वत नहीं रहेगा। जैसे-जैसे पिछड़े वर्ग के लोग विकसित और समुन्नत होते जायेंगे वैसे-वैसे उन वर्गों के लिए यह आरक्षण समाप्त होता जाएगा। आर्थिक दृष्टि से बहुत कमजोर युवकों-युवतियों को नियोजन देने के लिए विशेष कार्यक्रम बनाये और चलाये जायेंगे।[12]

Further, on 21 March, 1978 the State Cabinet approved the decision to reserve 26 per cent of Government jobs for other backward classes, with income limit of 12,000 per annum.[21] It was only for initial appointment not in promotion. The reserved seats and posts were divided between Annexure I and Annexure II in the ratio of 60 and 40 per cent.

The announcement led to an open confrontation between the backward castes and the upper castes. There were opened armed clashes, arson and destruction. A caste-based movement arose which was spearheaded by students belonging to the middle classes. The whole movement was actuated by caste consciousness. The caste-based reservation, thus, strengthened caste consciousness instead of class consciousness. The caste-war and class-war weakened the social environment.

The Janata Government's decision to reserve jobs for the backward classes seems to have been prompted by the Chief Minister's compulsion to consolidate his position among the backward castes. Karpoori Thakur was a member of one of the backward castes and he was regarded as the leader of the poor people in Bihar. He had defeated S.N. Sinha, a powerful leader belonging to one of the upper castes, in direct contest for the leadership of the Janata Legislature party in Bihar.

२०. पर्व पृष्ठ ३३६।

21. *Indian Nation*, 22 March, 1978.

Karpoori Thakur was opposed both by the upper castes and by the advanced sections of the backward castes. He, therefore, went ahead with the policy of reservation to unite the backward caste legislators behind him.

Bihar, thus, moved into an ugly phase of caste riots over the question of reservation. In contrast the other states were seeking to settle the question of reservation through a legal process. Bihar became the scene of street fights. Karpoori Thakur faced opposition not only from students belonging to the upper castes, who outnumbered backward caste students in schools and colleges, but also from the bureaucracy, which was dominated by the upper castes.[22] It was the pro-reservationist, who happens to be deprived groups in society, agitated first for their betterment. On the contrary, it was anti-reservationist who cornered all available opportunities for long time and nurtured hopes for socio-economic advancement with better education and Government jobs provided social basis for agitation.

The pro and anti-reservationist movement have been compared to the Quit India Movement of 1942 and the JP movement of 1974. Buses and railway trains were burnt down, post-offices and telephone exchanges were razed to the ground, telegraph and telephone lines were snapped, Government offices were raided, public property was looted, places of learning were desecrated, fish-plates were removed from railway tracks, railway wagons were derailed. All universties were closed, rail and road traffic was disrupted, there were ever-increasing group clashes in which the victims were generally Harijans and other weaker sections. Curfew was imposed on many towns.[23]

Karpoori Thakur had never imagined that the upper castes would unite so firmly to oppose his reservation policy. Even

22. "Design to Divide People on Caste Lines", *Link* (New Delhi), 26 March 1976.
23. *Economic Times* (New Delhi), 6 April 1978.

those young men, who had been quite happy over the defeat of S.N. Sin ha, now went on a rampage destroying Government property.

The backward castes also came together, however temporarily, to fight the anti-reservationists. Some of the leaders of the backward classes criticized Jayaprakash Narayan for suggesting the economic criterion in place of the caste criterion. Angry young men of the backward classes threw chappals and stones at the ailing leader at a function held on 12 March 1978 at the Patna Gandhi Maidan to celebrate his seventy-fifth birth anniversary (*Amrit Mahotsav*).[24]

In the tense atmosphere[25] seventeen Janata legislators, Jai Narain Mishra, Vikram Kunwar, Ram Prit Paswan, Md. Sahabudin and others belonging to the upper castes, Harijan and Muslim, warned the Bihar Government about fermenting explosive situation if economic backwardness was not adopted as the basis for the reservation of posts in Government service. They suggested that the Government might reserve all Government jobs, if it wished, for the economically poor after drawing a line of demarcation between the haves and the have-nots of society. But the Government turned down this suggestion.

The Caste/class based organizations through caste conferences' seminars and meetings have underlined the aspirations and opinions of their members. They shape decision-making in certain matters at the national and States levels. They also act as pressure groups.[26] In Bihar both the Forward Castes League and the Backward Castes Federation were formed for their respective cause in 1977 and have worked as pressure groups in regard to the reservation policy. These organisations were

24. *Times of India* (New Delhi), 13 March 1978.
25. *Hindustan Times* (New Delhi), 14 March 1978; and *Times of India* (New Delhi), 16 March 1978.
26. M.S.A. Rao, "Political *Elite* and Caste Association : A Report of a Caste Conference", *EPW*, 18 May 1968, p. 779.

organising demonstration, bandh and destroying Government properties. Their activists were engaged in caste war. In the Legislative Assembly and Legislative Council they voiced pro and anti-reservation views. Some of the legislators were engaged in lobbying Central leaders in favour of their viewpoints. These leaders pointed out that :

> "Some castes like Yadvas and Kurmis are economically better of than Brahmins in the Maithili area. The poverty of the Brahmins had to be seen to be believed.[27]

In October 1978 the pro-reservationists of Bihar came in touch with the leaders of the backward castes of South India. Some black-shirt leaders of the Dravida Kazhagam of Tamil Nadu visited rural and urban areas of Bihar.[28] They advised the backward castes to unite and fight for reservation. Narating their achievements, they said that it was only through united strength the backward classes of Tamil Nadu had been enjoying the benefits of reservation for the past fifty years. Their influence increased the intensity of the pro-reservationists agitation.

The legislators too fought, inside legislature in 1977-78 session, some for reservation and the others against it. They were doing active role in the Forward Castes League[29] and the Backward Castes Federation to mobilize people. These organisations opened branches all over the State to organise agitation even at Tehsil and district levels.

27. *Times of India* (New Delhi), 14 March 1978.
28. *Indian Express* (New Delhi), 20 October 1978.
29. The Bihar Forward Castes League was formed in 1977. Vikram Kunwar became President of the League, and Ram Jantan Sinha was elected Secretary. They were both Janata Party legislators. The Bihar Backward Castes Frederation was an organization of the backward classes. It was headed by Ramwadesh Singh, a Janata Member of Parliament. These organizations had branches all over the State.

The move of the Government to reserve jobs on caste basis had a long and deep impact on the society. It vertically divided the society into forward and backward castes groups irrespective of the fact who are really backward and who not. The concept of backwardness is vague. There are many families in forward castes who are academically and economically poor. Brahmans are passing their life by doing cook job. They are illiterate and ill-paid. Kayasthas do not possess land—their livelihood mostly depends on service. On the other hand Yadavas, Kurmis or Koiri, Bania, Marwari, Teli are well to do. They possess land and are good agriculturist. Many of them are engaged in business and are well off. They are educated. Therefore, any reservation policy mainly based on caste is illogical, unjust, unfair and unacceptable to the whole society, The demand to base reservation policy on economic ground is justified. Whosoever may be backward economically, academically and socially be allowed to get preference under reservation policy.

Finding their influence less effective inside the Assembly, the legislators started mobilizing the people for their cause. Public pressure began to take shape on both fronts. This was a unique phenomenon in the political development of Bihar. In 1974 a number of legislators from the opposition parties from Bihar had resigned from the House and participated in the student movement or the J.P. movement. The leadership from the hands of students passed into the hands of Jayaprakash Narayan. Joining national leaders, like Jayaprakash Narayan and others turned the picture of student's stir. It wrapped a big part of the country and soon took shape of a big political movement.

The reservation wave swept the whole state. Opinions for and against started coming in daily newspapers. Even legislators got divided on this issue. The legislators from forward group were not against reservation policy but they favoured to base it on economic ground rather than on caste ground. Whereas backward class legislators were favouring caste-based reservation policy. The differences gradually sharpened. They began to form orgnisations for protection of group interest. The Bihar Backward Class Federation had been functioning. It was headed by Ram Awadesh Singh, a Janata Party Legislator. In reply to it, the legislators of forward group formed Bihar Forward Castes League in 1977 under Presidentship of Vikram Kunwar and Secretaryships of Ram Jatan Sinha. The emergence of class based organisations, basically opposed to each other, showed the prevailing social environment created by reservation policy. The society was divided—hatred was created, heat was generated and class-stir was witnessed. No society can progress by class-war or caste-war. The long term evils of such policy must be kept in mind by the statesmen.

The Government decisions were not well thought of nor based on well accepted formula of backwardness. Consequently its decisions produced unforeseen consequences. The present crisis was the product of a number of factors. First, the Government failed to take the consent of the S.N. Sinha's faction of the Janata Legislature Party of Bihar. Second, the policy of reservation was not formulated or debated in the Legislative Assembly. Thirdly a few of the dominant backward castes were wrongly included in the list of backward classes. This infuriated the upper castes. Fourth, the policy of reservation was announced without dividing the backward classes into backward and most backward classes. Fifth, no step was proposed for checking the abuse of privilege by those sections of the backward classes which did not actually suffer from any special disability. Sixthly, the upper castes were placing hurdles in the way of implementation of the policy of reservation in order to check the emergent threat to them from the backward classes in the fields of technical education and Government service. And, lastly the emotions of all classes of people, both backward and the not-so-backward, were roused by the casteist rhetoric freely traded on the occasion.

The anti-reservationists belonged to a segment of society which was vocal and dominant socially and economically and which had traditionally controlled the economic and social life of the State. The pro-reservationists consisted largely of the newly prosperous backward castes, who wanted to control the State bureaucaracy with a view to their own social and economic development. The anti-reservationists were supported by the anti-Karpoori faction of the Janata Party and by the opposition parties in the Bihar Legislative Assembly. The anti Karpoori legislators of the Janata Legislature Party in Bihar sought relentlessly to exploit the situation for their own political ends. They were anxious to make him thoroughly unpopular and bring about a change in the leadership of the Janata Legislature Party in Bihar. The opposition parties were active for consolidating their own positions.

The State Government avoided to face the Legislative Assembly for quite some time. Karpoori Thakur announced his job reservation plan first during the bye-election in the Phulparas constituency in December 1977.[30] The electorate consisted predominantly of voters from the backward castes, particularly the Yadavas. The bye-election had been made necessary by the resignation of a Yadava member of the Janata Legislative Party, presumably to enable Karpoori Thakur to get elected to the Assembly. The Congress Party candidate was a Yadava, Ram Jaypal Singh Yadav, who sought to mobilize the Yadava vote in his own favour.

Karpoori Thakur was quite sure that the upper castes would vote against him on account of the policy of reservation. He, therefore, chose to please the backward castes by announcing

30. The bye-election was caused by the resignation of a Janata legislator to accommodate Karpoori Thakur in the Bihar Legislative Assembly to avert a constitutional crisis. Karpoori Thakur was a Member of the Lok Sabha at the time of his election as Leader of the Janata Legislature Party in Bihar.

his plan to reserve for them 26 per cent of the seats in educational institutions and jobs in Government service. Naturally he won by a big margin.

Unconstitutional Decision-Making Process

It is true that Bihar Government had constituted Backward Classes Commission for fact finding. The Report of the Commission was discussed in the Cabinet. The Janata Party in its election manifesto promised to implement the job reservation policy for other backward classes. But at last in the time of its implementation it tries to side track the State legislature.

Karpoori Thakur introduced the reservation policy by means of an executive order. The policy was not properly debated and voted for in the Legislative Assembly. The Government tried to win the support of the anti-reservationsist legislators but in vain. Karpoori Thakur, therefore, chose the expedient of an executive order.

These are certain laid down procedures of Government's decisions. Such issues are to be placed before the two houses for debate. The house should decide it on the basis of majority support. In a democratic society the Government, as true representative of public, must act according to mass majority view. Any deviation from this would be accepted as undemocratic way of functioning is condemnable action. It is in a sense betrayal of public and their support. Violation of set norms of decision making and constitutionat process.

There were altogether ninety-four legislators of the backward castes in the House, but they were not sure of the support of the legislators belonging to the Scheduled Castes and the Scheduled Tribes and of the Muslim legislators. By and large, all upper-caste legislators, regardless of their party affiliations, were against reservation. If a legislation had been debated and voted upon in the House, it might well have been lost.[31] It was, therefore, enforced by an executive order therefore, it can be described as the contempt of the House.

Gentral Leadership and Job Reservation Issue in Bihar

The elections held in 1977 brought the leaders of the backward castes into positions of national prominence for the first time.[32] They were dominating positions in the Janata Party. Controlling the affairs in several key Indian States they promised major initiatives to uplift their people. In the Centre Ch. Charan Singh emerged as the principal leader of the backward classes. His lieutenants highlighted plans for allocation of quotas for the backward classes in education and in Government service.

The President of the Bihar Pradesh Janata Party, S.N. Sinha, alleged that Karpoori Thakur had mishandled the reservation issue. He had not been consulted in advance. It was only when trouble started that Karpoori Thakur asked him to support the reservation policy. Reservation was part of the Janata Party election manifesto and it was, therefore, necessary to consult the Party President before any decision.[33] Karpoori Thakur had, however, allowed himself to be hustled into a decision in June 1977, by some leaders of the backward castes.

31. In 1953 a backward class leader of the Congress Party, Baijnath Singh had introduced a non-official bill in the Bihar Legislative Assembly which sought to reserve 25 per cent of the posts and job for the backward classes. But it failed to get the support of the legislators and the leaders. Later Baijnath Singh withdrew the bill owing to the pressure of the party leaders. Dev Saran Singh, a Congress leader, used occasionally to demand reservation for the backward classes. But they all failed to get a positive response. Thus the Government of Bihar in the Legisiative Assembly the nacessary legislation on reservation.

32. James Manor, "*The Revolt of India's Backward Classes*", New Society, 31 February 1980, p. 387.

33. Interview with S.N. Sinha, M.P., New Delhi, 30 May 1983.

They had not given him the necessary time to examine the issue in detail and to hold consultations and to win over the opponents of reservation within the party.

The way in which Karpoori Thakur's Government took decision on reservation policy, a most controversial issue, gives idea as to the procedure, manner, pressures operating in decision-making. The Chief Minister never thought to discuss it with the Executive Committee of the Political Party to which he belonged or with the Cabinet members or with the two houses. Either he did not realise the desirability of such a discussion or was afraid that he would not succeed in his attempt. Whatever the reason may be, he by-passed the normal decorum of functioning of a democratic Government. Such a way of functioning of the Government is not only unhealthy rather it is injurious to the cause of democracy and the whole society. The after-effects that wrapped the whole state into agitations and counter-agitations would not have taken place had there been cool, democratic and logical thinking, cross discussions and decisions taken thereafter.

When trouble started in Bihar, the leaders of the pro-reservationists and the anti-reservationists approached the Central leaders for their help. This brought Prime Minister Morarji Deasi and Party President Chandrasekhar into the picture. On the advice of Morarji Deasi, the Government of Bihar divided reservee quota into 60 per cent for the most backward classes and 40 per cent for the less backward classes. It also excluded income-tax payees from the benefit of reservation. The leaders of some of the backward castes, mostly the Yadavas and the Kurmis, opposed this move.[34] The

34. In 1951 the Government prepared a list of backward classes which divided the backward classes into "backward classes" and "most backwaad classes". The Mungeri Lal Commission approved this division. The Mandal Commission designated the more backward classes as Depressed Classes.

anti-reservationists too were not appeased for they were against all reservation.[35]

The pro-reservationists and the anti-reservationists kept up their agitations in Bihar. The situation was tense especially in Patna, Arrah, Chapra, Saran, Begusarai, Muzaffarpur, Samastipur and Sehars. A number of persons were assaulted, injured or killed by the police during the disturbances.[36]

The gradual deteriorating law and order situation was becoming a day to day problem. That forced the political parties to give fresh thinking on the whole situation—particularly on the main issue of reservation policy. No Government could function well in a continued atomsphere of poor law and order situation, dislocation of trade and business, social breakdown and general turmoil. Naturally this fast deteriorating situation of Bihar under the Janata Party Government compelled the Party leaders and the Government at the Centre to intervene.

The Janata Parliamentary Board on 13 March 1978, discussed the explosive situation in Bihar arising from the announcement of the reservation policy. It observed that the problems of unempioyment, land reform, inflation, slump in the price of cane, closure of jute mills, the indebtedness of agricultural workers, and others were being mixed up with the question of reservation for the backward classes in Government service. It made it clear that reservation would be limited strictly to initial appointments and admissions in technical institutions but not to promotion.[37] It advised the Government of Bihar to extend the benefit of reservation to those who were

35. Ishwari Prasad, "Job Reservation for OBCs in Bihar", *Janata* (Bombay), 23 April 1978, p. 9.

36. *Indian Nation* (Patna), 24 March 1978.

37. *Times af India* (New Delhi), 14 March 1978, *Indian Nation* (Patna), 22 March 1978.

economically poor among the upper castes and to exclude prosperous members of the castes, whose family income exceeded Rs. 5,000 a year, or whose families owned more than two hectares of land. It, further, advised the State leadership to frame rules in the matter and place before the State legislature for a full discussion.[38] The Government notification regarding reservation should be issued only after such discussion and after approval by the State legislature.

The situation was not favourable for the Chief Minister. He was not sure of getting the approval of the State legislature and so he preferred to issue an executive order. He thus, virtually arrogated to itself the powers of the State legislature. He, preferring to rule through ordinances rather than statutes passed by the legislature, showed his weak position in the house. He even by passed his own Council of Ministers.[39]

The President of the Janata Party, Chandrashekhar paid a visit to Patna on 2 April 1978 for discussing the problem with Jayaprakash Narayan, the Chief Minister and other important leaders. He asked the Janata legislators of the upper castes to support Karpoori Thakur's proposal.[40] The pressure from the President of Party was vehemently opposed. In utter disgust from the unwanten pressure from the top and undemocratic functioning of its Government, the legislators belonging to upper castes started getting ready to submit their resignations from the party. At a meeting of the Bihar Cabinet held in Delhi, the Ministers of the upper castes were asked to support reservation. They gave their consent to support any new modified reservation plan. Differences, thus, continued to plague the Bihar Cabinet. The Cabinet was divided into upper

38. P.C. Gandhi, "Proposals to Diffuse Bihar Situation", *Times of India* (New Delhi), 18 March 1978.
39. S. Sahay, "Bihar Constitutional Fraud", *The Stateman* (New Delhi), 6 October 1983.
40. *The Statesman* (Calcutta), 4 April 1978.

case and backward caste ministers. Even staunch socialists were against the caste criterion. Some of them did not want reservation of any kind.

The Central Parliamentary Board of the Janata Party discussed on 5 April 1978 three aspects of the job reservation issue at the meeting. First, should reservation be confined to those who belonged to the backward castes ? Second, should a reservation cover only those among the backward classes who were economically backward ? And, third, should reservation be extended to all those who were economically weak whatever their caste ?[41]

After long discussions, the party felt the necessity of further detail study of the problem. Consequently a committee with 27 members was appointed on 6 April 1978 under the Chairmanship of the Union Law Minister, Shanti Bhushan, to examine the demand of the pro-reservationists and the anti-reservationists and make recommendations. The Committee consisted of Central Law Minister, five party general secretaries of central organization of the party and eight Bihar's Cabinet Ministers and eight legislators from both the warring groups. It held a meeting in Delhi on 17 April 1978 to discuss the problem and put forward a new proposal. The Committee regarded caste as relevant factor but it could not be a sole factor. It took note of the social, educational and economic criteria and subsequently suggested[42] reservation of 11 per cent for the most backward classes, 6 per cent for the backward classes, 4 per cent for the economically backward among the upper castes; and 5 per cent for women. Thus, it also favoured reservation seats up to 26 per cent, but the leaders of the backward classes rejected the whole formula as inimical to their interests.

There is a strong apprehension that if separate quotas were not fixed for the backward and the most backward classes,

41. *Times of India* (New Delhi), 6 April 1978.
42. *Hindustan Times*, 18 April 1978; *Indian Nation*, 19 April 1978.

the relatively advanced backward castes like Bania, Kurmi, Koiri and Yadava would enjoy benefit from the reservation policy. Fixed quotas of this kind for different backward classes were in practice in Andhra Pradesh, Karnataka and Kerala.

Karpoori Thakur was in favour of reservation of 26 per cent for the backward classes, 5 per cent for the economically backward members of the upper castes, and 5 per cent for women, raising the reservation quota to 36 per cent. This was wholly unacceptable to the Central leaders and the State Cabinet. He was pressurized not to go beyond the limit of 26 per cent. The leaders of the backward classes resented this pressure. Thus, strong different views continued to operate in the State. Even the central leaders had no one opinion.

Change in the Decision, 1978

The reservation issues had gradually drawn the attention of the all sections of the people. Reservation compaign and anti-compaign arouse public consciousness. The pressures were operating from both sides. Academicians, particularly the experts of human resources and economists, remain busy in analysing pros and cons of proposed reservation policy. The politicians had a difficult task ahead. The legislators had a difficult time how to please voters of both forward and backward classes. The inter-class clash of intsrests posed problems for the policy makers.

Ultimately accepting a suggestion made by the Central leadership, particularly by Chandrashekhar, Karpoori Thakur declared a modified reservation plan[43] on 1 November 1978, effective from 31 October 1978. The plan contains reservation of 12 per cent for the most backward classes; 8 per cent for the backward classes, 3 per cent for the economically backward

43. *Indian Nation*, 2 November 1978.

among the upper castes, and 3 per cent for women. According to him, this plan would benefit the following sections of society :

1. Socially and educationally backward people.
2. Socially and educationally backward Muslims.
3. Women belonging to all castes and communities.
4. All poor people even if they were not otherwise backward.[44]

The Bihar Backward Classes Federation did not seem to be satisfied with a reservation of 20 per cent. It demanded reservation of 26 per cent of the jobs for the backward castes. It clearified that if the Government wanted to reserve jobs for women and other weaker sections, it should do so without touching the quota of the backward classes.

The new formula ensured that the well-to-do among the backward castes did not appropriate the benefits meant for the most backward classes. It benefited only those backward classes whose income did not exceed a thousand rupees a month. It thus, sought to prevent abuse of privilege by those sections of the backward classes which did not in practice suffer from any special disability.[45]

राज्य सरकार ने पिछड़े वर्ग के लिए, महिलाओं तथा आर्थिक दृष्टि से पिछड़े वर्ग के लिए सरकारी तथा जिला परिषद, नगरपालिका, अर्द्धसरकारी संस्थाएं, विश्वविद्यालयों एवं लोक उपक्रमों की सेवाओं में क्रमशः २० प्रतिशत, तीन प्रतिशत, तथा तीन प्रतिशत पदों को सीधी नियुक्ति हेतु आरक्षित करने का निर्णय लिया है (१९ मार्च १९७८), स्रोत-विहारः राज्यपाल का अभिभाषण १९४७-८२ (पटना, १९८२) पृष्ठ ३५० ।

44. *Bihar Gazettee Ertraordinary* (Patna), 31 October 1978; *Indian Nation* 2 November 1978.
45. Ishwari Prasad, n. 36 .

The economically dominant and politically powerful social group of upper castes legislators, thus, compelled the Chief Minister to change his stand on the reservation poliy. In contast the numerically larger but unorganized backward castes failed to maintain the *status quo* in respect of the reservation policy. This meant that in terms of organizational ability, technical knowledge, financial power, social daminance, and access to decision-makers, the backward castes were still no match for the upper castes. The decision-makers fovoured a sharing of Government jobs and educational opportunities rather than the establishment of a monopoly over them. A dispersion of economic power leads to a dispersion of political power and ultimately to a dispersion of Government jobs in favour of the backward castes.

It has been said that in liberal democratic societies, the Government institutions and their decision-making structures benefit the dominant social groups and that this looks legitimate to the less powerful and unorganized masses.

The new formula was certainly better than the earlier one, and more scientific. It took note of developments in the social, educational and political life of Bihar. It is wrong to equate caste with class. As social scentists say, the middle castes are the middle class.[46] Even among them the upper and the lower castes are in sufficient strengh. Now the upper castes are not exclusively upper class and the lower castes are not exclusively lower class. If one accepts Karl Marx's concept of class then economic conditions because the basis of division of the society. Any policy in a democratic society based on caste basis is unfair, unpractical and illogical. Castes does not determine economic position. If it is accepted, then why these are poor and backward people in so-called forward class on the one hand and rich

46. Sridhar V. Ketkar, *The Hsitory of Caste in India* (Ithaca, N.Y., 1909), Vol. 1, p, 28. Ketkar explains : "Class is synonymous with caste."

and prosperous people in backward class on the other hand. Even to maintain caste distinction in society for long is injurious for the society and great hurdle to its development. Individual is individual, he should be treated on economic position enjoyed by him rather than asked to maintain caste attitude. Further any priviledge granted to any caste would give an urge to maintain caste-system for ever. This will bite the society for ever allowing to caste conflict.

By agreeing to the new formula Karpoori Thakur showed his flexible approach. He had accepted the suggestions of the Central leaders and State legislators. He also witnessed the law and order problem of the State and accepted the deprivation of the poor section of the upper castes. At last he declared the new reservation formula within the limits of 26 per cent and divivided it acordingly. His new plan was good enough to satisfy all sections of people. Of course some Yadav and Kurmi leaders were unhappy about reservation being restricted to 8 per cent but excluding income-tax payees. On the other hand the upper-caste legislators kept up their demand for the implementation of the Shanti Bhushan formula which contained reservation of 11 per cent for the most backward classes; 6 per cent for the backward classes; 4 per cent for the economically backward among the upper castes; and 5 per cent for women.

One of the features of the reservation policy in Bihar was the inclusion of some Muslim groups in the list of backward classes. The Muslims never talked of oppression by those who were better placed among them though they confessed to differential behaviour based on differences in secular positions.[47] Mungeri Lal Commission listed some of castes from the Muslim community in the list of OBCs. They are also socially and educationally backward. In these circumstances reservation extended to them.

47. I.P. Desai, "Should 'Caste' Be the Basis for Recognising Backwardness?", *EPW*, 14 July 1984, p. 1106.

There was a controversy over the procedure to be adopted in implementing the reservation policy. The relevant natification said, simply, that the "procedure" would be the same as the one being followed in the case of the Scheduled Castes and the Scheduled Tribes. This meant that backward class candidates would be debarred from competing for the general vacancies. This, according to the leaders of the backward castes, was tantamount to granting 56 per cent reservation to the upper castes. The charge levied by the Backward classes that 56 per cent of seats were reserved for the upper class was misleading. Till now no where in the country posts or seats have been reserved for the upper class. There is free competition in which even backward class candidates do compete. And if the backward class candidates compete in open competition they are not counted in reserved quota.

Many recruiting agencies also misconstrued the provision for reservation as prescribing the upper limit for the intake of backward class candidates.[48] In July 1979, therefore, Bihar Government headed by new Chief Minister Ram Sunder Das made it clear that the reservation percentage indicated the minimum quota, not the maximum; and that candidates of the backward classes selected on merit should not be shown against the quota reserved for the backward classes.

New J.L.P. Leadership and Reservation Policy

Karpoori Thakur became a target of attack by different sections of society on the ground that he had divided the people on caste lines. The Janata Party legislators were demanding the resignation of Thakur. At last the Central leaders asked him to secure a fresh mandate on 19 April 1978 from the Janata Legislature Party. Karpoori Thakur lost the leadership of the Janata Party legislators by 105 votes to 135. His ministry was replaced by a new ministry headed by Ram Sunder Das.

48 *Report of the Backward Classes Commission*, (Chairman ; B.P, Mandal), Vols. I-II (New Delhi. 1981), p. 7,

Commenting upon the change of leadership of Bihar State Legislature Party S.N. Sinha commented that Karpoori Thakur had failed to provide a good, efficient and clean adminstration.[49] Although there were many allegations of corruption against his Cabinet colleagues, Karpoori Thakur had refused to take any action. In fact, he had stoutly defended his corrupt ministers. In the context of the reservation policy, Krishna Choudhary, a member of the Legislative Council, who had been elected on the ticket of the Communist party of India, had observed that "although he supported the policy of reservation, it was clear from the manner in which the policy was being implemented that the Janata Party was more interested in caste conflicts than in removing the backwardness of the people."[50]

On 21 April 1979 Ram Sunder Das was unanimously elected leader of the Janata Legislature Party. The meeting was attended by 168 member out of a total of 246. Of the 168 members who attended, 144 were Members of the Legislative Assembly. The replacement of Karpoori Thakur by Ram Sundar Das, a backward class legislator, was a political move of the forward class legislators. It was an indication of split in the Janata Party with class and caste colour. The reservation policy had become a major source of friction. Not the other legislators were against reservation policy but the manner in which it was announced by Karpoori Thakur was undemocratic and arbitrary. After the split in the Janata Party in August 1979 the group led by Karpoori Thakur demanded his resignation as he was not in a majority in the House. On two occasions, in August and December 1979, the Congress (I) had supported the Das Ministry during the trial of strength. After the elections to the Lok Sabha, when the Congress (I) decided to out the Janata Ministry, the Lok Dal, after its defeat in the Lok Sabha

49. *Current* (Bombay), 28 April 1979.
50. *Patriot* (New Delhi), 17 March 1978,

election, came to the rescue of the Das Ministry. Dr. Jagannath Mishra called it a double stand by the Lok Dal leadership. The Lok Dal supported the Janata Party Ministry during the trial of strength in the Legislative Assembly on 24 January 1980.

Ram Sunder Das was under consistent pressure from new Janata legislators for withdrawal of the reservation policy. Those legislators had played dominant role in changing state leadership of the Janata Party with the view that Ram Sunder Das would correct the reservation policy eliminating their objection. But he made it clear that since it was a matter of policy with the Janata Party, the question of withdrawal did not arise. This infuriated the leaders of the Forward Castes League. The withdrawal of reservation policy not easy as was thought off. Once a decision is announced by the Government, the people or organisation or class benefited by such announcement always remain vigilant for maintaining the status-quo. Pressures, for and against, operate, on the Government with arguments and counter-agruments. Further, the Chief Minister, Ram Sunder Das was a backward and was not willing to do any harm by withdrawing reservation policy.

Continuity of Reservation Policy during the Rule of Congress (I)

The Congress (I) Ministry, which succeeded the Das Ministry, accepted the policy of reservation. Dr. Jagannath Mishra, the new Chief Minister, even accepted the Mandal Commission's report when he was about to be replaced. The acceptance of Mandal Commission's report by Mishra Ministry had been interpreted in different ways. When Dr. Mishra apprehended downfall of his ministry, he had accepted Mandal Commission's report in order to win over the support of backward class legislators of Congress (I) party. He also showed his progressive outlook by accepting measures for upliftment of backward class. Really speaking Dr. Mishra's acceptance of report was more a political game than anything else. This reflects further the strength of the backward classes in the politics of Bihar. Indeed no political leader can dare to go back from the decison on the reservation policy introduced by the Janata Government 1977-78.

It is not the question of having a reservation policy or not ? There are no two opinions. All agree that a reservation policy is required for upliftment of backwards. The question, controversial in nature, is who are backwards? What are the rational criteria of backwardness? Is it caste or class or economic or educationl or else? It is clear that caste or class is not rational criterion. The backwardness should be decided on economic, social and academic basis irrespective of caste. The whole difference has surrounded on this point, which if accepted, would be the best solution.

The emergence of the backward castes into politics has a long history. The leaders of those castes succeded in building up a strong movement for upliftment of backward castes. But thoses castes are fragmented in different political parties from the Congress (I) to the Janata Party, then the Bhartiya Janata Party and the Bhartiya Lok Dal to the Communist Party of India. Among the advanced backward castes the Yadavas support legislators of their caste, whatever the party label. Bihar is a caste ridden state. Every issue is viewed from caste angle which does not allow the state to prosper. However, the issue of reservation brought them together trying to preserve their caste interest intact. Fortunately there has been no exclusive political party of any class, backward or forward. Each political party has members from all classes. The party aims to preserve interests of backward and weaker sections of the society. This aim of the party has strong political implications. Any political party would not like to displease the backward class and castes, which jointly represent major group of voters. But the political parties also would not like to lose the support of forward class and castes as they still are in forefront of political field. Reconciling the interests of both the groups as well as going ahead with development of the society including upliftment of backward castes and weaker sections are ticklish problems before the political parties in India and particularly the State of Bihar.

Why Anti-Reservationst Movement in Bihar ?

Bihar is part of the Gangetic heartland. It is a centre of Aryan civilization and Sanskritic, culture and the Aryan values are deeply rooted here.

For instance, the Brahmans are not the only twice-born caste in Bihar as in the South India. The twice-born castes in Bihar account for about 12.8 per cent of the total population (in 1931 as shown in Table No. 5). In contrast the Brahmans are the only twice-born caste in Tamil Nadu, and they account for just 3 per cent of the total population of the State. The movement of the Aryan people and of Sanskrit culture towards the South does not seem to have brought the locally dominant castes within the fold of the twice-born.[51]

TABLE 5

Upper Castes of Bihar in 1931

Castes	*Percentage*
Brahmans	4.7
Bhumihars	2.9
Rajputs	4.2
Kayasthas	1.0
Total	12.8

Source : *Census of India*, 1931, Vol. III, Part-II, p. 135.

51. L.I. Rudolph and S.H. Rudolph' *The Modernity of Tradition: Political Development* (New Delhi, 1969), p. 70.

The Brahmans, the Kajputs, the Bhumihars and the Kayasthas are the upper castes in Bihar and in many other North Indian States. They occupy higher social and ritual status. In contrast only the Brahmans have social and ritual status in the South.[52] The Brahmans are not the sole upper caste in Bihar; there are several other castes like Rajputs, Bhumihars and Kayasthas in that category. This makes the upper castes more numerous and hence stronger. They are capable resisting any move by the backward castes to end their domination.

Regional caste profiles affect the nature of political cleavage and mobilization.[53] In its early years the nationalist movement in the South was dominated by the Brahmans. The Brahmans also enjoyed the benefit of education and were conspicuous in the administrative field. Subsequently, other castes came into the picture. They felt that they were the equals of the Brahmans and resented being excluded from leading positions in political and professional life. They opposed the domination of the Brahmans by forming an anti-Brahman party called the Justice Party.[54]

In Bihar, the situation is quite different. The Kayasthas dominated the educational field in the early twentieth century. The Bhumihars and the Rajputs were in a better position in the political and economic fields. The leadership of the freedom struggle too was not in the hands of the Brahmans. As an intellectual caste the Brahmans devoted their time to English in addition to their traditional education. However, the Rajputs

52. Dominant castes like Vellalar, Mudaliar, Reddiar, Chettiar Naidu, and Kamma in Tamil Nadu and Andhra Pradesh are known as Shudra castes. In Kerala, the Nairs, who rank immediately after the Namboodiri Brahmans, are regarded as Shudras.

53. Rudolph and Rudolph, n. 52, p.77.

54. The Justice Party (South India Liberal Federation), the organ of the Non-Brahman Movement in Madras, was founded in 1916.

and the Kayasthas respected the superior social status of the Brahmans. It was only in the second quarter of the twentieth century that the Bhumihar peasant leader, Swami Sahajananda Saraswati, challenged the ritual superiority of the Brahmans and claimed that the Bhumihars too were Brahmans. Subsequently Bhumihars started enumerating themselves as Brahmans in 1921 and 1931 census. It leads to decline in the population of Bhumihars in 1931 in comparison to other castes. (See Table 5 and 6)

TABLE 6

Population of Certain Selected Castes of Bihar and their Educational Attainments 1891

Catse	*Population*	*Literate in*		
		Sanskrit	*English*	*Others*
Brahmans	12,00,269	25,080	4,463	148,175
Bhumihars	12,09,408	8,995	852	73,215
Rajputs	11,69,407	11,743	1,073	81,830
Yadavas	31,40,605	3,545	289	27,359
Kayasthas	3,89,585	17,620	686	85,969
Kurmis	11,27,324	5,148	276	2,447
Koiris	11,74,625	2,817	116	11,354
Dusadhs	11,68,521	660	190	4,259

Source : *Census of India*, 1891, Vol. V.

Table 6 shows that the Kayasthas were more English educated than the Brahmans and others. That is why in the early stages of the freedom movement the leadership went to them. They were also in the forefront of the movement for the separation of Bihar from Bengal. It is not sheer coincidence, as R.C. Prasad thinks, that the leaders of the movement belonged to the Kayastha community.[55] Even later, when the Bhumihars and the Rajputs wrested the leadership from the Kayasthas, the Brahmans were not in the frontline. This saved the Brahmans of Bihar from the hostility of the other castes unlike in South India. After Independence, the Bhumihars became the target of attack for they were the dominant caste in politics from 1937 to 1962.

It is only in North Bihar particularly in the Mithila region, the Brahmans were dominant.[56] Here it is the Brahmans who possessed most of the land. A Brahman family ruled the state of Darbhanga and it was the last ruling dynasty in the region. The Maharaja of Darbhanga was the leader of the Maithil Brahmans and of the Maithil Brahman Association. He contributed lakhs of rupees to the University of Calcutta and Allahabad although he did not open any college in Maithila itself. He thus, allowed the region to remain educationally backward.

With all their rituals and economic superiority, the Brahmans were not alineated from the other upper castes. There was, therefore, no anti-Brahman movement in the Mithila region.

The political leadership of Mithila was in the hands of Satya Narayan Sinha, a Rajput, from 1937 to 1970. When Binodanand Jha became the Chief Minister of Bihar, he mobilized the Maithil Brahmans in his own favour. During 1960s and 1970s they rallied behind L.N. Mishra and Dr. Jagannath Mishra. In the Mithila region generally and in the Darbhanga

55. R.C. Prasad, "Social Polarization and Political Instability," in Iqbal Narain, ed., State Politics in India (Meerut, 1976), Vol. 2. pp. 57-67,

56. Paul R. Brass, *Language Religion, and Politics in North India* (New Delhi, 1975), p. 50.

and Saharasa divisions particularly, there is at present conflict between the Maithil Brahmans and the Yadavas for dominance. The Yadavas are numerically, economically and politically strong. They may be regarded as the dominant caste in that area.

In Bihar there is considerable social intercourse among the upper castes. They have distributed power among themselves and control the political, social and economic systems. It is the infighting among the upper castes which has paved the way for the emergence of the backward castes in politics.[57] The fight of the backward castes is not so much with the Brahmans as with Brahmanical theology which countenances or sanctions the dominance of the upper castes.

In South India the differences between the Scheduled Castes and the Scheduled Tribes on the one hand and the backward castes on the other are not large. They were all united, in fact. in the first half of the present century. In Bihar, however, the upper backward castes were also among the traditional oppressors of the Scheduled Castes. The Scheduled Castes, therefore, depend more upon the upper castes than on the backward castes. This is borne out by the recent atrocities on the Harijans. In 1977-79 there were twenty major outrages on the Harijans and as many as fifteen of them were perpetrated by the Yadavas and the Kurmis.[58] The backward castes are also divided among themselves as there are differences among them in economic and social status. In the Nalanda District the main rivalry in the political field is between the Yadavas and the Kurmis, and the two frequently clash. The upper castes generally keep away from such clashes. In fact the backward castes are not a monolithic entity in Bihar.

57. W.H. Blair, n. 10, p.70.

58. "North Reacts Move to Job Reservation", *Patriot* (New Delhi), 10 April 1983.

Another fact, one which the Mandal Commission also noticed, is that the feudal and semi-feudal traditions in Bihar enable the upper castes to "keep tight control" over the smaller backward castes and to prevent them from joining the main-stream of the backward classes movement. Till recently, under the *zamindari* system in Bihar there was a paternal-filial relation ship between the landlords and the peasants. This kind of relationship was unknown under the *ryotwari* system of South India. Also in Bihar the backward castes were never oppressed and humiliated in the same degree as in the South. This helped to prevent any anti-upper castes feeling from assuming menacing proportions. It is only now for the sake of the political benefits that the Hindu-educated backward-caste leaders of the upper and upper-middle classes have inflamed such feeling.

The industrial establishments, public and private sectors, employ a fair percentage of working hands in Bihar. There are big industries—the coal, the iron and steel, the sugar, the power, the transport and many others. Big factories like TISCO, Bokaro Steel Plant, TELCO, HEC provide good employment where reservation policy is not applieable. Tha Government services, though provide not much employment opportunities but the status and power add importance. The power to rule the status attributes much importance. This importance of Government jobs has been most pinching factor for those affected by reservation policy. In Bihar the jobs are confined by and large to the Government sector. Young men of the upper castes are, therefore, unable to accept reservation. It is an immediate threat to their prospects in life.

Bihar has all through been a State of political upheavals. It is more politicized than other States. The Quit India Movement had moved students to fight for independence. Bihar's role in this movement was significant. Young men were politically trained in the J.P. movement in 1974-75. Jayaprakash

Narayan built up cadres in Gandhian fashion. He called upon students to boycott examinations. Students responded to the call with enthusiasm.

The social movement of the backward castes and the protest movement of the upper castes were not limited just to the big cities; they affected even small towns. Students participated in the students' movement of 1974 for the sake of society. In the anti-reservationist movement of 1977-79 their own particular interests were at stake.

The Tata Institute of Social Sciences, Bombay,[59] went into the same problem formulating the following hypotheses :

1. If the communal reservation scheme has had a long history, retaliation by the forward castes is likely to be absent;
2. If the upper castes are divided among themselves, the chances of retaliation would be much less;
3. If the backward classes and the Scheduled Castes do not get on well with each other, retaliation by the upper castes is likely to be stronger;
4. If the backward castes are deeply politicized and well organized, retaliation by the upper castes is less likely;
5. if the upper castes are suddenly faced with the prospect of losing their political and economic position, i.e., if a reservation scheme is likely to bring about a sudden rank disequilibrium, the chances of retaliation by such castes are very high;
6. If people belonging to the sub-castes of the major upper castes can pass off as backward-caste people, the likelihood of retaliation is less;

59. *Mandal Commission Report*, n. 49, p. 31.

7. If the State as a whole has experienced a kind of revivalism is mobilized against outside symbols, the backward classes movement is likely to be less powerful;

8. The capacity on the part of the backward castes to retaliate is a function of :

   (*a*) their numbers;

   (*b*) political consciousness;

   (*c*) dominance; and

   (*d*) perceived lack of alternative opportunities; and

9. If the Non-Government tertiary sector is expanding retaliation by the upper castes is less likely.

CHAPTER VII

Debate on Reservation Policy

Preferential treatment was accorded to the oppressed sections of the society in Bihar in the matter of admissions into educational institutions and appointments in Government service in order to enhance social status, improve economic condition, raise them to the level of the advanced sections of society, and thereby integrate them into the national mainstream. Policies of compensatory preference are part of the process of disestablishment of the traditional caste hierarchy and are, thus, meant to bring about an unprecedented transformation of the core structure of Indian society.

General View

The benefits of compensatory discrimination are available to three major classes. The first two classes are the Scheduled Castes and the Scheduled Tribes; and the third class consists of the backward classes (or the other backward classes, or OBCs for short), a heterogeneous category, varying greatly from State to State. Reservation for the backward classes, however, has been challenged in the courts time and again. It has become a debatable issue. Who should be given benefits under this policy? What should be the rational criteria for deciding eligibility or giving benefits? How long the benefit should be granted?

How much posts and seats be reserved? How to preserve the society from evil effects of reservation policy? How to maintain efficiency of services even after introducing reservation policy? These questions have arouse public attention. Heated discussions have been witnessed in and out of the house. It has also given birth to protest movements in many Central, Northern and Western Indian States.

One also witnesses some differences in the reservation policies for the Scheduled Castes and the Scheduled Tribes on the one hand and the backward classes on the other. Reservation for the backward classes is just twofold—i.e. in educational institutions and in Government and semi-Government service. For the Scheduled Castes and the Scheduled Tribes, however, it is threefold; seats are reserved for them in the legislatures too. The backward classes are now politically mobilized enough to ensure their due representation in the legislatures even without reservation.

Students of the backward classes are not in a position to compete on the strength of their merit with those of the advanced classes for admission into technical and professional institutions. Nor can candidates of the backward classes compete with success for jobs in Government service with those of the advanced classes. This is so largely because they generally lack the environment, intellectual and cultural, which is so necessary for the purpose. They allege also that experts from the advanced classes on the selection committees favour candidates of their own classes. Executives connected with developmental projects are also partial to the advanced sections of society. The backward classes are, therefore, anxious to secure due representation in the bureaucracy to protect their interests.

If preferential treatment is being accorded to the backward classes today it is because of the introduction of adult franchise which in its turn has facilitated the political emergence of the backward classes and given them capacity for manoeuvre. Compensatory discrimination in favour of the backward classes has led to much heart-burning among young men belonging to the advanced classes. The anti-reservationist movements are all due to a feeling of deprivation engendered in the young men of the advanced classes because of the rising percentage of reservation for the backward classes in the professional and technical institutions and in Government service.

In the 1950s and the 1960s the policy of reservation was not regarded as a social or political problem. There were job opportunities for all educated youth. The spread of education among all sections of society has fostered keen competition in the job market. Unemployment is an acute problem. This is way young men of the advanced classes think that reservation in favour of the backward classes is a great hindrance to them in their search for jobs and for better education. The concept of free labour market has been changed with adoption of reservation policy. Failure to get a job even in face of best result and better ability has created job consciousness amongst free job seekers. On the other hand young men belonging to the backward classes think that the young men of the advanced classes are out to corner all available opportunities. These mutually antagonistic feelings have led to the pro-reservationist and anti-reservationists movements in different parts of the country.

Nirmal Mukherjee rightly opines that the rise of the anti-reservationist feeling is a direct result of the sudden and massive success achieved in the implementation of the policy of reservation during the 1970s.

> "Upto the latter '60s there was steady but slow progress in the representation of SCs and STs in Central appointments. It began to appear that the system of reservation operated until then was not good enough to achieve adequate representation for these groups in a short time-span. No adverse

feelings were generated against reservations for the simple reason that the SC and ST entrants into Government service were too few and too junior to pose any kind of threat to the entrenched interests of the upper castes."[1]

The policy of reservation was not implemented seriously in the 1960s, and young men of the advanced classes were able to avail themselves of the seats as reserved for the Scheduled Castes and the Scheduled Tribes, as well as the backward classes. He, further, observes that reserv..tion for the Scheduled Castes and the Scheduled Tribes was raised from 12½ per cent and 5 per cent to 15 per cent and 7½ per cent respectively in 1970. The period for carrying forward unfilled vacancies was also extended from two to three years. And the benefits of reservation were extended to cover promotions as well. In December 1977 the number of seats reserved together with the number of seats carried forward exceeded 50 per cent of the total seats available. This led naturally to better representation for the Scheduled Castes and the Scheduled Tribes in Government service. As a corollary it also led to a spurt in the anti-reservationist feeling among the advanced classes. Next table explains the present proposition.

In the context of the backward classes the 1970s and the 1980s have witnessed the appointment of Backward Classes Commissions in different Indian States and the adoption of a policy of reservation for them in Bihar, Gujarat, Madhya Pradesh and Uttar Pradesh. This led to a reservation of 50 per cent or more of the available vacancies. The advanced classes took it as a great challenge to them in their search for a livelihood.

The policy of reservation is not based on the principle of equality. It implies that those who are better qualified and

1. Nirmal Mukherjee, "Perspective of a Policy", *Semenar* (New Delhi), December 1981, p. 16.

TABLE 1

Postal Inspector Jobs Reserved for Scheduled Castes and their Occupation

Year	*Vacancies for SCs*	*SC Applicants*	*Selected SC candidates*
1955	25	196	11
1956	45	215	7
1957	49	121	35
1958	48	111	4
1959	59	172	22
1960	65	237	23
Total	301	1052	102

Source : *Report of the Commissioner for Scheduled Castes of Scheduled Tribes*, 1960-61, Part I (New Delhi), p. 282.

thus more deserving stand excluded in favour of the less qualified and thus (in a strict sense) not deserving. Indeed, as in *Padmaraj Samendra* Vs *State of Bihar* the High Court of Patna has put it, "to allow the less qualified and the less deserving to fill up a majority of seats (or vacancies) is to destroy equality."[2]

Mukherjee argues that while there may be need for reservation to secure social and economic justice to the weaker sections of society, it is necessary to ensure that qualified and deserving candidates are not denied admission into higher educational institutions. Sometimes a student of one of the upper castes is

2. AIR 1979, Patna, p. 266.

denied admission into a medical college even if he has secured 80 per cent of the marks, but a student of the reserved category is admitted even if he has received no more than 35 per cent of the marks. This leads to low standards of education; so much so that many students are unable to follow what is taught in the class-rooms.

A large number of candidates of the backward classes are capable of competing with candidates of the advanced classes. For their upliftment, therefore, reservation is necessary. It is, however, only a means to an end, which is to secure social and economic justice to the weaker sections of society. Basically reservation is a measure devised to help circumvent "insurmountable obstacles to ensure equality of opportunity."[3] The more advanced sections in terms of standard of living, profession and level of education among the Scheduled Castes and the Scheduled Tribes and the backward classes misread the motives of the decision-makers and exploit the policy to their own narrow advantage. They tend to monopolize the benefits of reservation for ever. True to the theory "once backward, always backward," they perceive a "vested interest" in the retention of these privileges which is against the intention of the constitution makers. Sons and daughters of senior bureaucrats, Governors, and Ambassadors of the Scheduled Castes and the Scheduled Tribes get the benefit of reservation at the cost of meritorious but poor candidates of the general categories. A learned judge of the Andhra Pradesh High Court once observed :

> "The Constitution could never have intended the use of scarce resources of this poor nation to be used to benefit in advantage of those individuals who are already well advanced."[4]

3. *State of Kerala* v. *N.M. Thomas* (AIR 1976, Supreme Court), p. 574.
4. AIR 1980, Andhra Pradesh, p. 104.

The advanced classes accepted reservation up to some extent in the matter of initial appointments or admissions. When the roster system was introduced and the policy of reservation was made applicable to promotions as well, their resentment coupted into a strong protest movement. That is why many scholars, who are in favour of reservation at the time of initial appointments etc., are against reservation in the matter of promotion. The policy of reservation in promotion has long term implications. Higher the posts, greater are the responsibilities, power and duties. The proper discharge of responsibilities and duties require proper knowledge and experiences. The human engineering scientists have evolve promotional policy based on merit or length of service or merit-cum-length of service. The modern promotional policy has combined merit with length of service for maintaining efficiency and capability of employees. Any deviation from this policy would under efficacy with long range effects. The less capable persons, if promoted, would not be able to supervise, guide and control his subordinates who are better in many respects. Further, supersession on the basis of reservation policy would have deep psychological implications. The experienced and capable persons would feel demoralised lowering his efficiency and damaging his willingness to work. On the other hand the promotee would feel shaky in providing good leadership. These arguments have strengthened the stand of anti-reservationists movement.

The pro-reservationist and anti-reservationist movements are projected in terms of backward classes versus the advanced. As reservation restricts the opportunities available to job-seekers from the advanced classes, the rival social groups have come forward for and aganist the theory and practice of reservation. In general the backward-caste spokesmen have favoured reservation, and those of the advanced classes have opposed it. At the level of the legislature, legislators belonging to the advanced classes are against the reservation policy; legislators belonging to the backward classes are opposed to it.

Arguments of the Pro-Reservationists

The pro-reservationists argue that the superiority of the Brahmans and the other upper castes and the low social ranking of the backward castes and the shudras are ideas rooted in the Hindu scriptures. They point out how even today a poor Brahman enjoys a higher status socially than a rich man belonging to one of the backward castes. They, therefore, feel that caste is a relevant criterion in the determination of backwardness. They want to compensate members of the backward castes for their age-old social handicap by giving them better representation, better opportunities and better facilities.

They further argue that ritual status[5] is a predominant criterion of social stratification and that the acquisition of economic and political power does not in itself assure the upward movement of a social group on the social ladder. Further they point out how, if economic backwardness is everything,[6] the framers of the Constitution would not have taken the trouble of using the words "socially and educationally" in Article 15 (4). They would have been quite brief and used just the word "economically".

Dr. B.R. Ambedkar, the spokesman of the Scheduled Castes an the Scheduled Tribes, was familiar with the social persecution, economic discrimination and political deprivation suffered by those classes. As the Chairman of the Drafting Committee of the Constituent Assembly, therefore, he introduced certain political and constitutional safeguards for them in the Constitution to help them overcome the cumulative disadvantage

5. N. Radhakrishnan, "Units of Social, Economic and Educational Backwardness : Caste and Individual," *Journal of the Indian Law Institute* (New Delhi), Vol. 7, July-September 1965, p. 263.
6. M.N. Srinivas, *Social Change in Modern India* (New Delhi, 1982) p. 3.

suffered by those at the bottom of the social hierarchy. To promote the advancement of the untouchababables, tribals, and other "socially and educationally backward classes", the Constitution allows "protective" or "compensatory" discrimination in their behalf.[7] The pro-reservationists regard this as the acceptance of caste as a criterion for determining backwardness in the implementation of a policy of reservation. It is true that the advanced sections of the Scheduled Castes and the Scheduled Tribes have unduly exploited caste based reservation. And it is also true that the advanced sections among the backward castes also do so. Even then some scholars[8] are in favour of the continuance of reservation for the sons and daughters of IAS and other senior officers belonging to the Scheduled Castes and the Scheduled Tribes. They say that it would give moral support to the downtrodden.

Similarly, some scholars are not in favour of excluding the more advanced among the backward castes from the benefit of reservation. The Government of Tamil Nadu and Gujarat have not excluded the highest income groups among the backward castes from the benefits of reservation.

The national leaders, policy-makers and academicians must reconsider the whole thing in the existing conditions and the facts placed above. How far it would be fair to let the well to do families of so-called backward groups to enjoy the benefits of reservation policy ? The family of an IAS is definitely enjoying better economic position, high prestige in the society, high academic attainment and his status. It would be misnomour to call him backward any more. The society must take into account the changes brought in the last 4 decades of reservation policy. If today an I.A.S. officer's family deserves to enjoy benefits of reservation—will it not generate class conflict, class hatred and class movement ?

7. Mare Galanter, *Competing Equality* : *Law and Backward Classes in India* (New Delhi, 1984), p. 38.
8. Mukherjee, n. 1, p. 15.

Further, the leaders of the backward classes in Bihar allege that 85 per cent of the State Government jobs are in the hands of the upper castes, who constitute only 13 per cent of the population of the State.[9] Social prestige and recognition go with a Government job. According to one survey, 83 per cent of the bureaucrats at different levels in Bihar belong to the upper castes. Just about six per cent of the college students belong to the backward classes.[10] How can only few per cent of employees from reserved categories are responssible for bringing down the efficiency, standard and merit ? It must be due to upper castes monopoly.

It is widely accepted that birth in a backward family should not be allowed to put the seal of backwardness on an individual for ever.[11] At the same time it is equally true that in the given economic and political context one's birth in a particular family by and large determines one's life's chances. Not only have the so-called upper castes enjoyed control over resources for centuries, but they have also dominated the culture of the masses.

The leaders of the backward classes point out the Brahmans have stayed at the top for centuries and how this has helped them in acquiring certain progressive values.[12] Although the lower castes are now determined to raise higher, the upward movement is much too slow. The Brahmans and the other upper-caste people have thus a cultural advantage which helps even the poor among them in striving for worth-while goals.

9. *National Herald* (New Delhi), 24 March 1978.

10. Ghanshyam Shah, "Reservation for Backward Castes and Classes," *Economic Times* (New Delhi), 14 June 1978.

11. Ghanshyam Shah, "Caste, Class Reservation," *Economic and Political Weekly* (Bombay), 19 January 1985, p. 134. This periodical is cited hereafter as *EPW*.

12. Satish Kumar Kalra, "Caste, and Achievement Values", *Journal of Social Work* (Bombay), Vol. 27, Nov. 1, April 1976, p. 25.

This type of mental horizon and social make-up is not available to the backward classes. Reservation, therefore, is the only remedy for social and educational backwardness.

The pro-reservationists declare that it would be ridiculous to put poor Brahmans and poor Harijans on the same footing. The Brahmans have better access to jobs, they are better educated, and they have well-placed relatives to help them. They are brought up in a culturally superior social environment which is conducive to development of self-confidence. These facilities are not available to the backward classes. This is why they deserve reservation. Reservation will solve to some extent the rising unemployment problem among the backward classes.

The main motive behind the policy of reservation is to bring the downtrodden into the national mainstream. Government jobs give status; they imply power that is more valuable than more economic benefits. On this view, again, the problem of backwardness is social, not economic.

The leaders of the backward classes deny that caste-based reservation strengthens the caste system. They claim that students and employees of the backward classes have been the worst victims of casteism. The upper castes have always helped only their own people. If all castes and communities get their due representation in educational institutions and in Government service, it will make short work of parochial loyalties.

In support of the policy of reservation Devaraj Urs once urged that casteism of one hue could be fought only by casteism of another hue.[13] Why should anybody say that if the lower castes and the underprivileged fought for their share in Government, it was tantamount to casteism? If the upper castes

13. Devaraj Urs, "The Only Way," *Seminar*, December 1981, p. 27.

dominated the political scene and appropriated unto themselves a very large percentage of jobs in the Government, was it not tantamount to casteism ? Urs added that, after all, the social structure in which one grew up was basically an unequal one. And unless the State intervened, that set-up would continue for all times.

Shah also points out that upper-caste intellectuals did not raise the bogy of casteism when people of their castes were cornering all Government jobs, political positions, etc.[14]

The leaders of the backward classes say that intellectual merit and efficiency should not be the only criteria for distribution of jobs. The merits theory, according to them, is being used to exploit the weaker sections and deprive them of their share.

One must pause for a while for cool thinking on this statement. Recruitment policy based on scientific approach, everywhere in the world, has based it on merit amongst the available job-seekers. It is not the case of India only. To change Indian management on this plea is a based version. No society, no service or productive establishment would service and compete by sacrificing merit. Neglect of merit would be a cruel jock with the society.

In context of merit theory I.P. Desai which he also supports and favours change of reservation policy from caste to class observes :

> "The high castes therefore, wish to prevent the mobility of lower castes and contain the discontent among the lower strata of higher castes by appealing to the concealed caste sentiment among them and speaking publicly against casteism, communalism, reservation and that in particularistic,

14. Ghanshyam Shah, n. 11, p. 136.

narrow and parochial. Thus although 'merit' appears to be a progressive slogan, it is in fact a weapon for defending moribund Hindu hierarchy and maintain social economic status quo."[15]

Ram Manohar Lohia, who advocated 60 per cent reservation for the Scheduled Castes, the Scheduled Tribes, the backward classes and women, said :

"If merit were to be the sole criterion for selection or appointments, the high castes with their 5,000—year-old tradition of specialization in mental pursuits would be unbeatable." He further observed that three characteristics "distinguished India's ruling classes :

1. high caste;
2. English education; and
3. Wealth.

Any two of these three factors make a man a member of the ruling classes." He concluded that the presence of the first factor, viz. high caste, froze the whole situation almost into an immobility; for over 90 per cent of India's ruling classes belong to high castes.[16]

There must be competition among equals and not among unequals. Competition among unequals leads to disproportionate representation to certain castes and communities and to inadequate representation to certain other castes.

Further, the pro-reservationists argue that to run the administration efficiently one does not need to be a genius.

15. I.P. Desai, "Anti-Reservation Agitation and Structure of Gujarat Society" in I.P. Desai and others *Caste, Caste-Conflict And Reservation*, (New Delhi : Ajanta, 1985), p. 135.
16. Keshav Rao Jadhav, "Dr. Lohia on Reservation Policy," in B.A.V. Sharma and K. Madhusudhan Reddy, eds, *Reservation Policy in India* (New Delhi, 1982), pp. 37-38 and p. 40.

Common intelligence is sufficient if it is coupled with a high degree of honesty and a capacity to take decisions.[17] In recent years there has admittedly been a certain loss of efficiency in Indian administration. But this can hardly be attributed to officers of the Scheduled Castes, the Scheduled Tribes, and the backward classes; for they constitute just 10 per cent of the higher echelons of the administration. According to the leaders of the backward classes one's merit is a product of the socio-economic conditions of one's family. The children of socially superior and prosperous parents do well in education and in the job market. The socio-economic conditions of the backward castes have not improved. They are, therefore, entitled to reservation. Reservation, they, declare, does not lead to any decline in administrative efficiency. On the other hand it integrates the political and social systems and ensures social equality. It strengthens the faith of the backward classes in the political system. This in its turn promotes national integration.

The advanced sections among the backward castes object to the division of the backward castes into "backward" and "more backward" although it is freely conceded by all concerned that there are significant differences between caste and caste in socio-economic conditions. They cite the judgement of the Patna High Court of 1964 which called this division illegal. Eighty per cent of the leaders of the backward castes interviewed by the present author, has endorsed this point of view.

Arguments of the Anti-Reservationists

With the conforcement of land reforms, a large number of people among the neo-forward castes became small and medium farmers. This enabled them to acquire property and to snap

17. P.C. Chatterji, "In Defence of Reservation", *Patriot* (New Delhi), 23 April 1985.

their links with money-lenders. The only challenge that they were then lest with lay in the sphere of jobs where the upper castes still held away by virtue of their superior education. The anti-reservationists on the other hand regarded reservation as a long-term political strategy on the part of the backward classes to steel a march over them and to prosper at their expense.

The anti-reservationists point out that reservation has tended to increase rather than reduce disparities between and within target groups.[18] For example, the general mass of Harijans have been let down by their own people and only the prosperous among them have cornered all the benefits of preferential treatment.[19] This argument has valid ground. Under reservation policy who are the beneficiaries. Obviously only those persons have enjoyed benefits who can afford to send children for education and consequently after education can get job as well as promotion. Naturally the economically weaker families are out of the picture.

It is true that in the traditional Indian society there was a class correspondence between the caste hierarchy and the economic hierarchy;[20] so much so that the backward castes also constituted the backward classes. However, in the course of the last four decades or so, certain significant changes have taken place causing a number of traditional backward castes to move up socially and a number of traditional advanced castes to move down. In view of this development there is no need for reservation to ensure the upward mobility of the backward castes. They are now capable of furthering themselves.

18. "Forever Backward," *The Statesman* (New Delhi), editorial, 21 December 1980.
19. Janardan Thakur, "There Cannot Be Reservation for All Times," *News Time* (Hyderabad), 15 March 1985.
20. P. Radhakrishnan, "Discrimination and Other Backward Classes", *The Hindu* (Madras), 28 December 1982.

From the economic point of view the backward classes are by no means backward. They are basically agriculturists and artisans in the rural areas. They own land, cows and buffaloes. They lend money to the poor villagers and charge usurious rate of interest. They hoard surplus a grain, wait for the price to rise and then sell it at great profit. By consuming little money they save to educate their children in schools and colleges. They realize the value of education and are no longer steeped in illiteracy and backwardness.

The anti-reservationists, further, hold that the traditional system of social stratification has undergone a metamorphosis in recent times. A number of factors are responsible for this metamorphosis such as universal education, wide-ranging social legislation affecting age-old institutions and inequalities, land reforms, urbanization, industrialization, and the consequent diversification of occupational structures.[21] In this situation inferior occupations like artisan, landless labourer, cultivators and others would be the correct test of backwardness in place of caste.

Yet another argument is that the demand for reservation is due to lack of jobs. The problem of educated unemployment has assumed alarming dimensions in our country in view of the rapid expansion of education on the one hand and the slackening rate of economic development on the other. This problem can only be solved by creating more jobs, not by alienating any percentage of the existing jobs in favour of any caste or community. This can be better understood by having a glance over educated unemployment in Bihar as shown in Table No. 2.

21. D.L. Sheth, "Caste and Politics," in Rasheeduddin Khan and others, eds, *Political Dynamics* (New Delhi, 1976), p. 9.

TABLE 2

Educated Unemployed in Bihar, 1967-1972

	Matriculation	*Under graudates*	*Graduates, including Engineers & Doctors*	*Post-graduates*
31 December 1967	52,301	17,513	14,079	1,318
31 December 1970	77,376	26,517	27,916	2,653
31 December 1972	198,806	68,800	66,000	

Source : *Government of Bihar, Planning Department, Special Employment Programme for Unemployment in Bihar* (Patna), July 1972.

In June 1981 unemployed applicants[22] on live register of 64 Employment Exchange went upto 21,39,336. The employment opportunities in Bihar are limited only to Government sectors. Private concerns are not developed enough to provide jobs and case the problem of employment to any appreciable extent. The following table no. 3 gives an idea of the prospects of employment :

In a big State like Bihar 23,000 jobs a year are like a drop in the ocean. In July 1980 to June 1981 only 23,475 employment were provided. And if 50 per cent of even these jobs are reserved, what is left there for the well-educated and undoubtedly talented young men of the upper castes ? How can the State contain their frustration ? The anti-reservationists, therefore, feel that reservation would only aggravate the unemployment problem in the State. It will increase rate of brain-drain-affecting the State for long.

22. Radhanandan Jha, ed., *Origin and Development of Bihar Legislature* (Patna, 1982), p. 55.

TABLE 3

Total Number of Vacancies each Year in Bihar, 1977

Names of agencies	*Number of jobs every year*
State Government Departments	2,000
State Public Sector Undertakings	4,000
Local Bodies	2,000
Central Government Undertakings	15,000
Total	23,000

Source : Ishwari Prasad, "Job Reservation for Backward Classes in Bihar", *Janata* (Bombay), 23 April 1978, p. 10.

Members of the advanced sections of the backward castes are better off both economically and politically than many of the upper castes in many areas.[23] For instance, the Brahmans and other upper castes in Nalanda, Patna, Nawada, Rohtas, Saharsa, Madhepura, Khagaria and a few other districts in Bihar are dominated by the advanced backward castes. Their economic and educational superiority is on the decline. They have lost their dominance. In fact all that they have today is their ritual superiority.

Different political and social groups of Bihar had opposed the idea of reservation on different grounds. Legislators belonging to the Janata Party were themselves divided on the issue. Some of them were totally against reservation, saying that it would discourage merit and make for inefficiency in the

23. P.C. Gandhi, "Job-Reservation in Bihar Playing for Higher Status," *Times of India* (New Delhi), 20 April 1978.

administration. They feel that the young men of the upper castes should not be made to suffer for the misdeeds that their forefathers might be said to have committed in previous years. They also feel that the according of proferential treatment to the backward castes is against the principle of equality. Others were opposed to the criteria chosen for the determination of backwardness. They were less opposed to the idea of favouring only those who had been listed as "more backward."

Academics like Andre Beteille too have pointed out that the number of jobs that can be reserved is much too small in comparison with the population of the backward classes (whether in a broad or a narrow sense) and that it would be absurd to expect any significant redistribution of income among castes to follow directly from reservation.[24] He observes that reservation can do little to bring about a social revolution in India. Further, there can be no real change in the mental horizons of people. We shall remain eternally stuck with the very divisions we have inherited from the past unless we are able to move towards a different conception of backwardness, one that relates it to the needs of individuals rather than to the demands of castes and communities.[25]

If the caste system is to be destroyed or if its sanctity as a legitimizer of exploitation is to be undermined, one must deal with sources of exploitation on which the caste system thrives.[26] E.M.S. Namboodiripad[27] observes that in making the demand

24. Andre Beteille, "The Problem," *Seminar*, December 1981, p. 10.
25. Ibid., p. 13.
26. Dipankar Gupta, "Caste, Infrastructure and Super Structure A Critique," *EPW*, 19 December 1981, p. 2093.
27. E.M.S. Namboodiripad, "Caste Conflicts v. Growing Unity of Popular Democratic Forces," *EPW*, annual number, February 1977, p. 336.

for reservation the working people belonging to the "forward" communities are being pitted against the backward communities and that class unity on the basis of communities slogans and demands for democracy are being sacrificed for the sake of "unity" between the exploiters and the exploited.

The radicals[28] are also against reservation. They believe that piece-meal changes cannot ameliorate the conditions of the poor. They favour structural changes that can create enough job and educational opportunities. Reservation, according to them, snuffs out the revolutionary spirit of the have-nots.

Janata Party legislators in Bihar belonging to the anti-reservationist group, in a letter to the Shanti Bhushan Committee in 1978, had placed the following arguments :

1. The proposal for job reservation was politically motivated;
2. Economic conditions rather than caste should be the criterion of backwardness; and
3. If 50 per cent of Government posts were reserved for the backward castes, it would affect administrative efficiency in the State in the long run.

They were also of the opinion that it might result in the perpetuation of backwardness as a vested interest. The affluent sections of the backward castes were the immediate beneficiaries of the policy of protective discrimination, and they had a stake in an indefinite continuation of that policy. Further it would create a tendency to be called as backward for ever in order to avail benefits of reservation policy.

Backwardness ultimately is a matter of socio-economic opportunities, missed or denied, and illiteracy is one of its basic

28. K.S. Sharma, "Marxist Approach to Reservation Policy", in B.A.V. Sharma, and K. Madhusudhan Reddy, eds, *Reservation Policy in India* (New Delhi, 1982), pp. 43-57.

manifestations.[29] The anti-reservationists, therefore, advocate economic development and spread of education rather than reservation as the need of the hour. President Sanjiva Reddy[30] once said that there were several Brahmans, who were far below the poverty-line in spite of being members of an advanced community. "Is it not unjust to deny such Brahmans Government assistance ?", he asked. This question haunts all secular-minded intellectuals and critics of the compensatory discrimination policy. Such statement of the President of India has important bearing on reservation policy. He realized necessity of amending the policy for upliftment of backward and weaker sections of the society irrespective of caste. Granting protection to one and deny it for other is a discriminatory policy. This has strengthened the arguments placed by anti-reservationists, who demand reservation on economic basis.

D.A. Deasi, a learned Judge of the Supreme Court observed the same viewpoint.

> "If economic criterion for compensatory discrimination or affirmative action is accepted, it would strike at the root cause of social and educational backwardness, and simultaneous take a vital step in the direction of destruction of caste structure which in turn would advance the secular character of the Nation."[31]

He further explained the twin constitutional goals of this approach.

> "One, to strike at the perpetuation of the caste stratification of the Indian Society so as to arrest progressive

29. "Backward and Forward," *Indian Express* (New Delhi), 13 August 1982.
30. "Help the Poor and Forward Castes," *The Hindu*, 12 October 1978.
31. *K.C. Vasanth Kumar v State of Karnataka*, AIR 1985 S.C.P., 1496.

movement and to take a firm step towards establishing a castessless society; and two, to progressively eliminate poverty by giving an opportunity to the disadvantaged sections of the society to raise their position and be part of the mainstream of life which means eradication of poverty."[32]

The cultural and structural differences between caste groups are getting increasingly narrowed through acquisition of a new occupational status and similar economic interests. If, in this circumstance, caste is made the criterion for identifying backwardness, we would only be legitimizing the caste system by State action as the British and the pre-British Indian rulers did even though the system itself is no longer what it was, say, even forty years ago. I.P. Desai feel that the life chances of a citizen are determined by his economic condition and not by his membership of a particular social group.[33]

The pro-reservationists' claim that Articles 15 (4) and 16 (4) of Indian Constitution, entitle the backward classes to preferential treatment. Actually, it is not so. In the Balaji case[34] the Supreme Court described Articles 15 (4) and 16 (4) as only enabling provisions which do not impose any obligation on the State to act in a particular way. The use of those provisions, according to it, is a matter left to "the discretion of the State." It is not a constitutional duty cast upon the Government to make reservation. It is a discretionary power. Even if the Government uses the power to make reservation, it cannot destroy the interest of others.

32. Ibid.

33. I.P. Deasi, "Should 'Caste' Be the Basis for Recognising Backwardness ?", *EPW*, 14 July 1984, p. 1113.

34. Parmanand Singh, "Equal Opportunity and Compensatory Discrimination : Constitutional Policy and Judicial Control," *Journal of the Indian Law Institute*, vol. 18, April-June 1976, p. 303.

Devaraj Urs noted a number of points against reservation :

1. Reservation creates a vested interest in backwardness; it is a convenient means by which more and more sections of the community would try to wangle the concessions available;
2. The benefits do not percolate down to the broad masses of the backward classes. They reach only a tiny *elite* group. This group, in its turn, creates a gap between itself and the less fortunate sections of its own community. Members of the group copy the manners and life-styles of the advanced communities, a process which the sociologists have christened Sanskritization; and
3. Reservation does injustice to many meritorious candidates.

More often than not, these candidates are found to belong to the advanced communities.[35]

Instead of caste, I.P. Desai has suggested class criteris along with the following alternative criteria :

1. The unit must be completely secular.
2. It must be in consonance with the new society that has emerged and is developing.
3. The new society is based on a recognition of the individual as a citizen, and his rights and obligations are defined by secular political authority.
4. The class to which an individual belongs can be identified by the activity he engages in for earning his livelihood.[36]

He observes that social and educational backwardness need

35. Srs, n. 13, pp. 25-26.
36. Desai, n. 33, 1113.

not necessarily co-exit,[37] An individual belonging to one of the higher groups in the caste hierarchy may be educationally backward; and an individual who is educationally advanced may be socially backward. Similarly, an individual belonging to one of the lower castes may not belong to the socially and educationally backward class because of his caste. In a secular status system he may not be considered backward.

In support of the I.P. Desai view and negating the fear raised by Ghanshyam Shah about change of criteria for identifying other backward classes from caste to class, Upendra Baxi says that,

> "If the poor can be operationally defined, categorised and sub-categorised and reservation benefits be stratified accordingly, would the scenario still haunt us ? I think not."[38]

The arguments of I.P. Desai and Upendra Baxi is quite logical and looks secular, but not applicable and identifiable. All these are designed for the few per cent of poor people among the upper castes and ignoring the miserable condition of the large section of backward classes. Even the Baxi suggestion will not solve the fear raised by Shah in context of change in reservation policy from caste to class. He observes,

> "Now if the Government changes the criteria of reservation from caste to class, persons from the upper strata of the lower castes who are otherwise not able to compete with the upper strata of the upper castes despite the reservation will be excluded from the white collar jobs. And the persons from the lower strata of the lower castes will not be able to

37. Ibid.

38. Upendra Baxi, "Caste, Class, and Reservation," *EPW*, 9 March 1985, p. 428.

compete with their counterpart of the upper castes. They too will be excluded."[39]

Thus Shah suggest : "Caste/class social groups model, for the persons belonging to poor strata of the low castes/social groups of different religions. Shah advocates determination of beneficiaries in sub-regional exclusion of advanced backward castes from the benifit of reservation.[40]

In this circumstance we have to evolve a more scientific criteria which will benefit the deprived castes as well as the poor sections of the society. It also require to exclude the advanced backward castes from the list of the OBC's. The only combition of caste, class and occupation will be answer.

Summing Up

The arguments placed by pro and anti-reservationists groups have valid grounds. A comparative and analytical analysis of arguments seems desirable. In a democratic socialist country the upliftments of backward and weaker sections in the society is the responsibility of the State and the public. Measures for upliftment are to be adopted for a certain period—which may be economic, educational, cultural, social and political. The measures adopted should not have reverse impact on other groups for long. Further the backward and weaker sections must avail the limited benefits made available to them. The measures must be such as to check the undesirable use of privileges.

The reservation policy should be based on rational basis—which must eliminate caste basis. Any policy based only caste would provide fertile soil for germination of caste hatred and war which would be injurious for the society. Thus, it calls for

39. Ghanshyam Shah, n. 11, p. 136.
40. Ibid.

a well thought rational policy in order to provide opportunities for upliftment of those who are backward economically and socially. The continued demand for a change in reservation policy both in the Parliament and out of it—has logical force behind it. It has been supported through individusally by many members of the backward classes commissions, academicians, statemen, various organisations etc. Unless the present reservation policy is changed it would turn into further unbalance; well-to-do families in backward castes would grow and weaker families of forward castes would further become weaker. Such will be gross injustice against weaker sections of forward castes. The society would witness stir after stir which would be deterimental for all. Let a new thinking be infused to save the society as well as to provide opportunities for development.

CHAPTER VIII

Conclusions

Job reservation for the backward classes in Bhiar had two important consequences. First, it divided the whole society of Bihar into two camps—the upper castes and the backward classes or castes. Second, it influenced politics and the voters' decisions. The Congress (I) was able to exploit the sentiment of the upper castes on this issue and capture their votes and active support. The solidarity of the backward castes did not prove to be of a premanent nature. They were divided among different political parties. Their votes were fragmented, and this helped the Congress (I) to regain political power in the elections to the Legislative Assemblies held in 1980 and 1985. Indeed, in the elections of 1985 it increased its tally of seats from 167 to 194.

In their manifesto during the Lok Sabha Elections of 1984, the Dalit Mazdoor Kisan Party (Lok Dal) and the Janata Party pledged to implement the recommendations of the Mandal Commission for reservation of 26 per cent of the jobs in the Central services for the backward classes. However, they failed to mobilize total support of the backward castes in Bihar.

On the other hand the Congress (I) pledged to increase the percentage of reservation for the backward classes in

Gujarat and Madhya Pradesh. It was able to win impressive electoral victories. However, the moment it set about the task of implementing its electoral pledge, it found that it had stirred up a nest of hornets. A mighty wave of protest arose and a situation reminiscent of the anti-reservationist movement in Bihar was precipitated.

In the elections to the Assembly in 1985, Karpoori Thakur again made job reservation an issue. He announced his intention to reserve 36 per cent of the jobs in favour of the backward castes if returned to power. Even then his party could manage to win only forty-five seats in a House of 224 members. The motive behind the announcement was to make sure of their support for political gain. The issue of reservation was more political and emotional than socio-economic. If the political decision-makers were really interested in the upliftment of the downtrodden, they would have used the method of inclusion and exclusion in the lists of backward classes. They were not ready to oppose dominent social groups among the backward classes.

Whatever the value of caste-based reservation, it was not the only remedy to our socio-economic malaise. Bihar's greatest promblem was economic backwardness, but the mounting pressure for enhancing the percentage of caste-based reservation added to the delay in the implementation of land reforms and the much-needed development work, including irrigation and industrial development.

In fact it created one more acute problem, viz escalating social discontent

Even if the Government of Bihar had found in the reservation policy an important way of solving the age-old problem of social inequality and deprivation of the backward classes, it failed to shore it up with a proper infrastructure; for without a large number of scholarships, hostel facilities, and extra coaching to the students of the backward classes were not going to benefit from the policy of reservation. If the educational standard of the backward classes did not improve, they would not be able to utilize the benefit of reservation of Government jobs. Most probably it would be enjoyed by the advanced sections among the backward classes.

The social and political factors forcing the appointment of Backward Classes Commission in Bihar in 1971 and the impementation of its recommendations have been examined. The Legislative Assembly of Bihar has been taken as a reference group for judging the upward mobility of the backward classes in the social and political spheres. The upward mobility or political emergence of the backward classes was manifest in the adoption of the policy of reservation in the face of stiff opposition from the upper castes. It reflects the social and political advancement of the backward classes. They are politically mobilized and doing well in all spheres of life. In this circumstances the advanced backward castes do not require any protective discrimination. In the light of the study, the seven hypotheses have been re-evaluated.

Hypotheses Re-examined

1. Bihar has vast deposits of minerals. Giant steel plants are located in the State. Raw materials are available in abundance for feeding these industries. And yet per capita income in the State is desparately law. Large number of people are languishing in poverty. About 60 per cent of the people are living below poverty-line. Agriculture is the basic source of income, and about 80 per cant of the people depend on it entirely. Agriculture is not mechanized. Distribution of land is unequal. Land reforms have failed to bring about any signficant change in the countryside. Green revolution has not much contributed in its development.

The benefits of such progress, as Bihar has made since independence, are being cornered by certain groups favoured by the age-old, hierarchical social structure. They have failed to reach the toiling rural masses. All the fruits of development, innovation and invention are just a fairy tales for the ignorant and illiterate rural poor. The main reason for this is that political power is still in the hands of the upper-caste, upper-class politicians and their political parties. These politicans are least interested in brining about any socio-economic transformation. These social and economic inequalities have made life of millions miserable.

The escalating economic crisis and the rampant corruption and inefficiency led to the J.P. movement. The Janata Party Government in Bihar, with all its progressive slogans, failed to fulfil its promise of economic reforms. In the economic field it followed the Congress (I) culture by making big promises during election time and dragging its feet about redeeming the promises later. Politics during the Janata Party period was dominated by the policies of social equality, not economic equality. The party failed even to implement the different land reforms effectively.

The people did not forgive the Janata Party for its failure on the economic front. They switched to the Congress (I) in the elections held in 1980 and 1985. Earlier, the pro-reservationist and anti-reservationist movements shook the State. The economic crisis made matters worse. Taking all these social, political and economic factors into account, we may safely state that our first hypothesis has proved to be correct.

2. The Governor in an address to the joint session of the two Houses of the State legislature in June 1977 announced the Government's reservation policy for the backward classes irrespective of their economic condition. The condition of large sections of some of the advanced sections of the backward classes was better than that of the lower and middle classes of the upper castes. These classes latter depended heavily on Government jobs for their livelihood. The poor economic

conditions of some sections of the advance classes forced them to raise voice against reservation policy on purely castes basis. The changing conditions necessitated change in reservation policy. That is why they opposed the reservation policy.

Neither the upper castes nor the backward castes are homogeneous. Among the upper castes, some enjoy a higher social status and command greater economic resources. Among the backward castes, too there are social and economic differences. It is, therefore, necessary to try and avoid the pitfall of relying wholly on caste as the basis of reservation and offer a helping hand to all needy individuals irrespective of their caste or class affiliation. Among equals the law should be equal and all should be treated alike. Thus, our second hypothesis too is found to be correct.

3. The policy of reservation was not the result of any process of decision-making in the Legislative Assembly. It was not the decision of the legislature in 1971 to appoint a Backward Classes Commission. The implementation of the policy was effected by means of an executive order of the Bihar Governor and not by an Act of the Bihar Legislative Assembly. It was announced by the Governor at a joint session of the Bihar Legislative Assembly and the Legislative Council.

The Government of Bihar modified its policy of reservation a number of times, but it preferred to announce all the modifications from public platforms, never in the Legislative Assembly. This may even be regarded as amounting to contempt of the legislature. The Government of Bihar avoided facing hostile legislators in the Legislative Assembly. It preferred to get the support of the people into two hostile camps.

Instead of supporting the Government, a number of Janata legislators belonging to the upper castes openly criticized the reservation policy and participated in the anti-reservationist demonstrations. The legislators of the backward classes participated in the pro-reservationist demonstrations. The pressure tactics used by the legislators compelled the Government of Bihar to modify its policy and make it broad-based. Thus, it can be said that the Government of Bihar used the limited rationality method of decision-making and benefited from the feedback. It did not take the Legislative Assembly into its confidence before making this vital decision. Our third hypothesis, therefore, is valid. It was a strategic mistake made by the Government which generated only opposition.

4. The decision of Bihar's Government to implement the recommendations of the Backward Classes Commission mobilized all the backward castes behind the Chief Minister for the time being. The pro-reservationist movement consisted of students, legislators and bureaucrats of the so-called backward castes. They belonged to the upper and middle classes of the backwards. This meant a change in the traditional balance of power relations, altering the social and political superordinate subordinate relationships. The numerically strong, economically prosperous and politically conscious backward castes like the Yadavas and Kurmi refused to own their subordinate status.

The backward castes cast off their subordinate position in the social hierarchy and joined together to oppose the protest movement of the upper castes. For the first time after independence the Government's reservation proposal brought about the mobilization of the people and the legislators in Bihar. In the Legislative Assembly most of the legislators worked as a united caste group irrespective of political affiliations, That is why the mobilization of the backward classes to support the Government decision can be considered a social movement although it was dominated by the upper and middle classes belonging to the backward castes.

Before independence education and Government jobs were mostly patronised by the upper castes. After independence, the phenomenal expansion of educational facilities provided opportunity to the backward castes to get higher education. The number of Government jobs did not increase in proportion to the development of higher education. About 80 per cent of the limited jobs available were cornered by the four upper castes, who constituted just 13 per eent of the total population. In the Legislative Assembly the upper castes accounted for 45 per cent to 60 per cent of the total strength during 1962-80. The backward classes in contrast constituted just 30 to 40 per cent in the Legislative Assembly.

The problems of unemployment, poverty and illiteracy among the backward castes generated a feeling of hatred among them against the upper castes. They started blaiming the upper castes for all their problems. Consequently, the politically conscious, economically sound, and educationally advanced men of the backward castes raised demand for their share in all spheres of life. In this process they snatched away some of those benefits in the name of preferential treatment or reservation policy.

Their newly acquired economic prosperity enabled some backward castes to control political power. They also sought to control the bureaucracy as that was an important means of acquiring social prestige and domination.

This validates our fourth hypothesis.

5. Class consciousness has not as yet emerged among the poorer sections of society. The formation of classes is a slow process. In India there has to be a caste revolution before there can be a class revolution. As long as the ritualistic, economic, and social superiority of the upper castes continues, they will generally be considered to constitute the upper classes. The lower and lower middle classes among the upper castes have no

feeling of affinity with the lower and lower middle classes among the backward castes.

Upper and upper-middle classes are in the process of being formed among some of the backward castes. They have social interaction with the upper and upper-middle classes of the upper castes, but this is not true of the lower and lower-middle classes of the two categories of castes.

The present reservation policy is a hindrance in the way of class stratification. If the social development policy based on preferential treatment fails to bring about the desired results, it would generate class-based politics. The privileges separately for the Scheduled Castes, Scheduled Tribes and backward classes do not allow them to feel of being one class. The proponents of class-based politics are seeking to consolidate their position among the deprived sections of rural agricultural labourers and the urban working class. Although they have failed to organize them as a class-for-istelf, they are becoming a class-in-itself. Caste is great barrier in the way of the emergence of class consciousness. It stops the working class from becoming a class-for-itself.

Caste is indeed a vital factor in the present backwardness of Bihar and it is also a bar to the development of the State in future. The caste system, which receives its sanction from the Hindu scriptures and social practices is an obstacle in the way of class stratification. When the society is not stratified on the basis of class, the reservation policy only on caste or class basis will fails to ameliorate the traditional social, economic and political domination of upper castes. If caste based reservation policy with certain modifications will continue for a few years will provide confidence among the backward classes and germinate class consciousness among the poor sections of the upper castes. The casteism of upper castes is counter-balanced by the casteism of backward classes. Presently this is in process in

Bihar and obstructing all round development of Bihar. Our fifth hypothesis is thus validated.

6. Bihar politics is dominated by the caste factor. Caste is taken into account before making any political decision, appointment or transfer. In the field of political recruitment this factor is especially important. There is no political party which can be said to have shaken off the shackles of casteism. In the functioning of the organizational set-up, in the selection of candidates for elections and in the distribution of patronage, caste considerations are paramount. The term "Casteist Marxism" is popular in Bihar politics. This factor is detrimental to class-based politics.

Further, if one wishes to develop a just, egalitarian, secular and progressive society, he shall have to eradicate caste consciousness from the minds of the people. However much people talk of checking casteism, it is gaining strength day after day. It is because now the backward classes are not balancer among the rival groups of upper castes, but it contend or power. It reflects the strengthing of caste consciousness.

The strength of the upper castes in the Legislative Assembly has been slowly declining while that of the backward classes has grown. Leaders of the backward classes have worked as Chief Ministers, Speakers and Cabinet Ministers time and again. Now in politics the backward castes are the equal partners of the upper castes, not their eamp followers as in the 1950s. The dominant position of the backward castes in Bihar politics today is due to their realization strength of population, growing education, growing general and political consciousness and increased representation in both houses. The political value of caste has increased very sharply.

The politics of job reservation initiated by the Janata Government in Bihar in 1977-78 divided society into two mutually hostile camps—one of the upper castes and the other of the backward castes. These groups fought for and against reservation, agitating at the level of the legislature and in public. The reservation controversy is still continuing. A large number of legislators were members of either the one or the other of these two antagonistic camps. Our sixth hypothesis is thus, borne out by our empirical investigation.

7. The Indian Constitution envisages only social and educational backwardness, not economic backwardness. The Constituent Assembly accepted the need for reservation for the Scheduled Castes and the Scheduled Tribes but turned down the demand for the institution of similar reservation for the other backward classes.

The national leaders were aware of the deplorable economic conditions of the Scheduled Castes and the Scheduled Tribes. These people were not only socially and educationally backward, but also economically backward. That is why they found it logical to employ the test of economic backwardness in identifying backward classes. Some of them even equated social backwardness with economic backwardness.

In recent years the leaders of the backward castes have worked as pressure groups to secure for their castes the same benefits of protective discrimination as those available to the Scheduled Castes and the Scheduled Tribes. In fact, thirteen states in India have already granted their demand, and they are now engaged in an effort to get such benefits in the Central services as well. In these circumstances, the anti-reservationists and those, who are in favour of rationalizing the reservation policy, have mounted their pressure upon the Government of India to use economic backwardness as one of the criteria of backwardness.

The list of backward classes being used by the Government of Bihar includes a number of trader castes. These castes such as Marwari, Baniya, Teli, Sonar etc.. are economically strong and control the trade and commerce of the province. In fact, in some other states like Gujarat and Uttar Pradesh, they are categorized as upper castes. The Yadavas, the Kurmis and the Koiris are agriculturist castes, and they are economically well-to-do. By any yardstick of social backwardness they cannot be called backward. To remove the injustice entailed in this, it would be necessary to consider economic condition along with social and educational backwardness. It would not do to ignore anyone of the three criteria.

This proposition has a strong basis at the level of the legislature too. A traditional society like Bihar cannot be stratified on the basis of class because caste is a big obstacle in the way of formation of classes. Millions of families in Bihar live in such miserable economic conditions, their way of life and their interests are so utterly different from those of the other classes, that they find themselves in hostile opposition to those other classes. Still, they are not in a position to form a class as stratified on the basis of caste and religion. Thus, it is not possible to formulate a policy of reservation only on the basis of economic condition.

If economic condition is to be the only criterion, reservation will be enjoyed fairly by a large number of those who belong to the upper castes. If social and educational backwardness alone is considered and the economic criterion is given the go-by, it would help only the prosperous sections of the backward classes, not the sections that are weakest.

After proving the validity of seven hypotheses, a few suggestions are placed for better implementation of the reservation policy. Views of a number of scholars on reservation policy have been collected and assessed. By and large they are opposed to the caste criterion and favour merit, economic backwardness and occupation as the right criteria for extending preferential treatment.

To limit reservation strictly to the most backward classes is the only way. The criterion of extreme backwardness excludes the advanced backward classes from the benefits of reservation and safeguard the interests of the most deprived sections among the backward classes. It is based upon the caste-cum-class criterion and also permits reservation of a few seats for the economically backward among the upper castes. It would satisfy the poor sections among the upper castes and thereby prevents the growth of any anti-reservationist feeling among them.

Suggestions for an Equitable Reservation Policy

1. Caste and Class as Criteria

Observation reveals that caste is still one of the important factors which determine the chances of an individual in life. The backward classes are socialized in a culturally inferior social situation and fail to learn about the new avenues and opportunities in life. They are represented much less than even the Scheduled Castes and the Scheduled Tribes in the Central services and in the service of the State Governments.

They are in no position to compete with the candidates of the upper castes. In view of this it is only fair that caste should be used as one of the important criteria for identifying backward classes.

However, caste cannot be the only criterion. The Indian Constitution talks about socially and educationally backward classes. All the Backward Classes Commissions and the different Indian States have considered these two variables in their reservation policies. They have, however, failed to recognize the importance of the economic criterion along with the caste criterion. Reservation should be extended only to the poorer sections of the backward castes and not to those who are advanced in respect of the economic and educational variables and backward only in the context of ritual status. An income limit of Rs. 8,000 per annum should be laid down for each family to be considered qualified for preferential treatment. This would exclude the advanced sections of the backward castes from the benefits of reservation.

This criterion is in practice in most of the Indian States. Gujarat and Tamil Nadu, however, do not lay down any income limit. The reservation policy in Bihar is based on caste as well as income limit.

2. *Check on Elite Benefit*

Certain advanced sections and families among the backward classes, the Scheduled Castes and the Scheduled Tribes have taken advantage of the reservation policy. This is also one of the causes of heart-burning among the lower and middle class categories of the upper castes. That demand exclusion of certain beneficiaries by adopting a new reservation policy. If certain castes, which are traditionally called backward, are not in fact socially, educationally and economically backward, then they should be excluded from the list of backward classes after a proper investigation. This would provide an opportunity to wider sections to enjoy the benefits of reservation.

This process would check the *elite* trying to corner all the benefits. It would help in containing the anti-reservationist feeling to some extent. It would also minimize illiteracy, poverty and ignorance in which the masses are sunk.

3. *Reservation Only for One Generation*

If the Government really desires to uplift the backward classes by means of the policy of preferential treatment it has to devise a way of excluding from the ambit of reservation all those families which have already benefited from reservation. The number of jobs is limited, but the number of aspirants is ever on the increase. There is also much bompetition among the candidates of the Scheduled Castes and the Scheduled Tribes. Sections of the Scheduled Castes and the Scheduled Tribes, which have already been benefited from reservation, tend to monopolize all the available opportunities. Other sections among them remain where they have always been.

It is a travesty of justice to provide special facilities to the kith and kin of highly placed officers of the Scheduled Castes, the Scheduled Tribes and the backward classes. It is necessary to place some checks on the present reservation policy. The benefits should be restricted just to one generation of backward castes. Subsequent generations should be made to compete with the general categories.

4. *Periodical Evaluation of Reservation Policy*

The reservation policy should be evaluated from time to time with reference to the number of people recruited. The results of this evaluation should also be made available to the public. Now there is general talk about the deterioration of administrative standards and efficiency. It is also true that students of the reserved categories are not able to pass medical examinations even after four or five attempts. Besides, only certain castes and families have cornered the benefits of reservation. If specific cases of such miscarriage of justice are brought to light, remedies can be hammered out.

5. *Reservation Never More than 50 per cent*

The policy of reservation is intended to achieve an egalitarian society. If so, it should not be pursued at the expense of merit and the stability of the social, political and economic systems. If reservation is made in proportion to the population even in the case of the backward classes, it would lead to a collapse of the social, political, and economic systems. That is why the Mandal Commission has not recommended that move than 50 per cent of the available vacancies should be reserved for the backward classes. A number of High Courts and the Supreme Court have also said that reservations should not exceed 50 per cent of the total number of vacancies.

6. *Reservation Policy should be Sanctioned by the Legislature*

In most Indian States it is customary to appoint a backward classes commission headed by a legislator. Later, on the basis of the recommendations of such a commission, the Government tries to implement its policy of reservation by means of an executive order. It avoids getting the reservation policy scrutiinized and debated in the legislature; it tries to bypass the legislature. This enables the ruling *elite* to formulate any kind of policy to suit its political ends. Sometimes this generates a public upsurge against the Government order.

If the reservation policy gets the sanction of the legislature after being duly debated in the House, it would get wide publicity, and the Government would also stand to gain from the feedback from the public. The legislation would then be more acceptable to all concerned.

7. *Need for Infrastructure*

Reservation cannot help in achieving an egalitarian society unless it is supported by a suitable infrastructure like adequate scholarships, hostel accommodation, educational facilities, extra coaching, pre-selection training, etc. These measures improve the merit and efficiency of the students of the backward classes and give them confidence. Education can then improve their socio-economic conditions and make them effective participants in the social and political systems. Reservation by itself can hardly benefit the backward classes.

8. *Cut off-Points*

It has been observed that in many Indian States students in the general category do not get admission into a professional educational institution or secure a coveted job even with 80 per cent marks. On the other hand candidates of the Scheduled Castes, the Scheduled Tribes and the backward classes with 30 or 35 per cent marks manage to make it. If this is what reservation is in practice, it would spell disaster for the country. There must be a reasonable cut-off point for giving benefit to the weaker sections. In any case, the cut-off point should not be more than 10 to 15 per cent for adimission into technical institutions or for appointment to Government or semi-Government jobs.

9. *No Roster System*

At present rosteres are maintained in the Central services and even in the State services for candidates of the Scheduled Castes and the Scheduled Tribes. If the vacancies meant for those categories are not filled up in a certain year, they are kept vacant for three years before being dereserved. In certain years 80 or 85 per cent of the posts are reserved for them. This facility is extended to the bacaward classes too in certain States. The anti-reservationist movement, which took place in Gujarat in 1981, was particularly the result of the inequity of the roster system. It has to be scrapped to check the anti-reservationists feeling among different sections of society.

10. *No Reservation for Promotions*

Reservation at the time of appointment is acceptable, but it is certainly unjust and unacceptable in the matter of promotions. It is in fact subversive of merit, efficiency and social justice. In the service all employees are equal, and they must be treated equally. If a man gets a promotion just because he is a Harijan or a member of a backward class and is placed above others, it would be unjust and would cause frustration among those who are passed over. It would also undermine efficiency. Demoralisation due to policy of promotional reservation has long range effects on efficiency of any service. An efficient, experienced and older person suffers humiliation to work under an inefficient, unexperienced and young person, if such person is promoted. Such a feature can be assessed by social scientists and not a Judge or a Chairman of a backward commission.

11. *Time Limit for Reservation Policy*

Backwardness has a tendency to perpetuate itself. To cheek this tendency, a time-limit has to be set. One view is that when the backward classes become the equals of the advanced classes, the reservation system should be scrapped. Another view is that it would continue for as long as the caste system continues. Our own view is that it must have a time limit of ten to twenty years. At the end of this period, it should be re-evaluated from the viewpoint of the desirability of its continuance.

12. *National Consensus*

Recently the issue of reservation generated a number of clashes among the different social sections. At the natianal level the spokesmen of the backward classes are continually pressurizing the Government for the implementation of the Mandal Commission recommendations. Instead of accepting the demand for such implementation some leaders have expressed the need for a national consensus on the reservation policy. There can be no such consensus unless the Government and the difierent political parties take a firm, rational and scientific stand—a stand not based on any political motive.

Reviews of reservation policy necessitates a change in policy particularly its adverse impact on efficiency of services. Efficiency should not be sacrificed as that would lead the economy into crisis. On the other hand upliftment of weaker section is also desirable. In such case it is advisable that the children of weaker sections should be provided full infrastructure, such as, free education, free boarding and lodging, clothes, tuition fee, books atc., so that they are provided better environment to learn, level of knowledge, ability to compete in the open labour-market. This would also force them to devote greater attention towards study than to mere talk about facilities and rights. The security of job through reservation policy does not encourage them toward study, ability and efficiency.

As stated earlier, there are five major schools of thought about the reservation policy. Different social sections have different opinions in line with their own interests. The upper castes and the upper classes are championing the theory of merit and efficiency, whereas the backward classes are in favour of the reservation policy. Some of them favour the economic criterion; and the others, the caste criterion. In these circumstances to achieve a national consensus is a very difficult task.

If the suggestions given above are taken into account in the formulation of a reservation policy, a consensus may be worked out. These suggestions are aimed at making the reservation policy more scientific. The policy should benefit the needy sections of society without undermining efficiency and merit. The policy should not allow the advanced sections of the backward castes to take undue advantage. The poor and the needy among the upper castes too should be anabled to secure relief. Nobody should be allowed to develop a vested interest in the name of backwardness.

Bibliography

PRIMARY SOURCES

Government of India Publications

All-India Agricultural Labour Enquiry Commission, *Report on Intensive Survey of Agricultural Labour, Employment, Under-employment, Wages and Levels of Living* (Delhi, Manager of Publications, 1955).

Backward Classes Commission : A Report (Chairman : Kaka Kalelkar) (Delhi, Manager of Publications, 1955), 3 vols.

Backward Classes Commission : A Report (Chairman : B.P. Mandal), (New Delhi, Controller of Publications, 1981), 7 vols.

Census of India, 1891, 1931, 1971 and 1981.

Commissioner for Scheduled Castes and Scheduled Tribes : Annual Reports, 1955 and 1978-81 (New Delhi, Manager of Publications, 1981).

Ministry of Home Affairs, *Memorandum on the Report of the Backward Classes Commission* (Delhi, Government of India Press, 1956).

———, *Memorandum on the Report of the Backward Classes Commission* (Delhi, Government of India, 1981).

Planning Commission, *The First Five Year Plan : A Draft Outline* (New Delhi, Manager of Publications, 1951).

Study Team Social Welfare and Welfare of Backward Classes ; A Report (Chairman, Renuka Ray) (New Delhi, Committee on Plan Project, 1959).

State Government Publications

Andhra Pradesh, *Report of the Backward Classes Commission* (Chairman : Manohar Prasad), (Hyderabad, 1970).

Bihar, *Report of the Bihar Backward Classes Commission* (Chairman : Mungeri Lal), (Patna, 1976), 7 vols.

———, *Bihar Welfare Manual : Compendium of Important Circulars and Letters Relating to the Programme for the Welfare of Backward Classes* (Patna, 1966).

———, *Speech of the Governor of Bihar 1947-82*, (Patna, Government of Bihar, 1982).

Gujarat, *Report of the Socially and Educationally Backward Classes Commission* (Chairman : A.R. Bakshi) (Ahmedabad, 1976).

———, *Report of the Socially and Educationally Backward Classes (Second) Commission* (Chairman : C.V. Rane) (Ahmedabad, 1984).

Jammu & Kashmir, *Report of the Backward Classes Committee* (Chairman : J.N. Wazir) (Srinagar, 1969).

———, *Report of the Jammu & Kashmir, Backward Classes Commission* (Chairman, Adarish Sein Anand) (Srinagar, 1977).

Karnataka, *Report of the Karnataka Backward Classes Commission* (Chairman : L.G. Havanir) (Banglore, 1975), 4 vols.

Kerala, *Report of the Kerala Backward Classes Reservation Commission* (Chairman : Nettur P. Damodaran) (Trivendrum, 1971), 2 vols.

Kerala, *Commission for Reservation of Seats in Educational Institutions* (Chairman : G. Kumara Pillai) (Trivendrum, 1966).

Mysore, *Report of the Backward Classes Committee* (Chairman : R. Nagan Gowda) (Bangalore, 1961).

Punjab, *Committee on Welfare of Scheduled Castes, Scheduled Tribes and Backward Classes, 1975-1976 : Fourth Report* (Chandigarh, 1976).

Tamil Nadu, *Report of the Tamil Nadu Backward Classes Commission* (Chairman : A.N. Sattanathan) (Madras, Director of Stationery and Printing, 1971).

SECONDARY SOURCES

Books

Ambedkar, B.R., *Who are the Shudras ? How they come to be the Fourth Varna in the Indo-Aryan Society* (Bombay, Thackers, 1970).

Baliy, F.G., *Tribe, Caste and Nation : A Study of Activity and Political Change in Highland of Orissa* (Manchester : Manchester University, 1960).

Banerjee, Anil Chandra, *The Making of the Indian Constitution 1939-1947*, vol. I (Calcutta : A. Mukherjee & Co., 1949).

Beteille, Andre, *Backward Classes and their Future* : Delhi, Oxford University Press, 1981).

———, *Siudies in Agrarian Social Structure* (Delhi : Delhi University Press, 1974).

Beteille, Andre, ed., *Equality and Inequality : Theory and Practice* (Delhi : Oxford University Press, 1983).

Bhambhri, C P., *Janata Party : A Profile* (New Delhi, National, 1980).

Bhatt, Anil, *Caste, Class and Politics* (New Delhi, Manohar, 1975).

Blunt, E.A.H., *Caste System of Northern India with Special Reference to the United Provinces of Agra and Audh* (Delhi, S. Chand, 1969).

Bottomore, Tom, ed., *A Dictionary of Marxist Thought* (Oxford, Blackwell, 1983).

Brass, Paul R., *Pactional Politics in an Indian State : The Congress Party in Uttar Pradesh* (Bombay : Oxford Uuiversity Press, 1966).

————, *Language, Religion and Politics in North India* (New Delhi, Vikas, 1975).

Brass, Paul R., and Franda, F. Marcus, ed., *Radical Politics in South Asia* (Cambridge, Mass : MIT Press, 1973).

Chhibar, Y,P., *From Caste to Class : A Study of Indian Middle Class* (New Delhi : Associated Publishing House, 1976).

Chitalely, D.V., *A1R Commentaries : The Constitution of India* vol. I (Nagpur, All India Reporter, 1970).

Cole, G.D.H., *Studies in Class Structure* (London, Routledge & Kegan Paul, 1955).

Dahrendorf, ..alf, *Class and Class Conflict in Industrial Society* (Berkeley, Calif, : California University Press, 1959).

Devis, Kingsley, *Human Society* (New York : Macmillan, 1967).

Deasi, I.P. and others, *Caste, Caste-Conflict and Reservation* (Delhi : Ajanta, 1985).

Diwakar, R.R., *Bihar Through the Ages* (Bombay, Orient Longman, 1959).

Dumont Louis, *Homo Hierarchicus : The Caste System and Its Implications* (Delhi, Vikas, 1970).

Dutt, R.C., *History of Civilization in Ancient India*, 2 vols. (Delhi, Vishal Publishers, 1972).

Dwaine, Marvick, ed., *Political Decision Makers* (New Delhi, Arvind Publications, 1972).

Franda, Marcus F., *Political Development and Political Decay in Bengal* (Calcutta, Firma K.L. Mukhopadhyaya, 1971).

Galanter, Marc, *Competing Equalities and the Backward Classes in India* (Delhi, Oxford University Press, 1984).

Gerth, H.H., and Mills, C.W., eds., *From Max Weber : Essays in Sociology* (New York, Oxford University Press, 1958).

Ghurye, G.S., *Caste, Class and Occupation* (Bombay, Popular Prakashan, 1957).

Giddens, Anthony, and Held, David, ed., *Classes, Power and Conflict : Classical and Contemporary Debates* (London, Macmillan, 1982).

Huntington, S.P., *Political Order in Changing Societies*, (New Haven, Conn. : Yale University Press, 1968).

Huttoh, J.H., *Caste in India : Its Nature, Functions and Origins* (Bombay, Oxford University Press, 1980), edn. 4.

Jayaraman, Raja, *Caste and Class Dynamics of Inequality in Indian Society* (Delhi : Hindustan Publications, 1981).

Jha, Dayadhar, *State Legislature in India* (New Delhi, Abhinav Publications, 1977).

Jha, Radhanandan, ed., *Origin and Development of Bihar Legislature* (Patna, Government of Bihar, 1982).

Jha, Sashishekar, *Political Elite in Bihar* (Bombay, Vohra Publications, 1974).

Lang, K., and Lang, G., *Collective Dynamics* (New York, 1969).

Leach, Edmund R., *Aspects of Castes in South India*, Ceylon and *North West Pakistan* (Cambridge : Cambridge University Press, 1960).

Lohia, Ram Mohan, *The Caste System* (Hyderabad, Navhind, 1964).

Low, D.A., ed., *Congress and the Raj : Facts of the Indian Struggle, 1917-1947* (London, Arnold-Heinemann, 1977).

Ketkar, Sridhar V., *The History of Caste in India*, (Jaipur, Rawat Publication, 1979).

Khan, Rasheeduddin, and others, eds., *Political Process* (New Delhi, Indian Council of Social Science Research, 1981).

Khan, Rasheeduddin, and others, eds., *Politicals Dynamics* (New Delhi, Indian Council of Social Science Research, 1976).

Klass, Morton, *Caste : The Emergence of the South Asian Social System* (Philadelphia, Pa : Institute for the Study of Human Issues, 1980).

Kothari, Rajani, *Politics in India* (New Delhi, Orient Longman, 1970).

————, ed., *Caste in Indian Politics* (Delhi, Orient Longman, 1970).

Marx, Karl, and Engels, Frederick, *Selected Works*, Vol. I to III (Moscow : Progress Publishers, 1977).

Mathews, Donald R., *The Social Background of Political Decision Makers* (New York, Random House, 1962).

Michels, Robert, *Politics Parties* (New York, Collier Books, 1962).

Narain, Iqbal, ed., *State Politics in India* (Meerut, Meenakshi Prakashan, 1967, 1976), 2 vols.

Narayan, Jayaprakash, *Total Revolution* (Bombay, Popular Prakashan, 1980), 4 vols.

Omvedt, Gail, ed., *Land, Caste and Politics in Indian States* (Delhi, Teaching Politics 1982).

————, *Cultural Revolt in Colonial Society : The Non-Brahmin Movement in Western India*, 1873-1930 (Bombay, Scientific Socialist Fducation Trust, 1976).

Poulantzas, Nicols, *Classes in Contemporary Capitalism*, David Fernach, trans. (London, Vessoń, 1974).

————, *Political Power and Social Class* (London, New Left Books, 1973).

Prasad, Kedarnath, *The Economics of Backward Region in a Backward Economy : A Case Study of Bihar in Relation to other States in India*, Vol. I (Calcutta, Scientific Book Agency, 1967).

Pye, Lucian, and Verba, Sidney eds., *Political Culture and Political Development* (New Jersy, Princeton, 1969).

Pylee, M.V., *Constitutional Government in India* (New Delhi, S. Chand, 1984).

Rao, M.S.A., *Social Movement in India*, Vol. I (New Delhi, Manohar, 1979).

Risley, H.H., *The Peoples of India* (2nd edn.) (Delhi, Orient Books, 1969).

Rudolph, L.P., and Rudolph, S.H., *The Modernity of Tradition : Political Development in India*, (New Delhi, Orient Longman, 1969).

Runciman, W., *Relative Deprivation and Social Justice*, (Berkeley, Calif. : University of California Press, 1966).

Sachchidanand, *The Harijan Elite : A Study of Their Status, Networks, Mobility and Role in Social Transformation*, (Faridabad, Thomson Press, 1977).

Saraswati, S., *Minorities in Madras State : Group Interests in Modern Politics* (Delhi, Impex India, 1974).

Shah, Ghanshyam, *Protest Movement in Two Indian States : A Study of the Gujarat and Bihar Movements* (Delhi, Ajanta, 1977).

Sharma, B.A.V., and Reddy, K.M., eds., *Reservation Policy in India* (New Delhi, Light & Life, 1982).

Singh, Charan, *Who Is Casteist ? : An Analysis* (Delhi, Kisan Trust Publications, 1982).

Singh, Yogendra, *Social Stratification and Change in India* (New Delhi, Manohar, 1980).

Sinha, A.N., *Mere Sanamaran* (in Hindi) (Patna, Kusum Prakashan, 1961).

Sinha, Sachchidananda, *Some Eminent Bihar Contemporaries* (Patna, Himalaya Publications, 1944).

Srinivas, M.N., *Social Change in Modern India* (New Delhi, Orient Longman, 1982).

———, ed., *Dimensions of Social Change in India* (New Delhi, Allied, 1977).

Truman, D., *The Governmental Process* (New York, Knopf, 1951).

Verma, G.P., *Caste Reservation in India : Law and Constitution* (Allahabad, Chugh Publications, 1980).

Weber, Max, *Theory of Social and Economic Organization* (New York, Free Press, 1965).

Weiner, Myron, *The Politics of Scarcity : Public Pressure and Political Response in India* (Bombay, Asia Publishing House, 1963).

Articles :

Abraham, A.S., "Promoting Equal Opportunity : Positive Discrimination Becomes a Farce," *Times of India* (New Delhi), 18 March 1978.

———, "Anti-Reservation Protest : Growing Clout of Backward Classes", *Times of India* (New Delhi), 14 March 1985.

Aditya, "Reservation and Its Effects", *Indian Nation* (Patna), 4 April 1978.

Balagopal, K., "Andhra Pradesh, Anti-Reservation yet once More" *Economic and Political Weekly* (Bombay), 6 September, 1986. This periodical is citcd here in after as *EPW*.

Baru, Sanjaya, "Marx Centenary : Karl Marx and Analysis of Indian Society", *EPW*, 10 December 1983.

Baxi, Upendra, "Caste, Class and Reservation", *EPW*, 9 March 1981.

Beteille, Andre, "The Problem", *Seminar* (New Delhi), December 1981.

Blair, W.H., "Rising Kulaks and Backward Castes in Bihar", *EPW*, 12 January 1980.

Budola, V.M., "Backward Classes : New Commission Faces Uphill Task", *Indian Express* (New Delhi), 29 May 1979.

Chatterji, P.C., "In Defence of Reservation," *Patriot* (New Delhi, 23 April 1985).

Chsuhan, D.S., "India's Underprivileged Classes and the High Public Services : Towards Developing a Representative Cureaucracy," *International Review Administrative* Science (Brussels), Vol. 42, no. 1, 1976.

Chittaranjan, C.N., "Beyond Class Conflict", *Mainstream* (New Delhi), 8 April 1978.

Das, Arvind N., "Bihar under the Raj : Roots of Under Development", *Times of India* (New Delhi), 30 October 1985.

Dave, P.K., "Promotion and Incentives in Public Services", *Indian Journal of Public Administration* (New Delhi), Vol. 12, 1966.

Deekshin, Welah, "Backward Classes Benefits and Social Class in India, 1920-70", 7 April 1979.

Desai, I.P., "Should Caste Be the Basis for Recognising Backwardness ?", *EPW*, 14 July 1984.

Gandhi, P.C., "Proposals to Defuse Bihar Situation", *Times of India* (New Delhi), 18 March 1978.

Gangarde, K.D., "Adult Suffrage and Social Change", *Social Change* (Bombay), March-June 1976.

Grover Daniel R., "Political Mobilization in India", *Asian Survey* (Berkelep, Calf.), September 1974.

Gupta, Dipankar, "Caste Infrastructure and Superstructure : A Critique", *EPW*, 19 December 1981.

Gupta, S.C., "Structural Causes of the Economic Crisis", *EPW* 18 January 1975.

Guru, D.D., "Bihar's Problem of Educational Jobless", *Economic Times* (New Delhi), 13 January 1975.

Harcourt, Max, "Kisan Populism and Revolution in Rural India", in D.A., Low ed., *Congress and the Raj : Facets of the Indian Struggle* 1917-1947 (London, Arnold-Heinemann, 1977).

Jha, Chetkar, and Jha, Shree Nagesh, "Some Aspects of Bihar Politics", *India Quartely* (New Delhi), July-September, 1967.

Jha, Prem Shankar, "Discrimination on Caste Basis Threat to Country's Unity", *Times of India* (New Delhi), 3 April 1979.

————, Jati and Jobs", *Illustrated Weekly of India* (Bombay) 2 April 1978.

Jha, Shree Nagesh, "Caste in Bihar Politics", *EPW*, 14 February, 1970.

John, MacDugall, "Dominant Caste and Rich Peasants", *EPW*, 24 March 1979.

Joshi, P.C., "Organising Rural Poor : Some Basic Issues", *Mainstream*, 12 August 1978.

Kalra, Satish Kumar, "Caste and Achievement Values", *Journal of Social Work* (Bombay), April 1976.

Katyal, K.K., "Politics of Job Reservation", *The Hindu* (Madras), 20 March 1978.

————, "Exercise to Perfect Old Reasoning" *The Hindu* 12 January, 1981.

Kothari, Rajni, "Restoring the Political Process", *Seminar*, July 1970.

————, "The Congress System in India", *Asian Survey*, December 1964.

Manwans, Yogendra, *News Time* (Hyderabad), 16 April 1985.

Manor, James, "The Rest of India's Backward Classes", *New Society*, 21 February 1980.

Murthy, Sachchidanada, "Everyone Wants backward tag, *The Week* (Kottayama) 19-25 October, 1986.

Mukherjee, Nirmal, "Perspective of Policies", *Seminar*, December 1981.

Nambcodiripad, E.M.S., "Caste Conflicts versus Growing Unity of Popular Democratic Forces", *EPW*, annual number, February 1979.

Nayar, Kuldip., "Rights or Privileges", *Indian Express* (New Delhi), 11 October 1978.

Ninam, T.N. and Menon, Amarnath, Andhra Pradesh Reservation Ruckm Sparking off an Anti-Reservation Agitation", *India Today* (New Delhi), 31 August, 1986.

Omvedt, Gail, "Class Struggle or Caste War", *Forntier* (Calcutta), 30 September 1978.

Oommen,T.K., "Sociological Issues in the Analysis of Social Movements", *Sociological Bulletin* (New Delhi), March 1977.

— ——, "Agrarian Classes and Political Mobilisation in India" *Sociological Bulletin*, March, September 1984.

———, "Strategy of Social Change", *EPW*, 22 June 1968.

Pande, S.V., "The Politicisation of Special Constitutional Provisions and the Perpetuation of Casteism", *Indian Political Science Review* (Jaipur), January 1980.

Pathy, Jaganath, "Politics of Reservation in India : A Case Study of Political Agitation in the States of Bihar and Gujarat", *Philosophy and Social Action* (New Delhi), April-June 1982.

Prasad, Ishwari, "Job Reservation for Backward Classes in Bihar", *Janata* (Bombay), 23 April 1978.

Prasad, Pradhan H., "Dynamics of Growth in Rural Bihar", *Times of India* (New Delhi), 17 March 1981.

———, "Caste and Class in Bihar", *EPW*, annual number, February 1979.

Prasad, R.C., "Educational Development in Bihar", *Seminar*, July 1968.

———, "Electoral and Political Violence", *Indian Journal of Politics* (Aligarh), December 1981.

Prasad., R.C., "Social Polarization and Political Instability", in Iqbal Narian, ed., *State Politics in India*, Vol. II (Meerut, Meenakshi Prakashan, 1975).

Radhakrishnan, N., "Units of Social, Economic, and Educational Backwardness : Caste and Individual" *Journal of Indian Law Institute* (Delhi), July-September 1965.

Radhakrishana, P., "Discrimination and other Backward Classes", *The Hindu*, 28 December 1982.

Rajappa, S., "Something For Everyone In Reservation policy" *The Statesman* (Calcutta), 16 October 1986.

Rao, D.Narasimha, and Ramchander, M., "Reservation of Backward Classes : In Search of Criteria", in B.A.V. Sharma, and K.M. Reddy eds, *Reservation Policy in India* (New Delhi, Light & Life, 1982).

Rao, M.S.A., "Political Elite and Caste Association : A Report of Caste Conference", *EPW*, 18 May 1968.

Roy, Ramashray, "Caste and Political Recruitment in Bihar" in Rajni Kothari, ed *Caste in Indian Politics* (New Delhi, Orient Longman, 1970).

Sahay, S., "Bihar Constitutional Fraud", *The Statesman* (New Delhi), 6 October 1983.

Saxena, N.S., "The Reservation Issue : A Possible Basis for a Consensus", *Times of India* (New Delhi), 3 May 1985.

Shah, Ghanshyam, "Caste, Class and Reservation", *EPW* 19 January 1985.

Shah, Ghanshyam, "Reservation for Backward Castes and Classes", *Economic Times* (New Delhi), 14 June 1978.

Sharma, K.S., "Marxist Approach to Reservation Policy", in B.A.V. Sharma and K.M. Reddy eds, *Reservation Policy in India* (New Delhi, Light & Life, 1982).

Sharma, K.K., "Caste and Class in India : Some Conceptual Problem *Sociological Bulletin*, March-September 1984.

Sheth, D.L., "Caste and Political", in Rasheeduddin Khan and others, eds, *Political Dynamics* (New Delhi, Indian Council of Social Science Research, 1976).

———, "The Great Reservation Debate", *Indian Express* (New Delhi), 12 May 1985.

Singh, N.K., "Job Reservation in a Socialist Democracy", *Indian Nation*, 16 April 1978.

Singh, Parmanand, "Equal Opportunity and Compensatory Discrimination : Constitutional Policy and Judicial Control," *Journal of Indian Law Institute*, April-June 1976.

Singh, S.P., "Behind Job Reservation", *Hindustan Times* (New Delhi), 6 June 1978.

Singh, Yogendra, "The Changing Pattern of Social Stratification in India", in M.N. Srinivas, ed., *Dimension of Social Change in India* (New Delhi, Allied, 1979).

Sinha, Arun, "The Caste Factor in Bihar", Indian Express (New Delhi), 12 January 1979.

———, "Class War in Bhojpur", *EPW*, 7 January 1978.

Sirstkar, V.M., "Caste and Politics", *Seminar*, June 1965.

Sivaramayya, B., "Equality and Inequality : The Legfil Framework", in Andre Beteille ed *Equality and Inequality* : *Theory and Practice* (Delhi, Oxford University Press, 1983).

Srinivas, M.N., and Panini, M.N., "Politics and Society in Karnataka", *EPW*, 14 January 1984.

Thakur, Janardhan, "There Cannot Be Reservation for All Time", *News Time* (Hyderabad), 5 March 1985.

Urs, Devaraj, "The Only Way", *Seminar* December 1981.

Verghese, B.G., "Kosi Kranti-I : Land Reforms in Bihar", *The Statesman* (New Delhi), 18 September 1977.

Wober, Max, "Class, Status and Party", in C.S. Hells, ed., *Structural Social Inequality* : *Reader in Comparative Social Stratification* (New York, Macmillan, 1969).

Weiner, Myron, "India : Two Political Cultures", in Lucian Pye and Sidney Verba, eds, *Political Culture and Political* Development (New Jersy : Princeton, N.J., 1969).

Wright, Erik Odin, "The American Class Structure", *American Sociological Review* (Bloomington, Ind.), December 1982.

M.Phil,/Ph.D. Dissertations/Theses (Unpublished)

Blair, W.H., "Caste, Politics and Democracy in Bihar State, India : The Elections of 1967" (Ph.D. thesis Duke University N.C., 1969).

Narayanay, N. Padmini, "Scheduled Caste Politics : A Socio-Political Study of Special Representation in Parliament" (Ph. D. thesis, Jawaharlal Nehru University, School of Sciences, New Delhi, 1980).

Roy, Ramashray, "A Study of the Bihar Congress Committee, Bihar India" (Ph.D. thesis, University of California, Beakeley, Calif., 1966).

Singh, Bameshwar P., "The Control of AICC Executive Control over Making of Congress Ministries in Bihar" (Ph.D. thesis Bihar University, Muzaffarpur, 1978).

Sinha, Lila, "Political and Administrative Aspects of the Green Revolution in Bihar" (Ph.D. thesis, Patna University, Patna, 1975).

Sinha, Sanjay, "Backward Class Movement in Bihar : Sociological Study" (M.Phil. dissertation, Jawaharlal Nehru University, School of Social Sciences, New Delhi, 1984).

Srivastava, Alok K., "Emerging Patterns of Caste Conflicts in Bihar : A Study of Post-1977 Period" (M.Phil. dissertation, Jawaharlal Nehru University, School of Social Sciences, New Delhi, 1982).

Sharma, Arjun, "Caste, Class and Politics : A Case Study of A Village Panchayat, Nawadah District in Bihar" (M.Phil dissertation, Jawaharlal Nehru University, School of Social Sciences, 1983).

Supreme Court and High court Judgements

1. *Balaji* V *State of Mysore*, A.I.R. 1963, S.C. 649.
2. *Balaram* V *State of Andhra Pradesh*, A.I.R. 1972, 1375.
3. *Champakam Droraijan* V *State of Madras*, A.I.R. 1951, S.C. 226.
4. *Chitralekha* V *State of Mysore*, A.I.R. 1964 S.C. 1823.
5. *Chhotelal Pandey* V *State of Uttar Pradesh*, A.I.R. 1979 Allahabad.
6. *Janki Prasad Parimoo* V *State of Jammu & Kashmir*, A.I.R. 1973, S.C. 930.
7. *K.C. Vasanth Kumar* V *State of Karnataka*, A.I.R 1985 S.C. 1495.
8. *Ramkrishna Singh* V *State of India*, A.I.R. 1960, Mysore, 338.
9. *Thomas* V *State of Kerala*, A.I.R. 1976, S.C. 490.
10. *Padmaraj Samarendra* V *State of Bihar*, AIR 1979, Patna.
11. *P. Sagar* V *State of Andhra Pradesh*, A.I.R. 1968, 165.

Newspapers and Press Clippings (1977-1986)

1. *Patriot* (New Delhi).
2. *The Economic Times* (New Delhi, Calcutta).
3. *The Indian Nation* (Patna).
4. *The Hindustan Times* (New Delhi).
5. *The Hindu* (Madras).
6. *The Searchlight* (*Patna*).
7, *The Statesman* New Delhi, Calcutta).
8. *The Times of India* (New Delhi).

Index